The Rise of K-Dramas

The Rise of K-Dramas

Essays on Korean Television and Its Global Consumption

EDITED BY JAEYOON PARK *and* ANN-GEE LEE

McFarland & Company, Inc., Publishers
Jefferson, North Carolina

Library of Congress Cataloguing-in-Publication Data

Names: Park, JaeYoon, 1973– editor. | Lee, Ann-Gee, 1977– editor.
Title: The rise of K-dramas : essays on Korean television and its global consumption / edited by JaeYoon Park and Ann-Gee Lee.
Description: Jefferson, North Carolina : McFarland & Company, Inc., Publishers, 2019 | Includes bibliographical references and index.
Identifiers: LCCN 2019017088 | ISBN 9781476677477 (paperback : acid free paper) ♾
Subjects: LCSH: Television programs—Korea (South)—History and criticism. | Television plays, Korean—History and criticism. | Popular culture—Korea (South) | Popular culture and globalization. | Mass media and culture—Korea (South)
Classification: LCC PN1992.3.K6 R57 2019 | DDC 302.23/095195—dc23
LC record available at https://lccn.loc.gov/2019017088

British Library cataloguing data are available

ISBN (print) 978-1-4766-7747-7
ISBN (ebook) 978-1-4766-3658-0

Front cover: (top, left to right) Song Joong-ki, Song Hye-kyo, Jun Ji-hyun and Kim Soo-hyun; bottom photograph by Atakorn Daengpanya (Shutterstock)

Printed in the United States of America

McFarland & Company, Inc., Publishers
Box 611, Jefferson, North Carolina 28640
www.mcfarlandpub.com

Table of Contents

Part 3. Co-Production and Adaptation

Preface

JaeYoon Park

Living and teaching in a small town in Arkansas, I did not expect to hear a Korean greeting, "*Annyeonghaseyo*," during a community event. I turned around and saw a young woman who then bowed to me in a Korean style. She was not Korean; she had never visited Korea before; nonetheless, she demonstrated an excellent maneuver of the Korean language and cultural knowledge. Even though we had never met, she readily knew by my name that I was originally from Korea. Later on, I met quite a few Arkansans like her. I found out that although there are no Korean classes taught anywhere nearby, they were all self-taught through various Internet and new media resources while listening to their favorite Korean popular songs (K-pop) and watching Korean dramas (K-dramas). They comprise just a small part of the Korean Wave (or *hallyu*) fans.

I recall the time when I heard "Gangnam Style" on a local radio station while driving in Kansas a few years ago. I was teaching at a mid-size university and living in a college town in Kansas. The song went viral on the Internet, and it was, in fact, the first time that any piece of Korean popular culture gained recognition in mainstream U.S. media. In the late 1990s, the Korean Wave (hereafter *hallyu*) began crossing national borders, primarily in East Asia first, then throughout the Asian region in general. I heard the news about *hallyu* reaching its influence all over the world, including Latin American countries, Europe, the Middle East, and even Africa. While living and teaching in Kansas, I occasionally met hard-core *hallyu* fans. Yet they were all young college students who usually became fascinated with Japanese or Asian culture first, and then somehow transferred their interest into a then-new phenomenon called *hallyu*. They were early adopters, somewhat isolated from one another. Even when "Gangnam Style" became sensationally popular throughout the globe, it was still deemed an exception—a viral sensation, not enough to revert the larger, transnational cultural flows. South Korea remained in the periphery as a regional center, although it was an increasingly powerful and influential producer and exporter of cultural products.

Yet, it feels different. Something has shifted in recent years. The more I travel around North America, the more I can sense a change. My Koreanness is often associated with a young, new, and trendy culture. "Korea" is "cool." Before *hallyu*, it was the military culture: people I met would talk about their grandfather's or father's stories when they fought during the Korean War; or they would tell me their experiences when stationed in South Korea as American G.I.s. Now, people want to talk to me about their addiction to Korean dramas, and they also ask me where to buy Korean beauty products. I became curious.

When putting out a Call for Papers for this particular collection, I was pleasantly surprised to receive interests from authors of diverse national origins and geographical locations. The contributors of this collection are not only from the U.S. and Korea, but also from the UK, the Netherlands, Taiwan, Japan, Turkey, and Brazil. This collection of essays thus provides various perspectives on the cultural phenomenon of passionately watching and consuming Korean dramas around the globe.

I would like to thank all the contributors in this book for collaborating so patiently and pleasantly. I am grateful to Dr. Tamara Falicov, Dr. Novotny Lawrence, and Dr. Yan Bing Zhang for their valuable advice and support. I am also appreciative of Natalie Foreman, associate editor at McFarland, for her support and belief in this book. I would also like to thank Dr. Ann-Gee Lee, my coeditor for this collection. Without her, this publication would not have been possible. *Kamsahamnida.*

Introduction

JAEYOON PARK

With the proliferation of global media on the Internet, Korean television dramas (hereafter K-dramas) have quickly become a popular phenomenon. Not just permeating Asia, but also appearing in the U.S., the Middle East, Europe, and Spanish-speaking countries among others, these dramas have led to fans scrambling to provide subtitles in their own languages. Along with being enthralled with characters and storylines, fans find themselves listening to soundtracks and following their favorite actors to other K-dramas. According to Y. Kim (2013) in the book, *The Korean Wave: Korean Media Go Global*, "Korean TV dramas are emotionally powerful and self-reflexive. While Korean producers do not pay particular attention to a global formula for the success of TV drama, nevertheless they have found its affective form useful to touch the sensibilities of disparate audiences" (p. 7). This goes to show that anyone can find a K-drama suitable to their tastes: they can select from Korean period dramas, comedy, romance, action, horror, sci-fi, crime/thriller, and so on.

Furthermore, K-dramas provide food for thought on numerous topics of study. The increasing popularity of K-dramas across the globe draws a great deal of critical attention from media scholars, fan studies, and cultural studies scholars alike. As J. Kim (2014) observes, "it is the most recent transnational television phenomenon in East Asia, one that has most lately produced the greatest commitment from the largest number of viewers and has been attributed with most profoundly affecting regional dynamics" (p. 7). Thus, this book raises the following questions: What aspects of K-dramas appeal to audiences across different cultures and national boundaries? What types of influences can this K-drama craze have over transnational, committed fans who are willing to spend their valuable time and money to consume K-dramas and *hallyu*-related products? What are the implications of the K-drama craze for changing regional and global dynamics?

Yet, K-drama's fandom and cultural impact are not the only areas that are worthy of scholarly investigation. K-drama content and themes explore a variety of topics related to urban, modern, and professional life in contemporary Korea as well as differing cultural values and beliefs among social groups, especially in regards to the clash between and amalgamation of traditional Korean values and imported Western standards. Y. Kim (2013) notes, "The Korean Wave culture embedded in dramas … is in essence all things hybrid—a fusion of local, regional and Western cultures, forms, styles, genres, narratives or identities, in part accelerated by the developments in information and communication technologies, yet without necessarily eliminating the best of Korea's distinct traditional values, emotional aesthetics and expressive performances" (pp. 16–17). Such K-drama topicality, in this sense, lends well to the exploration of identity constructions at different junctures of gender, class, age, sexuality, and nationality. With K-dramas' hybridity in terms of both content and form, also emerging are transcultural conversations and reconfigurations of identities.

Part 1 of this collection, "Fandom, Consumption and International Relations," examines the diverse ways in which K-drama fans consume, seek out, and respond to Korean culture. Ranging from foods and romance-inspired tourism to beauty and fashion products and a national image, the first part's essays explore the complex ramifications of K-drama fandom in the socio-cultural, interpersonal, economic, and political contexts. In her essay, Jennifer Rachel Dutch focuses on K-drama super-fans' obsession with and desires for a real Korean meal. Dutch examines such addictive fan activities in relation to the intertwined nature of cuisine with culture and identity. Drawing on online fan discourses, Dutch argues that K-drama addicts' search for the authentic Korean cuisine is not really about the food itself. Rather, it is a way of reinforcing their individual identity as super-fans while forging deeper connections with the on-screen characters as well as with others in the larger fan community.

Min Joo Lee focuses on fan-tourism motivated by international fans' desires to experience and find true love in Korea as seen on romantic K-dramas. Lee's discussion utilizes qualitative data gathered through ethnographic research and interviews with young *hallyu* tourists (mostly women) in their late teens and early twenties. Foreign fans' expectations about Korean men and masculinity along with the influence of K-dramas on the formation of transnational intimacies are the main concerns of this essay.

Ann-Gee Lee discusses K-drama fandom in relation to fashion and beauty industries by focusing on the Chinese phenomenon of *wanghong*. As female power-bloggers and online celebrities, *wanghong* are great influencers in the Chinese market when it comes to promoting and selling K-drama related products. Lee looks at various discourses surrounding the *wanghong* phenomenon while exploring how it cannot simply signify a female empowerment in the context of how complex China-Korea relations and women's socio-economic status are intrinsically tied to extreme consumerism.

Tony Tai-Ting Liu and Phyllis Wei-Lih Yeh focus on China-Korea relations in a different light. The authors explore how the political discourses involving the two countries affect the K-drama craze in China in the context of Korea's pop nationalism and China's traditional nationalism. Particularly, Liu and Yeh examine China's recent sanction on the *hallyu* phenomenon in order to demonstrate how "soft power" can be limited vis-à-vis provoked Chinese nationalism.

Part 2, "Identity Formation, Transformation and Gender Relations," consists of three essays. In the first essay of this section, JaeYoon Park examines the issues of aging and disability represented in a K-drama, *Dear My Friends* (2016), in relation to the notion of a socially constructed identity. Park argues that while the series foregrounds often-neglected topics such as gendered aging processes, women's issues, female friendship, and ageism as a form of social oppression, the issues of disabilities are marginalized and rendered as individual stories rather than social problems in the series.

Mary A. Sobhani looks at the paranormal storylines of two K-dramas, *Oh My Ghost!* (2015) and *The Master's Sun* (2013), from the perspective of a postsecular analysis. Sobhani focuses on the female protagonists' identity formation and transformation processes in the two series, in which these characters come to grips with their unwanted spirit-seeing talents in order to successfully navigate the mundane world of labor and love. Sobhani also explores the series' use of urban spaces and humor in an effort to demonstrate how both the spiritual and the material constitute an integral part of the twenty-first century's postsecular reality.

Sofia Murell examines the portrayals of soft masculinity in K-dramas focusing on the "flower boy" (or *kkonminam*) images. Murell stresses the multidimensionality of the *kkonminam* syndrome by analyzing three *hallyu* male stars in particular: Bae Yong-joon in *Winter Sonata* (2002), Lee Min-ho in *Boys Over Flowers* (2009) and Kim Soo-hyun in *My Love from the Star* (2013–2014). Although traditionally regarded as effeminate and weak, *kkonminam* embodies the deconstruction and hybridization of male and female identities in contemporary Korea while also conveying the desires and anxieties that Korean youth feel regarding the notion of beauty and proper gender roles. Combining media image analyses with ethnographic research conducted in Seoul, Murell provides a valuable insight into the connections and disconnections between media representations and "real life" encounters.

Part 3, "Co-Production and Adaptation," shifts the focus from fandom and identities to cultural exchanges occurring in the political-economic contexts of television co-production and adaptations. Elaine W. Chung investigates the influence of political economy on media contents through the analyses of two dramas co-produced by Chinese and Korean broadcasting companies—*Modern Family* (2002) and *Master Lin in Seoul* (2012). Chung states that these internationally co-produced dramas, despite the fact that they are produced ten years apart, still adhere to a China-centric discourse of multiculturalism, which promotes and reinforces the assimiliation of foreign individuals into China's dominant social order. According to Chung, they are predominantly Chinese stories that employ the familiar tropes of Korean women as ideal, virtuous wives as the co-productions primarily intend to localize the proven K-drama formula and aesthetics in the Chinese context, driven by a commercial motivation.

Daniela Mazur, Melina Meimaridis and Afonso de Albuquerque look into two Korean adaptations of U.S. television series—*The Good Wife* (2016) and *Criminal Minds* (2017). The authors maintain that the legal procedural and the police procedural dramas, respectively, have undergone a considerable amount of adaptations and cultural translations in terms of both format and content. The conventions and standard practices of the Korean television industry as well as the locality and specificity of Korean culture are the two main factors this essay examines in an effort to shed light on the cross-cultural adaptation processes.

In the last essay of this book, Yeşim Kaptan and Murat Tutucu analyze *Waiting for the Sun* (2013–2014)—the Turkish adaptation of the K-drama *Boys Over Flowers* (2009). Based on individual interviews with Turkish audiences, Kaptan and Tutucu explore the popular appeal of the original K-drama and its Turkish adaptation in terms of romanticism, class differences, and family relations. The authors focus on the hybridity of Turkish culture with its geographical and cultural connections to Europe, the Middle East, and Asia, and also problematize the notion of cultural proximity in their analyses of audience responses that speak to the commonalities, contradictions, and differences between Turkish and Korean cultural values.

Without a doubt, the ten essays in this book prove that South Korea has secured its status as a creator and exporter of meaning in the global television market as well as a cultural mediator across various borders on the local, regional, and global levels. This book intends to provide a better understanding of the socio-cultural-political dynamics of *hallyu* with a clear focus on the K-drama craze. While all the authors draw on scholarly appoaches and frameworks, this collection is ultimately dedicated to the fans of various K-dramas around the world. We are K-drama "aca-fans," and we are inspired by other fans and their activities. We hope that our fellow fans will find an essay or essays (or, maybe even the entire collection!) suitable to their tastes.

References

Kim, J. (Ed.). (2014). Reading Asian television drama: Crossing borders and breaking boundaries. New York: I.B.Tauris.

Kim, Y. (Ed.). (2013). *The Korean wave: Korean media go global*. New York: Routledge.

Part 1

Fandom, Consumption and International Relations

Consuming K-Drama Cuisine

The Intersection of Fans, Fandom and Food in the Search for a Real Korean Meal

JENNIFER RACHEL DUTCH

In *Fantasy Couple* (*Hwansangui keopeul*), a 2006 drama based on the 1987 American movie, *Overboard*, the lead character Na Sang-shil/JoAnna (Han Ye-seul) falls in love with Jang Chul-soo (Oh Ji-ho), the man who takes care of her after she loses her memory in an accident. She also falls in love with the unique flavor of *jjajangmyeon*, a dish of noodles slathered in thick black bean sauce. In scene after scene, Sang-shil devours bowl after bowl of the popular comfort food. She has *jjajangmyeon* delivered, eats *jjajangmyeon* in restaurants, and even cooks instant *jjajangmyeon* from a package, adding her own fresh vegetables to make sure that it looks just like the picture on the package.

Jjajangmyeon is an essential element in Sang-shil's character development. She transforms from JoAnna, a spoiled rich girl who spends most of her time alone, into Sang-shil, a woman who loves Jang Chul-soo, cares for her neighbors, and feels like she is part of the community. JoAnna only eats "rich people's food" like steak and champagne; Sang-shil eats foods she likes best which happens to be "poor people's food," such as *jjajangmyeon* or black-bean noodles and *makgeolli*, Korean rice wine. The prim and proper JoAnna has exemplary table manners, cutting tiny bites with her knife and fork, carefully chewing, and swallowing before taking another bite; Sang-shil shovels mouthful after mouthful of slippery *jjajangmyeon* noodles into her mouth, barely taking time to chew or even breathe before wrapping more noodles around her chopsticks and shoveling them into her mouth. Even when eating *jjajangmyeon* in front of others, Sang-shil is unconcerned when her lips and cheeks are covered in the sticky black bean sauce. She is so intent on enjoying her meal that she does not even bother with proper table manners. Even after Sang-shil regains her memory and returns to her life as JoAnna, what she craves is *jjajangmyeon* and *makgeolli*, not steak and champagne. The transformation of her personality is realized just as much through her appetite as through her romance with Chul-soo.

This example from *Fantasy Couple* is one instance in which food is integral to plot and character development in a K-drama. Whether the food is *jjajangmyeon*, *kimchi*, *kimbap*, *bibimbap*, *bulgogi*, *tteokbokki*, or something else, Korean foods are an essential element of K-dramas. In fact, the action of some K-dramas revolves around food, such as *Let's Eat* (*Shiksyareul hapsida*) from 2013, which chronicles the "foodie" culture among contemporary young adults in Seoul, or *Kimchi Family* (*Balhyogajok*) from 2011, which follows the story of a modern family trying to keep its kimchi-focused restaurant afloat.

Other stories, however, integrate food in more subtle ways. For example, the popular classic *Boys Over Flowers* (*Kkotboda namja*) from 2009 uses food to convey the transformation of Gu Jun-pyo (Lee Min-ho) as he falls in love with Geum Jan-di (Ku Hye-sun). Jun-pyo, the rich son of the owner of an international conglomerate, rules his school; Jan-di is the poor daughter of a working-class family at school on scholarship. Jun-pyo's feelings for Jan-di change from contempt to adoration. The development of his romantic feelings for Jan-di is marked by his encounters with working-class food. At the start of their relationship, he is shocked by the idea of eating street food or even *ramyeon* (ramen). By the end of the drama, he loves *ramyeon* and eats it piping hot from the *ramyeon* pot lid, an informal habit and common trope for working-class households in K-dramas. While the food scenes are not the core element of *Boys Over Flowers*, they illustrate how Jun-pyo's acceptance of Jan-di grows over time as he falls more in love with her and her working-class foods.

For South Korean viewers, these onscreen foods are familiar staples. As Na Sang-shil guzzles *makgeolli* or Gu Jun-pyo slurps *ramyeon*, South-Korean viewers instantly recognize the flavor of the food and the meanings of these dishes in Korean culture. For South Korean viewers, the fact that two rich characters are enjoying foods typically popular among the working-class signals ways those characters have begun to change to fit in with the lives of the "common" people that they now love. Most importantly, however, South-Korean fans of these popular dramas know the taste of these dishes firsthand. There is no mystery in the flavor of the thick brown sauce swirled in with the noodles in *jjajangmyeon*. The spiciness of *kimchi* is a familiar part of almost every meal. The brand name on the package immediately signals the exact level of saltiness for the instant *ramyeon*. For South Koreans watching these scenes, the foods and the flavors, textures, and eating experiences are everyday occurrences and very much a part of their identity as Koreans.

This connection between food and identity shows the significance of food goes beyond individual dishes and daily meals. Once dismissed as a mundane essential, the complex meanings constructed around food and meals have become an important focus of a range of scholars across multiple disciplines, such as history, sociology, anthropology, and within the burgeoning field of Food Studies (Belasco, 2008, p. 5–6). According to prominent food scholar Belasco (2008), culture and cuisine are intertwined as "food serves to express personal and group identities and to cement social bonds" (p. 15). What people eat (mashed potatoes versus *kimchi*), where people eat (seated at a kitchen table versus seated on the floor), how people eat (with a knife and fork versus with chopsticks) and more are all guided by the rules and expectations developed by each culture. Belasco points to the work of Farb and Armelagos who "liken cuisine to a culture's language—a system of communication that is inculcated from birth, if not before, and is hard to change or learn once you are grown. Even if you migrate elsewhere, you will likely retain the 'accent' of your native cuisine" (qtd. as cited in Belasco, 2008, p. 16). The "accent" of Korean food comes through in all aspect of the meals served in K-dramas. For example, traditional Korean food played a key role in the 2003 smash hit, *Jewel in the Palace* (*Dae jang geum*), which helped to spread the Korean Wave across the globe. Telling the story of an orphaned girl who trained in cooking and traditional medicine in order to serve the King, this series gave a global audience a glimpse of *hansik* or traditional Korean food and dining (Xin, 2017, p. 83). The methods of preparation and presentation highlighted in this drama are quintessentially Korean and, according to Xin (2017), "the meticulous and traditional ways of preparing Korean cuisines and the creative food presentation have captivated many audiences" (p. 84). While the lavish palace feasts from *Dae jang geum* captured historic and formal Korean foods, other K-dramas present more recent and informal Korean meals. For example, the widely popular *My Love from the Star* (*Byeoreseo on geudae*) (2014) featured the main female character, a famous actress who had to watch her weight, indulging in cheat meals made up of eating chicken and drinking beer together, an indulgent snack known as *chimaek* in Korea. According to Xin (2017), not only was *My Love from the Star* a popular K-drama, but *chimaek* helped to drive up sales of chicken and beer, even in other countries outside of Korea. Xin writes, "*Xinhua* reported that the *chimaek* trend has revived China's poultry industry in 2014, which languished after the onset of the H7N9 avian flu" (p. 85). As these two examples demonstrate, K-dramas speak with the "accent" of Korean cuisine and include an intertwining of food and identity that is uniquely Korean, which non–Korean K-drama fans yearn to taste.

Non-Korean K-Drama Fans and the Search for Identity in Korean Food

For non–Korean K-drama fans, however, the flavors, textures, and experiences that make up the "accent" of Korean cuisine are unknown. As Korean popular culture spreads across the globe as part of the Korean Wave, more *hallyu* fans have no connection to South Korea other than the fact that they have fallen in love with the country's music, movies, and K-dramas. Most of these worldwide fans "are not Korean, have never been to Korea, and are not familiar with the country in any other way" (Schulze, 2013, p. 387–388). For these international fans, watching K-drama characters gorge on *jjajangmyeon*, savor *kimchi*, or devour *ramyeon* raises one important question: What do these foods taste like? Without having tasted the foods for themselves, foreign K-drama fans are left wondering about the flavors of these foods. Is *jjajangmyeon* sauce sweet and spicy or savory and rich? Is *kimchi* unbearably spicy or just right? Do Korean *ramyeon* brands taste the same as the ramen packages in the fan's home country, or are the noodles thicker and the broth spicier? With very little or no frame of reference in their own cultures' cuisines, many worldwide fans are left drooling as the characters in their favorite dramas eat and eat while they themselves have no real notion of the actual flavor, texture, or experience of eating those foods.

For the most dedicated K-drama fans, ignorance about the flavor of Korean foods is untenable. These self-styled "K-drama addicts" go beyond simply watching K-dramas, becoming obsessed with all aspects of South Korean culture including language, music, and, of course, food. Janey, who blogs about her K-drama obsession at *Asian Fixations*, identifies the number one "side effect" of "Korean Drama obsession" as "an insatiable craving for Korean food." She declares, "The struggle is real especially when it's 1 a.m. and you're suddenly craving for Korean barbeque and a bottle of soju to go with it. All while watching an episode of the latest tvN drama, of course" (Janey, 2014). This connection between TV portrayals, K-drama fandom, and food is a common theme running through many fan discussions of what it means to be a "K-drama addict." These fans do more than binge-watch K-dramas; they begin binging on Korean food.

As illustrated by the monumental growth in the consumption of *chimaek* in China, for many fans, being a "K-drama addict" includes the desire to get off the couch in order to find and consume a "real" Korean meal. This sentiment is expressed by addict-blogger Devon (2017) that a common occurrence for K-drama fans is watching a food scene and suddenly craving the food. Devon exclaims, "Your stomach realizes that it's a hollow cavern, and that THING ON THE SCREEN is the only thing that will satiate it! This happens to us Kdrama fans all the time. We see something in a drama that looks unbearably delectable, and we. must. devour it." This craving for K-drama food—a desire to eat the same food as the K-drama character and find out the taste of the food—leads to the quest for the real version of the foods that they have only seen onscreen. This drive to eat "real" Korean food inspired by K-dramas sets super-fans apart from other, more casual, K-drama viewers.

Less dedicated K-drama viewers are more likely to watch K-dramas passively. The more "addicted" a fan becomes, the more they seek out other experiences with South Korean culture: listening to K-pop, buying Korean cosmetics, or eating Korean foods.

This ever-widening interest in South Korean culture has also helped to spread the Korean wave. In an article discussing the ever-expanding boundary of what elements of South Korean culture can be considered part of *hallyu*, Choi (2015) proposes a "flowchart" that "illustrates how the boundary of Hallyu shifts" (p. 35). This progression is "listening to K-pop → watching K-dramas → joining online fan clubs for Korean popular cultures in general → trying Korean food → learning Korean language → purchasing Korean cosmetic/electronic goods → studying abroad in Korea → making Korean friends → picking up cultural idioms and local, traditional customs → launching personal blogs on Korea → working for Korea-related institutions of various sorts" (p. 35). The same type of progression can also represent the progression of the development of the K-drama addict, whose obsession beyond K-dramas to incorporate more and more aspects of Korean culture.

This desire to go from passively watching K-dramas on a screen to participating actively by speaking Korean, wearing Korean clothes, or eating Korean food is part of what Jenkins (2006) identifies as "participatory culture" (p. 3). In participatory culture, fans move beyond "older notions of passive media spectatorship" and take an active role in their fandoms and with the object of their obsessions (Jenkins, 2006, p. 3). This is particularly true in today's media-saturated, online environment. According to Jenkins, today's fans create "convergence culture" a space where "old and new media collide, where grassroots and corporate media intersect, where the power of the media and the power of the media consumer interact in unpredictable ways" (p. 2). In convergence culture, fans do not sit and wait for media to come to them. "The circulation of media content," Jenkins writes "—across different media systems, competing media economies, and national borders—depends heavily on consumers' active participation" (p. 3). Convergence culture happens within K-dramas when Korean media corporations release new episodes, which are then spread around the globe—both through legally licensed sites such as dramafever.com or viki.com or through illegal, unlicensed streaming sites—and fans begin adding subtitles, writing recaps, or creating mashup tribute videos. In fact, the intersection of corporate production of K-dramas and fan distribution, translation, and manipulation of these products have been essential to the growth of *hallyu*. As Lee (2014) confirms, the ability of fans outside of Korea to enjoy Korean popular culture "is facilitated greatly by media convergence and participatory consumption. Digital technologies and online communications ease fans' access, not only to cultural texts but also to up-to-date information on those texts and help them to take part in communities where various fan activities online and offline are conducted and shared. The fandom may be nurtured by top-down distribution of Japanese or Korean popular culture by local importers such as TV stations or publishing houses; however, its main feed is a wide range of contents unofficially disseminated via online communications among fans across borders" (Lee, 2014, p. 197). Participation is an integral component of *hallyu* and the "K-drama addict" fan experience.

However, participation is not isolated to watching K-dramas and communicating with other fans. Participation includes consuming other aspects of Korean culture. Lee also (2014) confirms that K-Pop, and by extension K-Drama, "fandom is highly inter-media, cutting across film, TV drama, TV comedy show, pop music, online games, animation and characters. The fans' desire is not limited to a particular medium or genre but often seems overarching across different aspects of Korean popular culture, or 'anything Korean'" (p. 200). Part of being a "K-drama addict" and participating in K-drama fandom is expanding interest beyond K-dramas themselves and into other aspects of Korean culture. Therefore, K-drama addicts' participation in K-drama fandom extends to eating Korean food. Maryx, a K-drama fan, shares how her K-drama obsession extends to Korean cuisine in a post on the fan forums at Mydramalist.com (2011):

> When I watch dramas and movies one thing that's always fascinated me was the [K] orean cuisine that we see these characters chowing down [all] the time. Their food and the way they eat everything from the dishes, utensils, floor tables, side dishes, ramen pots and more.

Anyone else?

> There are two things I really want to try. One is kimchi, [be]cause it's just traditional. And the other is kimbap [be]cause it looks like [so] much fun. Of course there's other stuff, but those two are on the top of my list.
>
> Has anyone else tried or wants to try [K]orean food?
>
> p.s. even the ramy[u]n looks great [Maryx, 2011].

This post reveals two of the key themes of participatory fan culture and food in the "K-drama addict" experience. First is a very personal desire to find out for herself what the dishes she has seen onscreen taste like. Her own "list" of foods to try includes *kimchi* and *kimbap*. By expressing the desire to try these foods, she has moved her own personal fan experience away from passive reception and into active participation. Second is the invitation for other fans to share their experiences with Korean food. This invitation reinforces her membership in the "K-drama addict" fandom and strengthens the ties between her experiences and others'. In this case, finding out the flavors of Korean food is both a very personal experience to satisfy "curiosity" and a public demonstration of dedication to K-drama fandom. For Maryx, the pleasure of her fan experiences comes both from her experience and other fans'; the enjoyment of her fan identity is both personal and communal.

In fact, many fans' enjoyment of fandom is both highly personal and interconnected with other fans. Initially, many foreign fans are drawn into watching K-dramas because they represent a culture that is very different from their own while Korean K-drama fans' enjoyment comes from viewing characters whose fictional lives are very much like their own real lives. Chua (2008) explores the question "How does an audience watch/read an imported cultural drama series?" (p. 73). Although the article focuses mainly on an East-Asian audience viewing K-dramas, Chua's discussion of the audience's experience can be expanded to include foreign fans watching K-dramas around the globe. What Chua notes is that part of the attraction that K-dramas have for audiences outside of Korea is the "'foreignness' of the TV drama programme to the audience" (p. 74). This "foreignness" is both central to the audience's interest in these programs and the ways they experience them. The fact that K-dramas represent a culture that is not their own is what makes them interesting and pleasurable for fans outside of South Korea. For foreign fans, according to Chua, much of the pleasure of viewing these K-dramas comes from the push and pull between the familiar and the unfamiliar that the audience feels as they watch the action onscreen. Chua explains that the process of watching/reading the foreign program creates "a process of identification and distancing" (p. 79). Familiar elements within the program help the viewers consider the characters and situations are "like me/us" while unfamiliar elements within the program push the viewer to consider the characters and situations "unlike me/us" (p. 79). However, Chua declares, "in the case of watching/reading an imported programme [sic] this identification/distancing process is complicated by the audience's awareness of the foreignness of the [program] which raises hurdles to identification and facilitates distancing" (p. 79–80). In other words, the identification and distancing that takes place when the foreign audience views K-dramas can be a source of "pleasure," but it can also be a source of discomfort as the audience moves between seeing the characters onscreen as like themselves or as very different from themselves.

Forging Fandom by Finding Food

This leads to another aspect of K-drama fandom that can provide fans with pleasure: the fandom itself. The pleasure derived from participating in K-drama fandom is not unique to international fans; K-drama fans within South Korea also create fan networks and derive enjoyment from participating in fan culture with other fans. Oh (2015) explores the notion of "discursive consumption" among K-drama fans in South Korea (p. 133). According to Oh, discursive consumption of television dramas occurs when "viewers actively share the experiences of drama watching, discuss stories and characters, collaboratively create parody texts for amusement, collectively provide meals and presents to the production staff, and suggest hoped-for plots and endings" (p. 133). This "discursive consumption" means that "television dramas become a source of collective discussion, collaborative production of secondary texts, and interactions among people" as "audience groups virtually gather and create, share, and exchange ideas and pleasures from talking about television dramas" (p. 134). The "pleasure" comes not from simply watching the drama individually, but coming together with other fans to participate in watching the drama and creating the fandom. International fans of K-dramas also experience pleasure from participatory fan culture. "Through spaces of social network services," writes Lee (2015), "fans of Korean TV dramas around the world set up online fan communities and share their knowledge, affections, and translations with other members, no matter what their nationalities are" (p. 183). This phenomenon is what Baym (2000) has identified as the "pleasures of collaborative interpretation" (p. 93). For Baym, fandom is both personal and public. Examining soap opera fandoms, Baym noted that

> one core practice in interpreting the soap is personalization, whereby viewers make the shows personally meaningful. They do this by putting themselves in the drama and identifying with its situations and characters. They also bring the drama into their own lives and making sense of the story in terms of the norms by which they make sense of their own experiences [p. 71].

Another aspect of fandom, however, is moving beyond the personal and into public participation in the fandom. Fans do this by sharing information about and interpretations of the program with other fans. Merging personal enjoyment with public participation enhances the pleasure of the fan experience. This means that, as K-drama fans move further away from passive viewing and closer to active participation in fandom as "K-drama addicts," the sense of "foreignness" or "exoticism" that once made K-dramas attractive may be replaced with the desire to become more personally involved with the object of their obsession. That is why "K-drama addicts" yearn to incorporate aspects of Korean culture, like music, food, and clothes, into their own lives and then share those experiences with other fans.

Food is one of the aspects of K-dramas that can increase the distance between the fans' lives and the lives of the characters for foreign K-drama fans. While the foreign fan may identify the gusto with which a character on a K-drama wolfs down a bowl of *bibimbap* after a bad day, the actual taste of the bowl of rice mixed with various ingredients and a spicy red condiment remains unfamiliar and reinforces that the fan is "not like" the character onscreen. Closing the distance between the character onscreen and the fan's own experiences by actually eating *bibimbap* is one of the cornerstones of the "K-drama addict" fan experience. The super-fan is able to show their dedication to K-dramas by making the unfamiliar dish part of their familiar repertoire of dishes and gain pleasure from making the personal experience of eating Korean food part of their public fan activity. For example, Auch (2015), a K-drama addict, begins sharing her experience of trying *bibimbap* on her blog, *The Ahjummas: Asian drama blog and reviews*:

> So let's pretend you're a [K]-drama character. Something has gone horribly wrong in your life, and all those looming catastrophes have finally come crashing down on your head. THE PLOT CONFLICT HURTS.
>
> What do you do? If you were American, you might go for the tub of ice cream. But if you're a [K]-drama character you grab...
>
> Bibimbap! Of course you do."

The opening to Auch's blog post makes the push and pull of the "like me" and "not like me" continuum clear. As an American viewer of K-dramas, she identifies with the emotions that the characters onscreen feel after having a bad day; in that way, she is "like them." However, as an American, her instinct would be to soothe her feelings with ice cream while K-drama characters reach for something unfamiliar: *bibimbap*. To close the gap between her own experiences and the experiences of the K-drama characters to make herself more "like them" and be able to "pretend" to be a K-drama character better, Auch needs know what *bibimbap* tastes like by eating it herself. And that is exactly what she did: "I've been curious about how this stuff tastes ... because honestly, it looks amazing. It's all moist and chewy, and you can grab giant spoonfuls of it to drown your problems" (2015).

To ensure she has the "real" bibimbap experience, Auch consults with a Korean friend named San and finds just the right ingredients. Auch explains, "The important thing you need—if you can find it—is the sauce that makes it that orange color. [Gochujang]. I just happened to find it at a pricey market near my house, so we were good to go" (2015). For Auch, the experience of mixing up the ingredients and eating real *bibimbap* just like she saw onscreen exceeded her expectations. Auch declares:

> After we mixed it all up, it looked exactly like the bibimbap I saw in dramas. And man was it GOOD. Better than I imagined, actually. It's really fresh (depending on the ingredients of your choice of course. Bibimbap just means mixed rice, so if you throw goldfish and doritos in there it probably won't taste the same. Fair warning.), and the spicy go ju jang sauce gave it the perfect kick of heat. I will definitely be making this again very soon!! [2015].

This experience of making and eating *bibimbap* fulfilled two desires for Auch. First, she was able to satisfy her curiosity and discover exactly what *bibimbap* tastes like. Second, she was able to recreate the experience that she had only viewed onscreen previously: K-drama fantasy became lived reality. This means in the future, she can watch her favorite K-dramas and relate to the characters on a more personal level. By eating *bibimbap*, Auch has become a little bit more "like them" and can not only understand the emotions that would drive a K-drama character to eat *bibimbap*, but also recall the spicy kick of the *gochujang* sauce tickling her own taste buds.

Seeking opportunities to eat Korean food and discover their taste serves as a new twist on what folklorist Long (2004) identifies as "culinary tourism" (p. 21). According to Long, culinary tourism is "the intentional, exploratory participation in the foodways of an other—participation including the consumption, preparation, and presentation of a food item, cuisine, or eating style considered to belong to a culinary system not one's own" (p. 21). The twist is that, while culinary tourism represents the exploration of "an other," the international K-drama fan is aware of being "the other" themselves. South-Korean media corporations produce K-dramas initially for Korean audiences in South Korea and diaspora. While these companies may have an awareness of *hallyu* and the possible profit earned through a global audience, many of these products are developed firstly with domestic consumption in mind. This means that international audiences viewing K-dramas can be fully aware that they are not part of the intended viewing audience and the culture represented onscreen is not their own.

As Chua noted, this sense of the "foreignness" of the television program, or, in other words, awareness of their own "otherness," is one of the key factors that draws in audiences from outside of South Korea to K-dramas. However, the push and pull of "foreignness" is not the only determining factor in drawing an international audience to K-dramas. Sexton (2017) warns against understanding international fans' attraction to foreign cult films based on their "exoticness." Sexton notes that much of the research surrounding "transnational cult cinema" has focused on "how non–Western cult films are celebrated by fans from Western locations, with many scholars focusing on the ways that the cultists' love of such films arises from a dubious process of exoticization" (p. 5). However, for Sexton, this represents "a problematic tendency amongst some to *assume* that fans are drawn to films from other regions largely because of their exotic qualities, and to assume that exoticism is always negative regardless of the context" (p. 6). While Sexton concedes that "difference" may play a factor in drawing Western fans to non–Western cult films, "familiarity" may also be a factor: familiarity both with elements onscreen that are like themselves and familiarity with the common tropes within the genre itself (p. 11). Moreover, some of the attraction may also grow from curiosity that creates a desire to learn more about the culture of origin. Drawing on the work of Leon Hunt, to explore the appeal of Hong Kong's films to non–Western audience, Sexton explains, "The films can thus act, for some fans, as a means to discover more about different cultural traditions. In this sense, rather than retaining a neo-imperialist, distanced relation to the texts, these fans use the films as a means of moving closer to the cultural terrain that fascinates them" (p. 14).

It is this drive to learn more about a different culture, and adopt those cultural elements in their own lives, that K-drama addicts share with Western fans of non–Western cult cinema. For many K-drama addicts, the pleasure is not simply in viewing television programs that show a different way of life. The enjoyment comes from shifting their perspectives from unfamiliarity to familiarity. They may fall in love with K-dramas at first because they are foreign, but they become "K-drama addicts" because they want to know more about South Korea and become more South Korean themselves.

Lee (2014) notes many transnational fans of K-dramas are "cultural consumers who deeply admire and feel attached to particular cultural and media texts to the level where their affection for the text plays a determinant role in shaping their identities and ways of life" (p. 196). These fans expand their fan experience to other aspects of Korean culture because they "feel attached" to that culture and want to incorporate more of its products into their individual lives and identities. This means that their "culinary tourism" of trying Korean food for themselves is not simply about eating Korean cuisine as an exploration of "an other," but becomes an effort to enhance familiarity with Korean cuisine so that they are themselves less of "an other" when compared to the characters in the K-dramas they watch.

Moving from a Real Korean Meal to a Taste of K-Dramaland

In fact, in many ways, K-drama fans' searching for a taste of the foods they see in K-dramas are not actually searching for a real Korean meal. Instead, they are looking for a real "K-drama" meal. Schulze (2013) argues that many foreign fans do not necessarily attempt to understand what they see onscreen as authentically Korean, but define the unfamiliar in terms of the patterns of K-dramas themselves. Schulze reveals that fans "often explain the happenings in K-Dramas by making reference to K-Dramaland—an emic term that refers to an imagined world created through the collective activity of the writers, directors, actors, and viewers of K-Dramas—and not to 'Korean culture' or 'society'" (p. 373). Certain patterns, or "narrative tropes" or "clichés," recur again and again in K-dramas and, for fans, these patterns make up "K-Dramaland" (p. 377). Schulze notes, "Happenings in K-Dramaland are then often explained exactly with these clichés or laws. A character's behavior is understood according to the way K-Dramaland rules require him/her to behave, or her/his reaction are questioned in the realm of K-Dramaland" (p. 378). According to Schulze, while some K-drama fans may take the leap and exclaim that what they see onscreen represents Korean culture as a whole, "most international fans don't want to risk defining what 'Korean culture' *is*. But what they know very well are the narrative tropes that constitute the K-drama genre" (p. 378). Therefore, it may not be assumed that every South Korean citizen chows down on a big bowl of *bibimbap* when upset, but it is a familiar sight in the realm "K-dramaland" and that onscreen experience is what many K-drama addicts want to recreate in their own lives by eating Korean food.

Therefore, what K-drama fans may be searching for is not a true taste of Korea, but the real flavor of K-Dramaland. As Kdrama Culture (2013) wrote on the fan blog, *The Problematic of the Unproblematic*, "Restaurants in Korean Dramas are as ubiquitous as the evil Mother-in-law. From humble to elegant, they can set the stage for either cute moments or disastrous scenes." These opening lines make the connection between K-drama tropes like the "evil mother in law" and K-drama food clear. This connection is reinforced in the description of "Street Food" in the body of the post. As the blogger notes, "This is probably everyone's favorite part—savory finger foods that just beg to be devoured while strolling your honey down Restaurant Row, or doing a bite-shot-bite-shot at your favorite p'macha, hand-held snacks can be some of the best local flavors you can find when you travel" (KDrama Culture, 2013). In this description, the goal of travel is not to experience authentic Korean cuisine by eating street foods on real Korean streets. Instead, the goal is to recreate the scenes from K-dramas. Seeing characters stroll hand-in-hand while exploring food stalls and other shops at the local market is a K-drama trope often used to demonstrate a budding romance. The image of a "bite-shot-bite-shot" would bring to mind many drama scenes in which a character sits in an outside food stall and eats a bite of food which is followed by a shot of *soju*, leading the character to get very drunk, often while nursing a broken heart (never fear, the romantic interest usually shows up with a taxi or piggy-back ride to make sure that their partner arrives home safely). In this case, eating these foods, even on the streets of Seoul, would help the K-drama addict recreate the fictional world of the dramas, not experiencing the real life of Korea.

Whether searching for a real Korean meal or hoping to sample K-drama cuisine, the experience of eating Korean food for foreign fans is often hampered by logistics. The difficulty of tasting real Korean food outside of Korea is illustrated by the cry for help from a K-drama fan living in Singapore. Posting on the message boards at Soompi, Mariemerong issues a cry for help in finding *jjajangmyeon*: "Ate it? Haven't and want to try? Knows where to buy? I've been searching for JiajangMyun (sic) since I watched Korean [d]ramas.

And I [l]ive in Singapore. And [y]et there isn't any sign of any here. Ate it before? What does it taste like? Do tell yeah. Any clue would be nice" (2008).

Other K-drama fans quickly responded. Cherishminx who commented the same day provides two of the most frequent strategies that K-drama addicts use to find the foods they crave: "[H]mm, for the instant type, you can get it at any of the [K]orean supermarts … or you can buy the black bean paste and cook it yourself. That[']s what I do, just cook the sauce, add some veggies and mix with Chinese noodles" (2008). Another respondent, Virvir1ll, reveals two other main strategies: "[I]f u want the jia jang myun from krn dramas. u have to go to korea [sic] for those stuff or a korean jia jia myun restaurant in the u.s. [errors in original]" (2008). These two responses illustrate strategies K-drama fans use to eat Korean food: cook at home, go to a restaurant, or visit Korea. Each choice differs in how much time and money must be spent to find and eat the food, the level of "authenticity" of the taste of the food consumed, and the amount of recognition that might be achieved within the fan community for the devotion displayed by that K-drama addict.

While cooking at home is an option, it can sometimes be difficult for foreign K-drama fans to find fresh ingredients. The only option for these fans may be to indulge in instant varieties. Ashling (2017) recounts her experience eating instant *jjajangmyeon* on her blog, *Adventures in Writing and Life*. Just like it occurs with other K-drama addicts, watching K-dramas made her curious about the tastes of the foods onscreen, but tasting *jjajangmyeon* proved daunting. Ashling exclaims, "It took me a long while to find out what exactly the noodles were and how to get them.… Basically the black bean noodles are everywhere in Korea, super common and easy to get (just as easy as pizza delivery). Not so abundant here in the states, unfortunately" (2017). Ashling rejected restaurant versions of *jjajangmyeon* because the dish contained onions, which ruined the flavor. Moreover, the noodles from scratch was "just way too complicated for someone who prefers mainly baking and slow-cooking things" (2017). Then, she discovered "instant powder mix" at the local Asian Market (2017). The option to use an instant mix met with Ashling's approval because the finished dish could be altered to suit her personal taste by omitting the onions and were not too much hard work. For Ashling, the fact that the noodles may not have tasted exactly the same as the fresh version was not as important as living the reality of eating the same food in the same way as the characters she had watched in her favorite K-dramas. Ashling declared, "The inner fangirl in me was squeeing the entire time. Look at those noodles. Seriously. They are messy, saucy heaven" (2017). Even though the ingredients in the dish had been altered to suit her personal preference, she was not concerned. The noodle dish "looked" right, which meant that she could enjoy them the same way that the characters on K-dramas did. "It was a dream for years and years, but that dream became dinner last night," Ashling concludes.

As a form of "culinary tourism," Ashling's exploration of *jjajangmyeon* was connected more to her view of K-Dramaland than of South Korea itself. She was happy to recreate the dish that looked like the one onscreen and had no concern that it did not taste the same as a more authentic homemade or restaurant version.

While Ashling may have been content to have the "real" K-drama experience without the "real" Korean taste, other K-drama addicts want the complete experience. This might mean cooking Korean food from scratch. Blogger hjlyon reveals that she is a K-drama fan and is "slightly obsessed with the Korean culture" ("About," 2014). Since her interest in K-dramas has moved beyond television programs, she has "started Korean lessons, cook[s] Korean dishes (as well as Thai, Japanese, Italian, American, etc.), and love[s] to share [her] obsession with friends" ("About," 2014). The key to her experience as a K-drama addict is trying to master onscreen dishes in her own kitchen. "I've been [in] love with Korean food since about day two of my drama addiction," hjlyon declares, "Since then, my kitchen has been used every weekend to try the next new recipe" ("Korean Recipes," 2015). Her dedication has meant not only making sure that "half my pantry [is] filled with foreign ingredients," but "learning how to read Hangul" in order "to be able to read the labels" ("Korean Recipes," 2015). For hjlyon, the most important part of the Korean recipe experience is making sure the flavor is right, and she chooses to make them "from-scratch" and not purchase pre-packaged or instant versions ("Korean Recipes," 2015). "Keep in mind," hjlyon writes, "…many of these things can be purchased at an Asian market. However, just like in America, these foods are so much tastier when homemade" ("Korean Recipes," 2015). While Ashling considered cooking *jjajangmyeon* from scratch as too difficult in favor of recreating the eating experience from her favorite dramas, it is the process of cooking Korean food herself through which hjlyon connects to the world of K-dramas. The recipe that hjlyon follows includes the same fresh ingredients, laborious preparation, and time-consuming cooking methods familiar in any Korean kitchen and, therefore, meets with her approval as a more authentic Korean meal.

The search for a real Korean meal sometimes makes K-drama addicts venture further than their own kitchens. For these fans, a Korean restaurant or food court might offer more authenticity than instant or from-scratch versions. Amanda, who blogged about her K-drama addiction at *Outside Seoul*, chronicled her own food adventure when she drove two hours to visit H Mart. "One of my favorite things about Kdrama," Amanda writes, "is how much attention it pays to the little details of life—how people eat, sleep, and even use the bathroom. Most shows leave me longing for more information, but as a resident of rural New England I haven't had much chance for reconnaissance" ("A Trip to Hmart: Stuff Edition," 2013). When she discovered that

H Mart, which "carries many of the things that appear in Korean dramas," was within driving distance of her home, Amanda decided that it was her best opportunity to experience the foods she had seen on K-dramas and had yet to find them anywhere else. Amanda explains,

> My local Korean restaurant carries only a few types of banchan, and the idea of making something at home that you've never had before seems weird to me. Even following a recipe, how do you know you did it right if you've never tried the finished product before? So of course I brought a cooler so I could get a bunch of things to try later. (Handily enough, Hmart provided bins of free ice that you could scoop into bags just for this purpose.) ["A Trip to Hmart: Stuff Edition," 2013].

Since her local Korean restaurant did not offer the wide array of choices she needed to discover the flavors from her favorite K-dramas, Amanda needed the authenticity of a Korean cook to know that the foods really tasted the way that they should. Wandering the aisles proved that Amanda's instinct had been right; visiting H Mart allowed her to bring what she had seen onscreen to life. First, she was able to see for herself that many of the items, such as the metal *ramyeon* pot that many K-drama characters use to make instant *ramyeon*, were actually real. Amanda reports, "During my travels, I spotted a number of drama curiosities that I've wondered about. It can be hard to be sure what's real and what has been crafted for television, but it seems that anything important enough to find its way into Hmart's limited space must be truly essential" ("A Trip to Hmart: Stuff Edition," 2013). In fact, the metal *ramyeon* pot is such an essential part of K-drama that she bought one for herself and confessed that she cooked *ramyeon* and ate it off the lid, just like many characters in K-dramas. "I did serve ramyun from it the other day," she writes, "and I swear that it really was tastier when eaten off the lid" ("A Trip to Hmart: Stuff Edition," 2013).

Most importantly, however, Amanda was able to finally try black bean noodles ("A Trip to Hmart: Eats Edition," 2013). Unfortunately, she accidentally tried "seafood black bean noodles" instead of the plain *jjajangmyeon*, but that was enough for her to feel like she had the real dish. Amanda reports, "I actually wanted the plain version of this dish that's shown in so many K-dramas, but an ordering fail meant this [seafood black bean noodles] is what I got. Not that I minded—it was savory, seafoody goodness with clams, squid, and several kinds of shrimp" ("A Trip to Hmart: Eats Edition," 2013). Amanda did not only enjoy the flavor of the meal, she also relished the experience of eating a similar type of dish to the ones she watched characters eat onscreen. Amanda exclaims,

> It also made me appreciate one of the most valuable chopstick techniques I've learned from dramas: the noodle grab. Because you're slurping up wiggly, saucy noodles rather than twirling them around a spoon, there can be some serious spatter issues when eating this kind of food with chopsticks. But if you use your chopsticks to grab

the noodles that dangle mid-slurp to steady them, things get a lot less messy ["A Trip to Hmart: Eats Edition," 2013].

By experiencing the seafood version of *jjajangmyeon* at the HMart food court, Amanda was able to bring her drama-viewing experience to life. She no longer needed to wonder what it felt like to eat sticky, saucy noodles. Due to her trip to HMart, she had the real experience for herself.

Perhaps, the most extreme quest for authentic flavor is when K-drama fans travel to South Korea, either on vacation, for study abroad, or to teach English. The phenomenon is so widespread that the official South Korean tourism agency offers "Themed Travel" packages, which include tours of popular K-drama filming locations ("Visit Korea," 2018). These types of drama-themed travel packages are designed to appeal to K-drama fans already enamored with South Korean culture, including Korean cuisine.

K-drama fan Jeanissi may have captured the sentiment of many K-drama addicts when she declared in a comment responding to Maryx's post on the MyDramaList Forums, "[Korean Food] is one of the main reasons I NEED to go to Korea. I want to eat my wat through the country! Why does almost EVERY drama have to show delicious food that makes me want to try every dish I see?" (2011). While a travelling to Korea might be too expensive for many K-drama fans, many aspire to take the journey and some are lucky enough to actually make the trip.

While Jeanissi may only dream of going to South Korea, that is exactly what the two Canadian bloggers from *Noonas over Forks* did in 2014, spending six days eating their way through Seoul, while exploring a variety of K-drama-related locations and other tourist attractions. The trip represented an exploration of Korean food and Korean culture as the two bloggers visited a wide array of famous Korean landmarks, such as Seoul Tower and the Demilitarized Zone, while satisfying their curiosity about Korean cuisine with meals ranging from simple *bibimbap* to *samgyetang*, traditional ginseng chicken soup. However, the pair discovered that, although they enjoyed their trip, the reality of traveling to Korea is much different from the fantasy of living in a K-drama. For example, the ginseng chicken soup was disappointing because it lacked flavor.

In fact, while many K-drama addicts find that sampling South Korean cuisine is a "dream" come true, some find unexpectedly unpalatable. The dishes that look delicious onscreen actually turn out to be disappointing or even disgusting in reality. Blogger waterrlilia shared her experience trying Korean food for the first time in a post on *Amino*. Visiting a Korean restaurant named Seoul Kitchen, this K-drama addict admitted that she was excited to try the food because "I'm obsessed with [S]outh [K]orea to be honest and the food in [K]orean dramas made me always curious how it would taste like" (2016). The experience was filled with surprises and unexpected flavors. For example, the appetizer was *misoguk*, which is "miso soup with tofu, seaweed and spring onions" (2016). While the soup was "tasty and a bit salty," waterrlilia reveals that she was "surprised by the taste" since it was her "first time trying tofu and seaweed" (2016). The main dish that she chose was *bibimbap*: the mixture of vegetables, egg, and rice included a hot pepper/chili sauce to mix in with the ingredients. Waterrlilia exclaims that after mixing the ingredients and taking the first bite, "it was a taste explosion in my mouth all ingredients mixed together, it was just awesome. I can't even describe in words how much I liked the dish" (2016). However, the experience also reinforced how different the flavors were from her usual fare. The spiciness of the foods available on the menu were very much outside her comfort zone. Therefore, she acknowledges that in order to really enjoy her next meal at the restaurant, she "probably should practice eating spicy things because most of the dishes on the menu were marked as spicy" (2016).

While waterrlilia ultimately enjoyed her Korean food adventure despite her aversion to spicy foods, some K-drama addicts find Korean food too different to be enjoyable. Responding to Mariemarong's inquiry about the flavor of *jjajangmyeon*, LiLLe divulged how her first and only time tasting it was "bleh." She claims it did not taste like barbecue, was a bit bland, and the noodles were chewy. She explains, "i had it once, i couldnt even finish the bowl before it started tasting bleh … it definately does not taste like barbeque … it tastes sort of bland and the noodles are very chewy. To me it only looks good on tv … but wouldn't mind some again, just not alot because i get tired of it fast [errors in original]." She told how they looked better on TV and may try them again, just not in large quantities (2008). LiLLe discovered that the thick, brown sauce looks rich and flavorful onscreen, but the reality is that the sauce can be bland for diners not used to the slimy texture. The reality did not live up to the flavor conjured up by her imagination.

Another K-drama addict, abbyinhallyuland, confesses that she does not really like South Korean food: "I think I'm weird but I'm not really a fan of some Korean food.… I love samgyupsal and japchae, but I was once traumatized when I ate bibimbap in Nami Island because I felt like I was eating grasses and leaves with spicy sauce … since then I go for the safe dishes" (2017). For this K-drama fan, even traveling to Nami Island in South Korea could not make the food meet the expectations built up from K-dramas. For this K-Drama fan, real Korean food was not "safe"—the foods that were "safe" were more in line with the foods that were familiar. Devonandcornwall, the original poster that abbyinhallyuland responded to, validated the idea that not all Korean food is palatable: "…I guess it could kind of feel like that, depending on what you put in your bibimbap! When I make it, I put pretty safe, American-like foods in it…" (2017). For K-drama fans who find real Korean food too spicy, too strong, or just too different for their taste, a real

Korean meal is just too "real." They may need to leave the food on the screen and enjoy eating the meal vicariously through the characters in their favorite K-dramas.

This clash between a fan's personal disappointment or dislike for the taste of Korean food and the fan's desire for approval from the wider K-drama fan community reveals the true nature of K-drama "culinary tourism." The physical experience of tasting real Korean food is not about the food itself. While the individual fan may quench their curiosity about the flavors of food shown in K-dramaland, the experience is just as much about the public display of the fan's belonging as part of the "K-drama addict" fandom. Consuming Korean food—even if they do not like the taste—can reap rewards for K-drama fans. "K-drama addicts" move from passive viewers to active participants and reaffirm their identity as a true fan and member of the fan community. Unknown flavors become familiar, drawing fans closer to the characters onscreen, making what was once unfamiliar and foreign something familiar and personal. At the same time, sharing stories about the adventures of searching for a real Korean (or K-Dramaland) meal unites fans. Hence, the "culinary tourism" of making K-Dramaland cuisine become real—whether through instant packets, from-scratch recipes, Korean restaurants, or travelling to Korea—helps K-drama addicts forge connections between the fans themselves, the K-dramas they adore, and the fandom in which they participate. For K-drama addicts, the successful search for real Korean food is about more than just the food; it is about the reinforcement of their individual identity as a super-fan; about forging connections as part of the wider fandom; and about growing a better understanding of the characters whose lives play out onscreen.

References

Amanda. (2013, April 30). A trip to Hmart: Stuff edition. [Blog post]. Retrieved from http://outsideseoul.blogspot.com/2013/04/a-trip-to-hmart-stuff-edition.html.

Amanda. (2013, May 2). A trip to Hmart: Eats edition. [Blog post]. Retrieved from http://outsideseoul.blogspot.com/2013/05/a-trip-to-hmart-eats-edition.html.

Ashling, S. (2017, April 6). Korean black bean noodles (jajangmyeon) and Kdramas. [Blog post]. Retrieved from https://seraashling.blogspot.com/2017/04/korean-black-bean-noodles-jajangmyeon.html.

Auch, A. (2015, January 30). Korean food—Bibimbap. [Blog post]. Retrieved from http://theahjummas.blogspot.com/2015/01/korean-food-bibimbap.html?m=1.

Baym, N.K. (2000). *Tune in, log on: Soaps, fandom, and online community.* Thousand Oaks, CA: SAGE Publications, Inc.

Belasco, W. (2008). *Food: The key concepts.* Oxford: Berg.

Cherishminx. (2008, August 18). Jia jang myun (Koreanblack bean noodles). [Online forum comment]. https://forums.soompi.com/en/topic/163275-jia-jang-myun-korean-black-bean-noodles/.

Choi, J. (2015). Hallyu versus Hally-hwa. In S. Lee & A.M. Nornes (Eds.), *Hallyu 2.0: The Korean Wave in the age of social media* (pp. 31–51). Ann Arbor: University of Michigan Press.

Chua, B.H. (2008). Structure of identification and distancing in watching East Asian television drama. In B.H. Chua & K. Iwabuchi (Eds.), *East Asian pop culture: Analysing the Korean Wave* (pp. 73–90). Hong Kong: Hong Kong University Press.

Devon. (2017, April 12). 5 foods all Kdrama fans want to try. [Blog post]. Retrieved from http://devoncornwallwrite.com/2017/04/12/5-foods-all-kdrama-fans-want-to-try.

Devonandcornwall. (2017, April 12). 5 foods all Kdrama fans want to try. [Blog post response]. Retrieved from http://devoncornwallwrite.com/2017/04/12/5-foods-all-kdrama-fans-want-to-try.

Hjlyon. (2014, January). About. [Blog post]. Retrieved from https://kdramaheidi.wordpress.com/about.

Hjlyon. (2015, December 1). Korean recipes. [Blog post]. Retrieved from https://kdramaheidi.wordpress.com/korean-recipes.

Janey. (2014, July 1). Help! I'm an addict: Side effects of Korean drama obsession. [Blog post]. Retrieved from http://www.asianfixations.com/2014/07/01/help-im-an-addict-side-effects-of-korean-drama-obsession/.

Javabeans. (2015, February 10). Healer: Episode 20 (Final). [Blog post]. Retrieved from http://www.dramabeans.com/2015/02/healer-episode-20-final.

Jeaniessi. (2011, April 26). Korean food. [Blog post]. Retrieved from https://mydramalist.com/discussions/general-korea-talk/100-korean-food?page=1.

Jenkins, H. (2006). *Convergence culture: Where old and new media collide*. New York: New York University Press.

Joynyash. (2006, June 16). 10 signs that you're a Kdrama addict. [Blog post]. Retrieved from https://aminoapps.com/c/k-drama/page/blog/10-signs-that-youre-a-kdrama-addict/6Pos_zujeBlEvj6a63vJ48owlqJ4xr.

Junggugeo Kaenada. (2014, September 19). Friday feature: Seoul searching days 1–3. [Blog post]. Retrieved from http://noonasoverforks.com/friday-feature-seoul-searching-days-1-3.

Junggugeo Kaenada. (2014, September 26). Friday feature: Seoul searching days 4–6. [Blog post]. Retrieved from http://noonasoverforks.com/friday-feature-seoul-searching-days-4–6.

KDrama culture: Restaurant food. (2013, February 27). [Blog post]. Retrieved from http://dr-myri-blog.blogspot.com/2013/02/kdrama-culture-restaurant-food.html?m=1.

Lee, H. (2014). Transnational cultural fandom. In L. Duits, K. Zwaan & S. Reijnders (Eds.), *The Ashgate research companion to fan cultures* (pp. 195–208). Burlington, VT: Ashgate Publishing Company.

Lee, S. (2015). From diaspora TV to social media: Korean TV dramas in America. In S. Lee & A.M. Nomes (Eds.), *Hallyu 2.0: The Korean Wave in the age of social media*. (pp. 171–191). Ann Arbor: University of Michigan Press.

LiLLe. (2008, August 19). Response to jia jang myun (Korean black bean noodles). [Online forum comment]. Retrieved from https://forums.soompi.com/en/topic/163275-jia-jang-myun-korean-black-bean-noodles.

Long, L. (2004). Culinary tourism: A folklorsitic perspective on eating and otherness. In L. Long (Ed.), *Culinary tourism* (pp. 20–50). Lexington: University Press of Kentucky.

Mariemerong. (2008, August 18). Jia jang myun (Korean black bean noodles). [Online forum comment]. Retrieved from https://forums.soompi.com/en/topic/163275-jia-jang-myun-korean-black-bean-noodles.

Mary-x. (2011, April 26). Korean food. [Online forum comment]. Retrieved from https://mydramalist.com/discussions/general-korea-talk/100-korean-food?page=1.

Oh, Y. (2015). The interactive nature of Korean TV dramas: Flexible texts, discursive consumption, and social media. In S. Lee & A.M. Nomes (Eds.), *Hallyu 2.0: The Korean Wave in the age of social media*. (pp. 133–153). Ann Arbor: University of Michigan Press.

Schulze, M. (2013 December). Korea vs. K-Dramaland: The culturalization of K-Dramas by international fans. *Acta Koreana*, *16*(2), 367–397.

Sexton, J. (2017). The allure of otherness: Transnational cult film fandom and the exoticist assumption. *Transnational Cinemas*, *8*(1), 5–19.

Virvirl11. (2008, November 30). Jia jang myun (Korean black bean noodles) [Online forum comment]. Retrieved from https://forums.soompi.com/en/topic/163275-jia-jang-myun-korean-black-bean-noodles.

Visit Korea. (2018). Themed travel: Filming locations. *Visit korea*. http://english.visitkorea.or.kr/enu/SI/SI_EN_3_4_2.jsp?sets=drama.

Waterrlilia. (2016, October 14). My Korean food experience. [Blog post]. Retrieved from https://aminoapps.com/c/k-drama/page/blog/my-korean-food-experience/lXGs_QugNWz0woNVw0Y3l7dmKZWJkRg.

Xin, L.W. (2017). Interlocking cultural relations between South Korea and its neighbouring countries. In L.P. Er & L.T. Wei (Eds.), *Politics, culture, and identities in East Asia: Integration and division* (pp. 77–86). Hackensack: World Scientific.

Desiring Asian Masculinities Through *Hallyu* Tourism

Min Joo Lee

They survive multiple car crashes, kidnappings, and even years of separation because their love for each other is that strong; this is a plot to the most popular Korean drama, *Descendants of the Sun (Taeyangui huye)* (2016). Not only did the drama create sensational fandom within Korea, but it was also popular beyond Korea. The drama has been exported to twenty seven countries including the United Kingdom, Italy, Germany, Sweden, Saudi Arabia, Iran, Cambodia, and the United States (Yoon, 2016). *Descendants of the Sun* is just one of many Korean dramas with transnational fandom; numerous dramas have garnered worldwide viewership via *hallyu*. Korean Creative Contents Agency (2014) estimated that more than 18 million *hallyu* fans regularly stream K-dramas online. They also noticed that these fans spend an average of ten hours a week watching these dramas, making them a considerable part of their everyday lives. Some viewers invest money and time into visiting Korea to experience the culture and drama-filming locations. Beginning in the early 21st century when *hallyu* started growing exponentially, international tourism to Korea increased three-fold from 62 million tourists in 2005 to more than 170 million tourists in 2016 (Choi & Kim, 2016). According to a survey conducted by the Korean Tourism Organization (2013), the tourists listed K-pop concerts and drama-filming locations as key reasons for visiting Korea.

Besides going to concerts and drama-filming locations, according to the research conducted for this essay, *hallyu* tourists also spend the rest of their time dating Korean men. The pool of *hallyu* tourists discussed in this essay are mostly white women in their late teens to early twenties from European or North-American countries. Official reports show the numerical outcomes of *hallyu* but not necessarily the emotions that drive the phenomenon. Analyzing *hallyu* through young female K-drama tourists' perspectives as case studies is important because it indicates that *hallyu* is not only a successful politico-economic phenomenon but also a transnational phenomenon of emotion in which romantic desires dictate the flow of money and people across geographical borders. By analyzing the romantic encounters between *hallyu* tourists and Korean men, the researcher argues that transnational media shapes female desire for "alternative" masculinities. The K-dramas concretize women viewers' desire for soft masculinity in opposition to what can only be identified as Western "macho" or aggressive masculinity. Therefore, Asian/Korean men—formerly maligned as emotionally and physically effeminate—become popular romantic partners for *hallyu* tourists for those exact same reasons; they and their soft masculinity become prized qualities by tourists due to the popularity of transnational media, in this case, K-dramas.

If femininity is a genre, soap operas and melodramas are the representative entertainments of such "feminine genre." Berlant (2008) argues that femininity is a genre created by patriarchal society and is perpetuated by women who participate in it. Here, genre is defined as "an aesthetic structure of affective expectation, an institution or formation that absorbs all kinds of small variations or modifications while promising that the persons transacting with it will experience the pleasure of encountering what they expected, with details varying the theme" (p. 3). Although highly critical of femininity as a genre, Berlant observes that the desire for participation in the genre of femininity comes from women who want a sense of belonging and acceptance. Soap operas and melodramas are perfect case studies of such genres as they provide the affective sense of acceptance that female viewers desire. Brunsdon (1997) states that soap operas carry ideas of a female spectator and operate with respect for women as audience while Modleski (2007) suggests soap operas have a feminine narrative form. Modleski connects the flow of soap operas to motherhood; the women viewers of soap operas are made to empathize with all the characters and are rendered helpless during altercations in the narrative similar to the positions of mothers when there is a dispute within the family. According to Kuhn (1999) "soaps and melodramas inscribe femininity in their address" (p. 230) because melodramatic and soap operatic narrative flows are similar to domestic activities of housewives. Though not necessarily escapist per se, these women's genres do provide a sense of escape and pleasure for the housewives (Ang & Couling, 1985). For example, the housewives use melodramatic texts to cross the boundaries between the "possible" and the "real"; they fantasize about the glamorous lives of drama heroines in order to temporarily forget their less-then-fortunate reality (Abelmann, 2003, p. 25). These seminal works on the relationship between housewives and soap operas contributed greatly to subverting social as well as academic stigma against such "low brow" women's entertainment.

However, the question arises: do K-dramas influence younger unmarried female viewers the same way they inspire middle-aged housewives? While K-dramas provide comfort and a sense of escape for housewives, the stories also inspire single young women's expectations for marriage and dating. A survey of nearly three hundred single university students reveals that viewing romantic television genres has a positive correlation to idealistic expectations of marriage and desire for marriage (Segrin & Nabi, 2002). In the case of K-dramas, both Japanese (Takeda, 2014) and Vietnamese (Vu & Lee, 2013) women have a more positive image of Korean men after viewing the dramas, seeing Korean men as eligible and ideal marriage partners. Creighton (2009) states "it is perhaps valid to state that Bae Yong-joon (Yonsama) has likely done more to contribute to positive relations between Japan and Korea than most of Japan's political leaders" (p. 16). This demonstrates how the soft masculinity of K-drama heroes has successfully garnered soft power for Korea as a nation in the Asian region, especially among Japanese and Vietnamese K-drama fans.

The concept of cultural proximity provides an important theoretical backdrop for explaining the *hallyu* phenomenon. Chua (2008) promotes the theory as a central framework for the circulation of popular media among Asian audiences. According to Chua, Asian audiences deal with foreign media from other parts of Asia by going back and forth between identifying with and distancing oneself from it. They identify with the Asian transnational media with the framework of "we are Asians" and distance themselves from it through their national identities. The reason K-dramas are successful in other Asian countries is because they are culturally proximate and share a sense of regional identity as Asians. As a case in point, Lin and Tong (2008) argues that Hong Kong and Singaporean women have shifted their interests from Japanese dramas to K-dramas because the former have become too westernized for the likings of Asian women. Lin and Tong claims the quality of "Asian us" in K-dramas is the reason for their transnational success. Furthermore, some researchers suggest Malaysian K-drama fans epitomize the unifying strength of the identity of Asian-ness; Malaysia, despite being a "Muslim Asia," enjoys K-dramas more than Western or Middle-Eastern dramas because the regionally shared identity of Asianness surpasses the differences between "Muslim Asia" and "Confucian Asia" (Hudson & Azalanshah, 2014). If cultural proximity is the reason for K-dramas' success within Asia, what are researchers to make of their success and wide fandom outside of Asia? Glynn and Kim (2014) discuss the example of *Jewel in the Palace* (*Dae jang geum*) from 2003 focusing on how it is extremely popular in Zimbabwe and Egypt (nations neither popularly nor academically considered a part of the "Asian us" framework) and urge for expansion of the academic scope of *hallyu* beyond Asia.

Analyzing *hallyu* outside of Asia is significant because it highlights the disparate intimate and romantic desires that propel the phenomenon. Researchers have observed in depth how Asian women perceive and desire Korean men; Chinese women sexualize male K-pop idols (Pease, 2009) and Singaporean women (Liew, Tay, Chan, & Xueli, 2011) as well as Japanese women (Creighton, 2009) desire Korean men based on their depiction in K-dramas. However, few studies exist on Western women's desires for Korean men. The studies that do analyze Western women's gaze towards Korean men observe the K-pop scene rather than K-dramas. Oh (2015) argues that the androgynous male dancing bodies of K-pop idols draw Western women's attention by going back and forth between images of "beast idols" and "flower boys."

Shin (2009) analyzes K-pop star Bi (Rain) and his failed attempts in Hollywood. According to Shin, Bi's masculinity, situated somewhere between pretty boyishness and macho laddishness, worked well in the Asian market, but was received poorly in the U.S. because it did not fit within Western masculine norms. Despite Bi's failure, K-pop idols have experienced their own success in the West: idol group EXO has garnered fandom around Europe; boy group BTS performed on the Grammys stage. However, the powerful masculine performances they purvey through their *kalgunmu* (perfectly-synchronized group dance) are different from the soft masculinity portrayed by K-drama heroes. Therefore, K-dramas, and their depiction of Korean men will be the primary focus of this essay. More specifically, this essay will look at how Western *hallyu* tourists' intimate desires are influenced by the image of Korean soft masculinity they see in the K-dramas.

Soft masculinity has been academically considered an alternative or nonhegemonic masculinity. With different terminology, scholarship on masculinity has observed the emergence of such nonhegemonic masculinities. Coles (2008) uses "soft masculinity" to describe a type of masculinity in which men "desire to express themselves emotionally and did not see this as being in any way effeminate" (p. 241). The study of soft masculinity has especially been prevalent in research on East-Asian masculinity. For instance, Louie (2012) analyzes the emergence of "pan-East Asian soft masculinity," pointing out that in the past few years, East Asian countries have experienced a massive popularity of soft masculinity, in which Asian women consume and create images of effeminate and girly men. In a detailed analysis, Charlebois (2013) highlights the rise of Japanese "herbivore masculinity." The men who embody the so-called "herbivore masculinity" physically groom themselves, form tight friendships with women, remain single, and are sexually passive to the point of never pursuing physical intimacy with women. In the case of Korean men, nonhegemonic or soft masculinity is equated with the term *kkonminam*[1] (flower boy) because of their pretty-boyish appearance, and effeminacy is a key component of such alternative masculinity (Jung, 2006; Maliangkay, 2013). These definitions highlight the traits of soft masculinity in non-romantic settings because men with soft masculine characteristics, as Charlebois (2013) notes, are not particularly active in the heterosexual romantic and sexual realm; they are basically considered honorary women. However, this essay will use the term "soft masculinity" in the context of heterosexual romantic desires. Soft masculinity, as it is used in this essay, is a term which describes men who make women's romantic dreams come true: they are emotionally expressive, sexually competent but not demanding, and all the while possess the "masculine" physical strengths to save women in peril.

Researching Western *hallyu* fans' desire for Korean men and the representation of masculinity in K-dramas is important because it epitomizes the K-drama's profound impact on the formation of transnational intimacies. Ong (1999) states that transnationality is a "condition of cultural interconnectedness and mobility across space" (p. 4). In particular, Yang (1997) argues that media is foundational in expanding such transnationality because it allows audience to travel without physically moving. Furthermore, Mankekar and Schein (2013) suggest that transnational media helps to refashion the cartographies of desire. According to them, desire is usually bounded to a place the person lives because one desires what one can see and consume. However, transnational media, especially transnational television, brings materials for consumption from afar. Through those images, the viewers come to desire transnationally rather than setting the boundaries of their desires within their physical locale.

From Appadurai's (1996) concept, transnational media creates "mediascapes" which influence the viewer's life. Creating mediascapes is one's ability to disseminate image-focused information to the world. Through such visual information, "the line between the realistic and the fictional landscapes they [the audience] see are blurred" (Appadurai, 1996, p. 35). What Appadurai means by this is that the farther the audience is from the origin of the transnational media they are consuming, the more likely they would create imagined worlds based on such images of the places that they have not experienced. Such is the case with U.S. women who fantasize about Asia after consuming the popular novel and film, *Memoirs of a Geisha* (Allison, 2013). They have never been to Japan and thus base their imaginations of Japanese realities on such fictional media. The slimmer the chance of actually experiencing the culture portrayed in the media, the more likely the imagined worlds take on an aura of reality for viewers. In such ways, transnational media creates imagined lives and imagined worlds for viewers that lead to transnational affective intimacy. However, as opposed to Yang's (1997) and Appadurai's (1996) argument that transnational media "substitutes" for actual physical movement across geographical boundaries, the researcher argues that transnational media, in this case K-dramas, "facilitate" transnational connections not just affectively but also physically. *Hallyu* fans, especially the young and mobile females, are not just satisfied with imagining worlds through images on K-dramas; they physically move as tourists to Korea to make their imaginations and desires a reality.

Since *hallyu* tourists predominantly hail from other Asian countries, academic research has also focused on Asian tourists and their desires. Han and Lee (2008) researched Japanese fans-turned-tourists due to the influence of the drama, *Winter Sonata* (*Gyeoul yeonga*). Kim (2010) also analyzed tourism as a result of *Winter Sonata* and focused his research on Nami Island, a place that appeared in the drama. The drama which started *hallyu* tourism in the early 21st century has now become less influential compared to more recent dramas like *My Love from the Star* (*Byeoreseo on geudae*) (2013), *Descendants of the Sun* (*Taeyangui huye*) (2016), and *Guardian: The Lonely and Great God* (*Sseulsseulhago challanhasin—Dokkaebi*) (2016) as motivators of *hallyu* tourism. Therefore, building on previous research, this essay not only expands *hallyu* studies to analyze non–Asian tourist desires and experiences in Korea but also references newer K-dramas as driving forces for *hallyu*-tourism. Through such comparative analysis, the research at hand will show how K-dramas configure transnational intimacies through women's desire for soft masculinity.

This research compares media with tourism and therefore utilizes two research methods: ethnographic field research and K-drama analyses. The first research method used for this paper is participant-observation and interviews. The researcher conducted field research during the summer of 2016 and for one year from July 2017 to June 2018. 123 *hallyu* tourists were recruited for this research; all of them participated in the interviews, and 50 also agreed to the participant-observation. The majority of the participants were heterosexual women in their late teens to early twenties. In addition to the 123 women who identified themselves as *hallyu* tourists, three men, who did not identify themselves as such but knew of K-dramas, also participated in the interview process. Among the total of 126 participants interviewed, with the exception of five participants, all of the participants were White tourists from Australia, Canada, Denmark, France, Germany, Russia, Sweden, Switzerland, Turkey, and the United States. Most of these *hallyu* tourists traveled to Korea alone or in a small group with one or two close friends who shared similar passions for K-dramas and Korean culture. For other non-*hallyu* tourists, Korea was just a short stop in their grand tour of Asia, but for the *hallyu* tourists Korea was the only destination in which they stayed for anywhere in between two weeks to three months depending on their economic situations. Furthermore, a significant number of the tourists were repeat-visitors to Korea, and at the time of the interview, they had already been to Korea two or more times and showed the desire to visit it again during their next school vacation.

To gain access to the *hallyu* tourists, the researcher stayed as a guest in hostels around Seoul mainly in Hongdae, Shinchon, and Gangnam where a majority of Seoul hostels are located. The duration of the stay in each hostel lasted from five days to two weeks during which the researcher recruited hostel guests as research participants and conducted interviews with the tourists who identified themselves as *hallyu* tourists. The researcher chose to stay in the guesthouses to build rapport with the tourists. Jennings (2005) emphasizes how important building rapport with the interviewees is, especially in conducting qualitative interviews: "The success of an interview depends on establishing rapport with the participant. This means that the interview time will need to include time to establish a social relationship, as well as trust and respect" (p. 107). Establishing affinity with tourists at the toured site during a limited time is difficult if not impossible; therefore, the researcher chose to stay in the hostels with the tourists to spend as much time as possible with them and bond with them. The interviews ranged from individual interviews to small group interviews depending on the schedules and preferences of the interviewees. Format-wise, the interviews were semi-structured revolving around questions of K-dramas and the tourists' dating lives at home and in Korea (See Appendix for interview questions). These sessions lasted between thirty minutes to several hours and usually occurred in the hostel living rooms, conducted in a mixture of English and Korean.

After the interviews, the researcher conducted participant-observation of some of the interviewees to compare interviews with actual activities. The researcher followed them to bars and clubs to observe which Korean men they were attracted to, how they approached Korean men, and how they interacted with each other including what conversations they had and whether they went on dates or just enjoyed casual hook-ups. Some interviews that began at cafes or hostels continued in these venues in between the participant-observations as the interviewees informed the researcher about their current feelings and desires (for Korean men) throughout the night. The data gathered through such participant observation was used in this research to buttress the contents of the interviews.

The second research method used was K-drama analyses. During the interviews with *hallyu* tourists, the one question that the researcher asked all the tourists was "What are some of your favorite or most memorable Korean television dramas?" Without exception, all of them listed one or a combination of these three dramas: *My Love from the Star* (*Byeoreseo on geudae*) (2013), *Descendants of the Sun* (*Taeyangui huye*) (2016), and *Guardian: The Lonely and Great God* (*Sseulsseulhago challanhasin—Dokkaebi*) (2016). All three dramas are romantic stories with different settings. *My Love from the Star* is a love story between a male alien (in the shape of a handsome Korean professor) and a top Korean actress while *Guardian: The Lonely and*

Great God is about a love story between a goblin (appearing in the shape of a handsome and rich Korean man) and a goblin's bride (a girl who sees ghosts). Finally, *Descendants of the Sun* is a love story between a Captain of the Korean army and a female doctor whose love life spans several years and multiple continents. Based on *hallyu* tourist preferences, the researcher conducted textual analyses of these three K-dramas with a focus on the male protagonists' romantic gestures towards the heroines. In this essay, the textual analyses of the dramas are juxtaposed with the data gathered from the *hallyu* tourists' interviews and participant-observations about dating Korean men. Through the comparisons between fictional tales and realities, the research shows how transnational K-dramas foster transnational intimacies through the appeal of Korean men's soft masculinity.

Parallels Between Korean Dramas and Tourism

The researcher finds three major themes that run throughout both K-dramas and the *hallyu* tourist interviews regarding Korean men. They are (1) being emotionally expressive, (2) being sexually and physically unimposing, and (3) being selfless and undemanding givers. Through these three qualities, *hallyu* tourists position Korean masculinity in opposition to aggressive masculinity of Western men. The following sections will compare K-drama scenes with *hallyu* tourists' responses in an effort to depict the complex ways in which intimate desires for Korean soft masculinity become shaped in between transnational media and reality.

Emotionally-Expressive Korean Men

Most heroes of K-dramas are not afraid to cry or to show their emotions. Alien Do Min-joon, the male protagonist of *My Love from the Star*, stares at the camera and tremors as if to withhold his sorrow (Episode 12). However, he is defeated by his emotions and begins to scrunch up his face and sheds copious amounts of tears while turning red in the face and shaking uncontrollably from sobbing. The scene continues without any lines, just showing alien Do's sorrow. It is just the beginning of many scenes of the protagonist crying while staring at the camera, alone, or in the company of his lover. Granted the heroine cries alongside the hero because their relationship is in peril due to the hero's identity as an alien. However, a rough count of the actual number and screening time of the crying scenes reveals that alien Do cries more than the heroine; he sheds tears in ten scenes while the heroine cries in nine scenes throughout the drama. He has only one reason for all the tears he shed: his love for the heroine, Cheon Song-yi. His display of emotionality is not because he is "weak" but because his love for the heroine overrides all social conventions that deem male emotionality as taboo.

Contrary to social stigma against male tears, the *hallyu* tourists express their desire for crying men. This discussion took place during an interview with four tourists: a man from the Netherlands and female *hallyu* tourists from Canada, France and Sweden. The male tourist from the Netherlands revealed, "I don't watch Korean dramas because I am afraid they will make me too emotional. I heard from my female friends that Korean dramas can make you cry. I don't want to cry. It is too … feminine, so I don't watch Korean dramas." A female *hallyu* tourist from Canada responded, "I don't think that is a good thing. Why are men so afraid to cry? Korean men cry all the time in the dramas. Being emotional is not a bad thing at all, but men think that crying and being emotional is not something men should do. It is ridiculous." A female *hallyu* tourist from Sweden added, "I agree being emotional is not a bad thing. It means you feel things. Sometimes, crying is better than holding it in." The interviewer asked, "So it doesn't turn you off? Men crying and being emotional?" The female *hallyu* tourist from France replied, "No, not for me. When I went on this one date with a Korean guy, he actually started crying saying how beautiful I am. I don't know why he was crying and I was worried but that didn't make me dislike him. I went on a few more dates with him afterwards and eventually it didn't work out between us but not because he cried." The man from the Netherlands who stated he did not watch Korean dramas was not a self-proclaimed *hallyu* tourist. However, he wanted to participate in the interviews because he knew a little about the dramas from hearing about it from his female friends back home. Echoing the popular social stigma against male emotionality, he resisted the entertainments that would make him break the taboo but the *hallyu* tourists encouraged him to let go of the "ridiculous" thought that men should not cry.

Ahmed (2014) states that "The fear of passivity is tied to the fear of emotionality, in which weakness is defined in terms of a tendency to be shaped by others" (p. 2). Being emotional is about being touched by others and being influenced by them; it signifies an intimate connection to others. The malleability of such prospect is fearful to some people; therefore, they push such vulnerable position of emotionality onto "others." Oftentimes, this dynamic is gendered whereby the "other" being deemed emotional are women while the ones pushing away from it are men. The male participant in the above interview stated that crying and being moved to tears by the dramas is "too feminine," pushing emotionality onto women. He refused to be moved by others and thereby refused to acknowledge that he is malleable to the influence of others. However, that is not the type of masculinity that *hallyu* tourists find desirable. They reference the Korean drama heroes as a case for why crying is nothing to be ashamed of. These signs of male emotionality are not a sign of weakness but a way of signifying their willingness to admit that they are influenced by and connected to others. Admitting one's intimate connection with others is the first step to creating the transnational affective intimacies which female *hallyu* tourists are seeking. From their perspective, Korean men who—from the way they are depicted in the dramas as emotional—are the perfect candidates to form such affective intimacies with the *hallyu* tourists.

The male protagonists in the dramas are not only tearfully expressive, they are even better emotional communicators when it comes to their romantic feelings. In *Descendants of the Sun*, the female protagonist, Dr. Kang Mo-yeon and the hero, Captain Yoo Shi-jin, have a quiet time alone after a disastrous earthquake. Captain Yoo said, "I missed you so much. I tried everything but whatever I do I could not stop thinking about you. I tried physical labor, drinking myself out of my mind and everything else possible but at the end of the day I still missed you. Is this confession unexpected for you? If so, then start thinking about it because that is the truth of how I feel about you" (Episode 7). Whenever they have a moment to talk to each other, Shi-jin always tells Mo-yeon how beautiful she is and how much he loves her. Similarly, Kim Shin, the hero of *Guardian: The Lonely and Great God*, tells the heroine, Ji Eun-tak, "Every moment I spent with you shined. Because the weather was good, because the weather was bad, and because the weather was good enough. I loved every moment that I spent with you" (Episode 6). When the drama aired, this line resonated with the viewers so much that it became one of the most frequently cited and parodied lines of the year among K-drama fans.

The heroes of these dramas are not afraid or embarrassed about expressing their romantic emotions truthfully and poetically. Masculinity is often dissociated with romance to the point where men who are "too romantic" are deemed foppish and effeminate (Giddens, 1992). Therefore, men are not completely opposed to romance; instead, men end up *using* romance. Based on Redman's (2001) research of romance among male students as well as one on the use of romantic rhetoric among rural Korean men (M. Kim, 2014), instead of it being an emotion that one "feels," romantic feelings become a tool that they "use" to validate their heteronormative patriarchal identities. Contrary to the results of such studies as well as the popular perception of masculinity and romance, K-drama heroes are not the type of men who "use" romance; instead, they "feel" it. It is not something used to prop up one's ego; instead, it becomes the emotional fodder for affective intimacy in which both women and men involved in such relationships are intimately feeling each other.

The *hallyu* tourists note how Korean men are more romantically expressive than men from other countries. A female French tourist said,

> When I first started dating Korean men I was really surprised because they kept saying stuff like "I miss you" and "I love you." I dated men from other countries like Japan and France and some other countries but none of them are as romantically

> expressive as Korean men. At first when you are dating Korean men, it feels just like dating a Korean drama male character because they are so cheesy. Even when we just met, they would call me up and say "I miss you" and always say "I love you."

At least in the beginning of the relationship, Korean men perfectly reflect their fictional images on K-dramas by being verbally expressive of their feelings towards the *hallyu* tourists. *Hallyu* female tourists essentially become heroines in their own romantic K-dramas through the Korean men's frequent utterance of "I love you" and "I miss you." A tourist from Germany said, "It was like having my own Korean television drama," in regards to dating her Korean boyfriend. For these *hallyu* tourists, love defines their transnational travel and hearing the "I love you" from the Korean men makes their travels worthwhile. Faier's (2007) research on Filipina migrant sex workers in Japan also points to how love defines Filipina transnational identities. These sex workers proclaim their love for their Japanese husbands. Here, the concept as well as the utterance of the word "love" is made meaningful through global processes; they generate new identities for the transnational subjects who are the Filipina sex workers in Japan. In this case, the women state their love for the men to justify their position in a foreign country as loving wives to their husbands. *Hallyu* tourists are similar in that their transnationality is defined by love. However, the primary difference is in that while the Filipina sex workers must proclaim their love to legally stay in Japan, the *hallyu* tourists are more privileged cosmopolitans who choose the rhetoric of love to define their identities. Love is not essential to their legal status in Korea, but they choose to seek it nonetheless. Furthermore, the tourists are recipients of love and the utterance of "I love you" instead of being the ones who need to proclaim the affects. As recipients of such statements, they become newly (if temporarily) identified as their own drama heroines. Their transnational travel is justified through it and transnational affective intimacy is formulated through soft masculine men who are willing to say those words to them every day throughout their relationships.

Sexually Unimposing and Undemanding Men

Many people travel to other countries to fulfill intimate desires that cannot be fulfilled at home. A whole genre of tourism exists called "sex tourism" or "romance tourism" in which people transnationally travel in order to become intimate with the "others" of their dreams. For instance, numerous scholars (Pruitt & LaFont, 1995; Taylor, 2001) analyze women tourists going to the Caribbean to have sex with local people who are stereotypically sexualized. Kelsky (1994) looks at Japanese women traveling to the U.S. to have sex with Western men and escape Japanese men's patriarchal treatment of women; Tornqvist (2012) studies women who travel to Argentina to fulfill intimate desires. Even though the research subjects in this paper are similar to participants in these studies in that they all travel abroad seeking ideal intimacy unfulfilled at home, they are fundamentally different in the type of transnational intimacy that they seek. While the women who go to the Caribbean or the U.S. are specifically seeking sexual intimacy, *hallyu* tourists who visit Korea want affective intimacy. In other words, while the former is transnationally connected through shared corporeal experiences, the latter desires emotions as the connecting thread between themselves and the Korean men.

Due to Korean broadcasting regulations, explicit sexuality is not permitted in K-dramas, which creates heroes less sexually inclined than ones in Western television shows. As a prime example, in *My Love from the Star*, the hero Do Min-joon has a medical condition preventing physical intimacy. Since he has a different immune system from humans, if he mixes bodily fluids with humans, he becomes ill. Due to his condition, for several hundred years on earth before he meets and falls in love with the heroine, alien Do does not even eat food at the same table as humans and resists all attempts by women to kiss him. His first kiss is with the heroine because she initiates the kiss. Alien Do carries drunk Cheon Song-yi into bed. The camera takes a close-up of the two as alien Do lovingly stares at Song-yi with one of his arms stuck behind her head. The camera takes an extreme close-up of his hand pinned behind her and cuts to a close-up of Song-yi's arms reaching behind alien Do's neck and pulling him towards her for a kiss (Episode 4). The hero initiates their second kiss, but in the aftermath of the kiss, he is more flustered than the heroine in part because of his physical condition, makes him sick, and in part because of his love for Song-yi (Episode 9). To show the different attitudes, after the kiss, the drama cuts to a split-screen of the hero and the heroine separately pondering the kiss in their bed. The bottom of the screen states, "one hour after the kiss" and "two hours after the kiss" to show the passing of time as well as a heart-rate monitor for the two protagonists. Over time, Song-yi falls asleep and regains a normal heartbeat; she snores and sleeps comfortably. On the other side of the split-screen, alien Do's heart rate keeps rising, and he sweats and grabs his heart until with a comedic "poof" sound, heart-rate monitors at the bottom of the screen show alien Do's heart rate bursting into flames. Thereafter, Song-yi is more enthusiastic about physical intimacy to the point where alien Do says, "What kind of a woman is this enthusiastic?!"

In K-dramas, Korean men are sexually unimposing to the point of being usurped by women as the ones with sexual and physical advantage. Similar to how they compare Korean men's emotional expressiveness with the emotionally-barren Western men, *hallyu* tourists compare Korean men's sexually unimposing and physically unintimidating attitudes with the masculinity and roughness of Western men. A female Swedish tourist stated,

> I like going to clubs in Asia and especially clubs that do not have many tourists. I am not saying they [Koreans] are weaker. but they … foreigners are more aggressive and rude. Even at home [Sweden], men do not take no for an answer so I had to actually punch some guys to get them to back off. I had my brother teach me how to fight so I won't get forced by guys back home.

Compared to "foreigners," Korean men are less physically intimidating especially when it comes to sexual situations. However, participant-observation has shown that is not always the case. The tourists occasionally experienced sexual harassment at the hands of Korean men. Multiple tourists disclosed that at clubs and bars, they have been forcibly grabbed by Korean men they had no desire to be intimate with. One *hallyu* tourist who went on a date with a Korean man even had bruised wrists by the time she returned to the hostel because he grabbed her too hard. However, the *hallyu* tourists, including the one who sustained the bruised wrist, maintained a firm belief that Korean men were much less sexually imposing than "rough and rude" Western men.

Elfving-Hwang (2011) analyzes, "For female viewers the *kkonminam* thus represent a 'safe' kind of masculine which does not threaten with violence or necessitate hierarchical submission" (p. 12). *Kkonminam* (flower boys) are men who are beautiful to the point of looking androgynous. Their relatively feminine appearances make them seem harmless in the tourists' eyes while being described as "weak." Even the bouts of aggression and the sexual inclinations they show towards the *hallyu* tourists were brushed off as insignificant incidents because the harmlessness and asexual character associated with *kkonminam* imagery makes the Korean men seem innately innocent.

In one case, a female *hallyu* tourist from Denmark expounded on the virtues of Korean men because the one man that she was interested in was willing to meet her despite being told that they could not have sex. She stated, "He came all the way and met me after work well past midnight. How sweet is that? Even though I told him we couldn't have sex he was willing to meet me. I think that shows that he is interested in me and not just my body." This could be because in the past decade, East Asian countries namely China, Korea, and Japan have experienced a rise in popularity of "soft males" (Louie, 2012). These men do not have traditionally manly characteristics like aggressiveness and sexual dominance, and thus do not treat women as mere sexual objects (Louie, 2012). Similar to the cultural proximity theory often used to explain the popularity of Korean pop culture in East Asia, Louie's analysis of women's desire for soft masculinity is explained through the shared identity of "CJK women," China, Japan, and Korea. This research reveals that such desires go far beyond the realms of "CJK women" to include women from the "Western" cultures as well. As indicated in the above interview, the "Western" *hallyu* tourist admired the "sweetness" of Korean men's gesture to care for and spend time with women who are not even sexually available. Ironically, the female Danish tourist stated that when they met, they had sex after all. Thus, it was not the actions that mattered in formulating the tourists' desire for transnational affective intimacy but the gesture itself which gave the tourist a sense of being valued for more than one's sexual availability.

Despite the *hallyu* tourists' remarks of how sexually unimposing the Korean men are and how they take women out on proper dates, based on the researcher's participant-observations, they have as many one-night stands as actual dates with Korean men. Therefore, what they mean by sexually unimposing and "timid" means that although the Korean men do not push or pressure the women into sex, the women do not consider Korean men to be sexually incompetent or asexual. When put to the task, the Korean men are sexually adept, but, like the Korean drama heroes, they do not make the romantic relationships all about physical intimacy; kissing and sex are seemingly afterthoughts for the "gentlemanly" Korean men who take the women out on "proper dates." The transnational affective intimacy that the *hallyu* tourists desire is not necessarily rooted in real experiences but instead on the television-inspired transnational imaginations of women which is so powerful as to sometimes override the real-life experiences with rough and sexual Korean masculinity.

Selfless and Undemanding Saviors and Givers

In all three dramas analyzed in this essay, the male protagonists save the heroine more than once and literally save the heroines from deadly harm. For example, in a key scene in *My Love from the Star*, the villain tries to kill Song-yi by drugging her and pushing her car over a cliff (Episode 7). Sensing that she is in danger, alien Do teleports and uses his body to prevent her car from going over the cliff. Before the incident, he was hiding his alien status from humans because nothing good would come out of revealing himself. However, in an effort to save her, he reveals his identity to the villain and even becomes injured in the process of blocking the speeding car with Song-yi in it with his body.

Captain Yoo Shi-jin in *Descendants of the Sun* not only saves Doctor Kang Mo-Yeon from falling over a cliff but also from a kidnapping. Mo-yeon is taken as a hostage by the villain, and Shi-jin defies commands from the military officials and goes to save her (Episode 12). "Trust me," he says to Mo-yeon, who is wearing a vest loaded with explosives with the villain holding a gun to her head. Shi-jin successfully kills the villains while covering Mo-yeon's eyes and then dismantles the bomb-vest to save her.

In *Guardian: The Lonely and Great God*, the gods tell Kim Shin (who is a demi-god himself) that if he does not die, then his lover, Eun-tak, will die in his place because their fates would not allow them to coexist. Eun-tak is the only one who can kill the hero, but she resists killing him because she loves him. However, in order to save Eun-tak, the hero makes her kill him while promising her that he would do everything in his godly powers to return from the dead and come back to her side (Episode 13). In this sense, the hero saves the heroine through his own death. The notable aspect of this themes of the hero saving the heroine is that the heroes do not ask for anything in return from the heroines; they are undemanding saviors who are just content with the mere existence and safety of the heroines. Alien Do, even when confronted by Song-yi, refuses to take credit for saving her (Episode 8). Both Captain Yoo and Kim Shin never even mention the fact that they saved the heroines let alone attempt to take credit for or get something in return for their efforts. Their sacrifices are purely motivated by their love for the heroines and demand no compensation.

In the *hallyu* tourists' narratives, a similar theme emerges of Korean men saving them from harm's way. Obviously the tourists' experiences of being saved are not as dramatic as that of the K-drama heroines (deadly situations do not happen as often in real life at it seems to in the dramas). Nonetheless, in the interviews with *hallyu* tourists, Korean men reflect the persona of the undemanding saviors similar to the drama heroes.

A female Canadian tourist said, "Foreigners are so rude. The other night, I was dancing at this club and one of them stuck their hand up my dress. This Korean guy saw it and made that f*cker get off me. He didn't even know me, like we weren't there together or anything like that but he saved me anyways." When the researcher asked about what had happened afterwards, the Canadian tourist replied, "Nothing. He didn't approach me or anything like that. He didn't have any alternative motive like thinking I was his. He just made sure the creep was gone, and he just went with his group of friends and had fun, and I went with my group of friends and had fun that was about it. They are gentlemen like that." Unfortunately, sexual harassment and assaults occur more in the clubs than ideally but in the interviews with the *hallyu* tourists, Korean men are portrayed not as the perpetrators but as the saviors from aggressive foreign men. The Korean men are not possessive nor are they demanding and thus they are "gentlemen." This notion is also linked to the previous theme of Korean men being sexually unimposing and undemanding.

By sexually not imposing their wishes on women even as a favor for saving their lives, Korean men become the type of men who do not treat sex as a currency; to them, sex is not something to be earned or bartered with. Based on such perception, Korean men value the physical intimacy and the women's affective desires driving those intimacies so they would not force their way with women. A female Swiss tourist recounted an incident in which a Korean man saved her from the unwanted sexual aggressions of a White man without demanding any sexual compensations of his own:

> One day, I was at a club dancing like this and really enjoying the music because I felt cute. But then I noticed this really big White guy staring at me from the side, and it was really creepy. I ignored him but he kept staring at me! And then all of a sudden, he comes up from behind me and starts grinding on me and trying to kiss me and touch my chest. I yelled that I have a boyfriend because if you say you have a boyfriend, those guys leave you alone. And I ran to the bar and grabbed this Korean guy and said he was my boyfriend. We did not know each other at all but he saved me. He put his arm on my shoulder and told the creepy guy to leave me alone and said I was his girlfriend. He asked me if I was ok. He was like a Korean drama actor! Such a gentleman!

When the researcher asked about what happened afterwards, the female Swiss tourist replied thusly:

> I go to that club a lot and he was there all the time too. When we see each other as a joke I would always say "My *namja chingu* (boyfriend)!" and he would smile at me and say "My girlfriend!" and buy me drinks. But he never tried touching me or sleeping with me. I actually wanted him because he was so handsome, but he wasn't like that. He was a real gentleman.

In these interviews, Korean men's actions are compared with that of the "foreign men" who are aggressive and sexual to the point of sexually harassing and assaulting the women. Korean men being aggressive and rough in real life as well as in the dramas during the process of saving the women is not a typical trait of soft masculinity which is marked by its "soft" attitudes. Nonetheless, such necessary roughness counts towards the appeal of Korean men because it is aggression aimed towards the ultimate villain whom the women would want to exact revenge against; it is not a force that would turn against the women.

Giddens (1992) states that the concept of "love" for heterosexual men is directly correlated with sexual access: "Men have tended to be 'specialists in love' only in respect of the techniques of seduction or conquest" (p. 60). This is not because men innately lack the ability to love but, as Giddens says, because gendered social upbringing prohibit men from developing emotional communications and connections. It creates a dynamic in which women want affective intimacies while men are unable to give it to them without linking it back to sexuality and sexual conquests. Therefore, even when men talk of romance and argue that they enjoy romance, in the same sentence they prevent themselves from sounding too romantic by using crude and nonchalant language (Allen, 2007). On the other hand, Korean men, from the *hallyu* tourists' perspective, have no sexual motives and are thus more accessible for affective intimacy than other men who cannot distinguish between the two. Hence, these tourists visit Korea from different parts of the world to create transnational affective intimacies with Korean men who, based on the portrayals in Korean dramas, appear to be more available for affective intimacies than other foreign men.

Conclusion

Through comparisons, this research has found three major themes that run throughout both the dramas and *hallyu* tourists' desires, which speak to the influence the dramas have on the formation of transnational intimacies between the tourists and Korean men. First, the K-dramas depict emotionally-expressive Korean men. The heroes cry as much if not more than the heroines. Echoing such depiction of soft "emotional" masculinity in the dramas, the *hallyu* tourists express a desire for men who have no qualms about crying or being "emotional" despite social stigma against male tears. Furthermore, in the K-dramas, the Korean men are unafraid of expressing their love towards the heroine. According to the tourists, dating Korean men in the beginning resembles dating a Korean drama hero because they constantly say "I love you" or "I miss you" to the tourists compared to men from other countries who, the tourists say based on their personal experiences, are not as affectionate. Second, the K-drama heroes are sexually unimposing; they prioritize emotional intimacy over physical intimacy. The tourists' description of Korean men they have dated also reflects the supposed sexually-unintimidating and "gentlemanly" soft masculinity of Korean men who do not push the tourists for sex. Third, within the K-dramas, the male characters become selfless saviors of the heroines. They save the heroines' lives multiple times within the fictional stories. Although real-life experiences of the *hallyu* tourists are not as dramatic as life-and-death situations that the drama heroines are put in, they nonetheless describe Korean men as saviors from macho masculine sexuality of "foreign men."

The study featured in this essay contributes to the study of *hallyu* in two ways. Numerous seminal *hallyu* studies focus primarily on Asian fans, while this study analyzes Western fans of K-dramas. While the research that focuses on Asian fans lean towards pan-Asianism as an explanation for the transnational success of K-dramas, the existence and the zeal of Western fans-turned tourists reveal that there might be something more to the appeals of K-dramas to transnational viewers than cultural proximity. Though it may be a factor in the exorbitant success of K-dramas around Asia, another huge factor of the drama's success is its truthful depiction of women's desires for a different kind of masculinity. *Hallyu* tourists make use of K-dramas to figure out what kind of qualities they desire in their future intimate partners.

The research also shows how K-dramas as transnational media create young cosmopolitan women who travel across half the globe to realize their romantic imaginations. The *hallyu* tourists desire a certain type of soft masculinity that they see in transnational K-dramas. The Western *hallyu* tourists travel across the world to Korea in order to experience the men of their dreams. They derive ultimate romantic satisfaction when the images of Korean men in the K-dramas match their own experiences as tourists. In essence, this essay shows the profound impact of K-dramas in formulating transnational intimacies across different cultural backgrounds of the *hallyu* tourists and Korean men. From within such transnational intimacies, the tourists navigate in between the ideal soft masculinity of fictional drama heroes and their personal experiences of dating Korean men in order to define an alternative masculinity to that of romantically unsatisfying masculinity back home.

Appendix

A list of interview questions

1. Do you watch Korean dramas?
2. Which drama did you watch most recently?
3. What is your all-time favorite Korean drama? Why?
4. What do you like about Korean dramas? Why do you watch them?
5. Why did you decide to visit Korea?
6. How long are you planning on staying in Korea?
7. What do you hope to do during your time in Korea? What have you done so far?
8. Have you dated Korean men before?
9. Have you gone on dates with Korean men while in Korea?
10. What did you think of the experience of dating Korean men? What do you think of Korean men?
11. What did you think of Korean men before you dated them? Did you have any preconceived thoughts about them?
12. Are Korean men different from men of other nationalities? If so, how are they different?
13. How do Korean men in real life compare to the depiction of them in the dramas?

These questions were simply used as the basic frameworks of the semi-structured interviews. Depending on the interviewees' willingness to respond to each question, some of the questions from the above list were excluded while other questions were added on a case-by-case basis.

Note

1. For more on this issue, refer to Sofia Murell's essay in this book.

References

Abelmann, N. (2003). The melodrama of mobility: Women, talk, and class in contemporary South Korea. Honolulu: University of Hawai'i Press.

Ahmed, S. (2014). *Cultural politics of emotion*. Edinburgh, UK: Edinburgh University Press.

Allen, L. (2007). "Sensitive and real macho all at the same time": Young heterosexual men and romance. *Men and Masculinities, 10* (2), 137–152.

Allison, A. (2013). American geishas and Oriental/ist fantasies. In P. Mankekar & L. Schein (Eds.), *Media, erotics, and transnational Asia* (pp. 297–322). Durham, NC: Duke University Press.

Ang, I., & Couling, D. (1985). Watching Dallas: Soap opera and the melodramatic imagination. New York: Routledge.

Appadurai, A. (1996). *Modernity at large: Cultural dimensions of globalization.* Minneapolis: University of Minnesota Press.

Berlant, L. (2008). The female complaint: The unfinished business of sentimentality in American culture. Durham, NC: Duke University Press.

Brunsdon, C. (1997). Screen tastes: Soap opera to satellite dishes. London: Routledge.

Charlebois, J. (2013). Herbivore masculinity as an oppositional form of masculinity. *Culture, Society and Masculinities, 5*(1), 89.

Choi, S., & Kim, C. (2016, November 22). Oegugin 1700manmyeongi Hanguge … olhae sasangchoedae (17 million foreigners visit Korea.… The largest number in Korean tourism history). *Chosun Biz.* Retrieved from http://biz.chosun.com/site/data/html_dir/2016/11/22/2016112200213.html.

Chua, B.H. (2008). Structure of identification and distancing in watching East Asian television drama. In B.H. Chua & K. Iwabuchi (Eds.), *East Asian pop culture: Analysing the Korean Wave* (pp. 73–90). Hong Kong: Hong Kong University Press.

Coles, T. (2008). Finding space in the field of masculinity: Lived experiences of men's masculinities. *Journal of Sociology, 44*(3), 233–248.

Creighton, M. (2009). Japanese surfing the Korean Wave: Drama tourism, nationalism, and gender via ethnic eroticisms. *Southeast Review of Asian Studies, 31*, 10–38.

Elfving-Hwang, J. (2011). *Not so soft after all: Kkonminam masculinities in contemporary South Korean popular culture.* Paper presented at the 7th Korean Studies Association of Australia Biennial Conference, University of New South Wales, Sydney, Australia. Retrieved from https://www.academia.edu/22503546/Not_So_Soft_After_All_Kkonminam_Masculinities_in_Contemporary_South_Korean_Popular_Culture.

Faier, L. (2007). Filipina migrants in rural Japan and their professions of love. *American Ethnologist, 34*(1), 148–162.

Giddens, A. (1992). The transformation of intimacy: Sexuality, love and eroticism in modern societies. Stanford, CA: Stanford University Press.

Glynn, B. (2014). Approximating cultural proximity and accentuating cultural difference: Cross-border transformations in Asian television drama. In J. Kim (Ed.), *Reading Asian television drama: Crossing borders and breaking boundaries* (pp. 47–74). New York: IB Tauris.

Han, H.J., & Lee, J.S. (2008). A study on the KBS TV drama Winter Sonata and its impact on Korea's Hallyu tourism development. *Journal of Travel & Tourism Marketing, 24*(2–3), 115–126.

Hudson, C., & Azalanshah, M. (2014). Women and television in Malaysia: Soaps, transnational pleasure and modernity. In J. Kim (Ed.), *Reading Asian television drama: Crossing borders and breaking boundaries* (pp. 125–146). New York: IB Tauris.

Jennings, G.R. (2005). 9 Interviewing techniques. In B.W. Ritchie, P. Burns, & C. Palmer (Eds.), *Tourism research methods* (pp. 99–118). Cambridge: CABI.

Jung, S. (2006). Bae Yong-joon, hybrid masculinity & the counter-coeval desire of Japanese female fans. *Particip@tions, 3*(2). Retrieved from http://www.participations.org/volume%203/issue%202%20-%20special/3_02_jung.html.

Kelsky, K. (1994). Intimate ideologies: Transnational theory and Japan's "Yellow Cab." *Public Culture, 6*(3), 465–478.

Kim, E. (Writer). (2016). Sseulsseulhago chanlanhasin—Dokkaebi (Guardian: The Lonely and Great God) [Television broadcast]. In E.-b. Lee (Producer). Seoul, South Korea: tvN.

Kim, E., & Kim, W. (Writers). (2016). Taeyang-ui huye (Descendants of the Sun) [Television broadcast]. In E.-b. Lee & S.-h. Baek (Producer). Seoul, South Korea: KBS.

Kim, M. (2014). South Korean rural husbands, compensatory masculinity, and international marriage. *Journal of Korean Studies, 19*(2), 291–325.

Kim, S. (2010). Extraordinary experience: Re-enacting and photographing at screen tourism locations. *Tourism and Hospitality Planning & Development, 7*(1), 59–75.

KOCCA. (2014). Miguk hangukkontencheu miguk sobijajosa-deurama gyeolgwa yoyak (14nyeon 22ho) (U.S. Korean content consumer research result–Drama result summary). Retrieved from http://www.kocca.kr/cop/bbs/view/B0000153/1824479.do?searchCnd=&searchWrd=&cateTp1=&cateTp2=&useAt=&menuNo=200911&categorys=0&subcate=0&cateCode=&type=&instNo=0&questionTp=&uf_Setting=&recovery=&option1=&option2=&categoryCOM062=&categoryCOM063=&categoryCOM208=&categoryInst=&morePage=&pageIndex=4#.

Korea Tourism Organization. (2013). Hallyugwangwangsijang josayeongu (Korea tourism market research). Retrieved from http://kto.visitkorea.or.kr/kor/notice/data/report/org/board/view.kto?id=421648&rnum=2.

Kuhn, A. (1999). Women's genres: Melodrama, soap opera and theory. In S. Thornham (Ed.), *Feminist film theory : A reader* (pp. 146, 156). New York: New York University Press.

Liew, K.K., Tay, J., Chan, B., & Xueli, W. (2011). Of Prince Charming and male chauvinist pigs: Singaporean female viewers and the dream-world of Korean television dramas. *International Journal of Cultural Studies, 14*(3), 291–305.

Lin, A., & Tong, A. (2008). Re-imagining a cosmopolitan 'Asian us': Korean media flows and imaginaries of Asian modern femininities. In C.B. Huat & K. Iwabuchi (Eds.), *East Asian pop culture: Analysing the Korean Wave* (pp. 91–126). Hong Kong: Hong Kong University Press.

Louie, K. (2012). Popular culture and masculinity ideals in East Asia, with special reference to China. *The Journal of Asian Studies, 71*(4), 929–943.

Maliangkay, R. (2013). Catering to the female gaze: The semiotics of masculinity in Korean advertising. *Situations, 7*(1).

Mankekar, P., & Schein, L. (2013). Mediation and transmediations: Erotics, sociality, and "Asia." In P. Mankekar & L. Schein (Eds.), *Media, erotics, and transnational Asia* (pp. 1–32). Durham, NC: Duke University Press.

Modleski, T. (2007). The search for tomorrow in today's soap operas: Notes on a feminine narrative form. In C. Brunsdon, and L. Spigel (Eds.), *Feminist television criticism: A reader* (pp. 29–40). New York: McGraw-Hill Education.

Oh, C. (2015). Queering spectatorship in K-pop: The androgynous male dancing body and western female fandom. *The Journal of Fandom Studies, 3*(1), 59–78.

Ong, A. (1999). Flexible citizenship: The cultural logics of transnationality. Durham, NC: Duke University Press.

Park, J. (Writer). (2013). Byeoreseo on geudae (My Love from the Star) [Television broadcast]. In T. Jang (Producer). Seoul, South Korea: SBS.

Pease, R. (2009). Korean pop music in China: Nationalism, authenticity, and gender. In C. Berry, N. Liscutin, & J.D. Mackintosh (Eds.), *Cultural studies and cultural industries in Northeast Asia: What a difference a region makes* (pp. 151–168). Hong Kong: Hong Kong University Press.

Pruitt, D., & LaFont, S. (1995). For love and money: romance tourism in Jamaica. *Annals of Tourism Research, 22*(2), 422–440.

Redman, P. (2001). The discipline of love: Negotiation and regulation in boys' performance of a romance-based heterosexual masculinity. *Men and Masculinities, 4*(2), 186–200.

Segrin, C., & Nabi, R.L. (2002). Does television viewing cultivate unrealistic expectations about marriage? *Journal of Communication, 52*(2), 247–263.

Shin, H. (2009). Have you ever seen the Rain? And who'll stop the Rain?: The globalizing project of Korean pop (K-pop). *Inter-Asia Cultural Studies, 10*(4), 507–523.

Takeda, A. (2014). Japanese-Korean international marriages through the Korean Wave in Japan. In V. Marinescu (Ed.), *The global impact of South Korean popular culture: Hallyu unbound* (pp. 35–46). Lanham, MD: Lexington Books.

Taylor, J.S. (2001). Dollars are a girl's best friend? Female tourists' sexual behaviour in the Caribbean. *Sociology, 35*(3), 749–764.

Törnqvist, M. (2012). Troubling romance tourism: sex, gender and class inside the Argentinean tango clubs. *Feminist Review, 102*(1), 21–40.

Vu, H.T., & Lee, T. (2013). Soap operas as a matchmaker: A cultivation analysis of the effects of South Korean TV dramas on Vietnamese women's marital intentions. *Journalism & Mass Communication Quarterly, 90*(2), 308–330.

Yang, M.M. (1997). Mass media and transnational subjectivity in Shanghai: Notes on (re) cosmopolitanism in a Chinese metropolis. In A. Ong & D. Nonini (Eds.), *Ungrounded empires: The cultural politics of modern Chinese transnationalism* (pp. 287–322). New York: Routledge.

Yoon, G. (2016). 'Taeyangui huye' 27gaeguk suchultt"suchul gukga gyesok neureona" (Descendants of the Sun exported to 27 countries.... Increasing popularity of the drama). *Yonhap news.* Retrieved from http://www.yonhapnews.co.kr/bulletin/2016/03/23/0200000000AKR20160323156200033.html.

Korean Dramas as Chinese "She-Economy"

Ann-Gee Lee

The popularity of Korean entertainment is a growing phenomenon. Nearly every *hallyu* fan understands that the experience of merely watching a Korean drama is not enough. Besides being enthralled with various characters and storylines and cultural values, *hallyu* fans listen to K-drama soundtracks repeatedly, follow their favorite actors' filmographies religiously, and eagerly await freshly-translated dramas to arrive on streaming platforms. However, it rarely ends there, especially for Chinese female fans. They aspire to have their engagement photos taken at television sets on which their favorite K-dramas were filmed. They snatch up the heroines' same lipstick color; they sweep the boutiques that sell the exact clothing or accessories worn by those heroines. For those that take fandom to the extreme, they surrender their own faces to plastic surgeons' scalpels.

In a *LinkedIn* article for *Invest Korea*, Rhim (2016) puts Korea's role in the global context: "Among the major players of the cultural content market, which include Europe, North America and Africa, Korea consistently ranks high despite its geographically small size." QZ reporter Huang (2016) supplied a statistic for the growth: "China has been one of the largest markets for Korean pop culture in the last decade, investing $275 million in Korean publications and broadcasting in 2015 alone." Moreover, a large body of Chinese female fans constitutes Korean *hallyu* tourists. For this reason and for the purpose of this collection, the researcher will focus on Korean dramas and how their merchandising relates to the Chinese She-Economy via tourism, beauty, fashion, and online celebrities.

Because of their popularity for the above-mentioned reasons, K-dramas obviously impact Korean tourism. In fact, the Korean Tourism Organization's official English website (2018) includes links to 68 specific dramas with synopses, character descriptions, and filming locations, facilitating tourists' desires. Coco (2017), a writer for *DramaFever*, listed some places *hallyu* fans should visit, including numerous spots on Jeju Island, which is a popular filming site, and other places in Seoul such as Suncheon, Namsan Seoul Tower, and Mapo District. These locations are especially attractive to Chinese tourists who consume K-dramas. In fact, some Chinese fans will even spend $4,000 U.S. dollars to have their engagement photos taken on K-drama sets (Zhang, 2015). In fact, "An estimated 10,000 couples from outside of Korea, mostly of Chinese ethnicity, go to South Korea to have their wedding photo shoots done" (CGTN America, 2015). To capture the look of certain actresses or K-drama characters, female fans even go so far as to undergo plastic surgery or purchase fashion and beauty products at duty-free stores, which is much easier and safer.

However, for those who wish to stay in the comfort of their homes in China, Chinese homemade Internet celebrities or *wanghong*—also known as "key opinion leaders" (KOLs), "microcelebrities," or "power bloggers" or a term more popularly used for fashion bloggers in the United States who have adopted the name, "influencers," capitalize by selling or promoting beauty and fashion products to help fans capture K-drama looks via blogs on Weibo, storefronts such as Taobao and Alibaba, or messenger-like apps such as WeChat, which has a billion active users (Tao, 2017). They may travel to Korea by themselves to purchase Korean beauty products and clothing more affordably either in bulk or wholesale and sell them on their storefronts for higher prices. Moreover, these self-made Chinese women are becoming extremely influential in the beauty and fashion industries. Their followers relate to them and trust them when they promote certain beauty products since the followers cannot test the products before purchasing them online. These new internet celebrities are often invited to be spokespeople for popular Korean companies or as guests at exclusive events. They could also be employees of the flurry of companies specifically in the market of creating online celebrities. Furthermore, these *wanghong*, with their thousands or millions of fans, contribute to what business experts call the "She-Economy" or female-driven economy. Asian marketing expert, Bierbower (2015) explained in her *China Skinny* blog that "Of China's huge population, 640 million are women consumers. Not only are they shopping, but [are] also creating change and driving China's economy." For any industry, ignoring such a large number of potential customers would be less than wise.

While the author of the essay is not against the idea of self-made women, she is also concerned that the revenue being made by these Chinese influencers as well as money lost during a political lull is not returning to South-Korean production companies, who have invested so much time and money into creating those dramas that the public knows and loves while most likely the revenue is returning through the K-beauty industry. Using cultural, political, and fan studies approaches, this essay covers the important roles the K-beauty and tourism industries play in conjunction with the K-drama industry in terms of attracting Chinese female fans.

The Rising Chinese She-Economy

Rein (2009) argued in a *Forbes* article, "Women have become a major driving force behind China's economic growth—yet they remain little understood in the West…." He mentions that since the late 1970s, Chinese girls who were not given up by their parents due to the one-child policy have been raised as little princesses (Rein, 2009), much as boys have been raised to be little emperors. He alluded to Chairman Mao's quote, "Women hold up half of the sky." This is relevant because Mao was the first to allow women to pursue education. While few women are allowed to become politicians, Chinese women have more power than ever. Chinese women nowadays are more able to afford luxury brands due to "higher education, equal employment opportunities, and financial independence" (Ni, 2012). Moreover, Chinese women consumers are willing to spend 40% of their annual salary on expensive skin-care products (Gentleman Marketing Agency, 2018), considering it an investment in themselves. Rein (2009) provided a hypothetical situation for a typical Chinese woman's spending habits:

> [She] might typically spend $100 in a shopping outing, as before, but now she'll buy not 10 items but six more expensive ones. She'll look for products like a handbag she can use daily instead of a shirt to wear once a month. She wants cosmetics that last longer. She is cutting back on impulse purchases, spending more time before entering a store to do research online on what she wants to buy, consulting blogs and search engines and Web sites like Sina and Baidu.

Rein (2009) also revealed, "Chinese women are emerging as one of the most confident bodies of consumers in the world. And they have the money to keep on spending. To be successful selling to them, you have to cater to their emotions and concerns more than ever before…." Vivienne Rudd, director of global innovation at market researcher Mintel, elaborated on the South Korean influence on Chinese women: "South Korean women are very much held up as the standard of beauty across Asia" (qtd. as cited in Shadbolt, 2014). Rudd added that another appeal could be due to the fact that South Korean cosmetics are less serious than their Western counterparts since "[t]hey are very quick to use catchy new ingredients, thick textures, and they're very careful with their pricing" (qtd. as cited in Shadbolt, 2014).

One way to examine the popularity of K-dramas and its associated merchandise is through the concept of symbolic consumption. Sirgy, Rahtz, and Portolese (2014) defined symbolic consumption as "the process through which consumers—on the basis of symbols—buy, consume, and dispose of products." They continued, "Understanding the effects of symbols can provide important insights into consumer behavior [because] consumers buy and use goods and services not just for their utility but for the things they represent. A great part of consumption is therefore symbolic [because] it reflects the personalities, lifestyles, and desires of consumers" (Sirgy, Rahtz & Portolese, 2014). Thus, it is important to recognize how it relates to experiences. In a study, Luna-Cortes (2016) discovered that "when customers think that one experience reinforces their identities, they perceive higher value… [W]hen customers want to materialize their experience, they use the basic tool of virtual social networks" (Abstract 39). This is where Internet celebrities and influencers come in.

Tying a little more closely to K-dramas, Cohen (2010) although she was referring to western romantic comedies, argued in a journal article that the genre allows female audiences to engage with it materialistically. In other words, they appeal to the "material girl" because they appeal to the female gaze. She continued, "Here, women gaze as women, disconnected from a conventional male economy of desire, whether or not a man has made the film or a patriarchal perspective informs it" (p. 80). In fact, according to her, "…women learn how to use the material world creatively and to assimilate things into a style of being that defines and empowers them" (p. 80). Similarly, Chinese women who admire Korean culture and style aspire to be like the Korean actresses and characters they see on their screens.

How K-Dramas Appeal to Chinese Women

Rahman of the *South China Morning Post* (2015) points out: "This intertwining of fashion, music, film and television has allowed Seoul to become arguably the most fashionable and culturally influential city in Asia, taking the unofficial title from long-time holder Tokyo." An unnamed representative from the Matches Fashion website based in the United Kingdom revealed, "Seoul has just taken over Hong Kong as its biggest Asian market and third biggest market worldwide" (qtd. as cited in Rahman, 2015).

To find out what draws Chinese viewers to K-dramas in 2013, researchers from Seoul National University interviewed 400 Chinese men and women from 20–50 regarding their attitudes towards K-dramas and dramas from other Asian countries. The study concluded that K-drama fans in China had "lower incomes and lower academic backgrounds compared to those who watched popular American and Japanese television dramas," according to a report from *Donga Daily* (qtd. as cited in Luo, 2013). Naturally, Chinese K-drama fans took offense to such assumptions. Perhaps the phenomenon can be better explained by a representative for iQiyi, an online video streaming site: "We share the same culture and cherish similar social values.... So Korean content naturally is easy to be understood and accepted by the Chinese audience" (qtd. as cited in Qin, 2015).

In an *Epoch Times* article, Hong Kong writer Chip Tsao described the top reasons for K-drama popularity more directly: "Firstly, [the dramas contain] beautiful packaging; the leads are pretty, the plot is romantic and the contents are straightforward and appealing" (qtd. as cited in Zhen, 2016). The "beautiful packaging" and "romantic plots" may refer to the picturesque scenes from various dramas; the "pretty leads" refer to beauty and fashion; and the "straightforward content" may align with certain Asian group's values, particularly the Chinese (qtd. as cited in Zhen, 2016). Laurence Lim Dally, founder of Hong Kong–based market research and consulting firm Cherry Blossoms asserted, "[hallyu] stars are sought after by mass-market advertisers in China because they offer a blend of familiarity, as fellow Asians, and aspiration, as Korea has a reputation for style and beauty" (qtd. as cited in Doland, 2014). However, according to Rudd of Mintel, it is simpler than that: "The success of South Korean brands has a lot to do with Chinese consumers copying the style of South Korean soap opera and music stars.... They'll even go so far as to get the particular products being used by these stars" (qtd. as cited in Shadbolt, 2014). Jessie Xie, a Chinese fashion buyer would add on to that idea through this point: "Right after the airing of each drama [in China], [online shopping site] Taobao would feature 'hot items' from different looks featured in the drama.... If one drama is showing in China, all the looks the actors are wearing, viewers will copy them exactly. The clothes they wear become hot items for maybe two or three months" (qtd. as cited in Tai, 2017). Still, according to a Nielsen study, Chinese consumers (compared to those in Hong Kong, Taiwan, and Singapore) "were more influenced by Korean television dramas and advertisements that feature Korean stars in making their shopping decisions" (Sun, 2015). Such materials appeal to fans because they can emulate their favorite heroines' styles and relive the scenes from their favorite K-dramas by dressing up as them. This also brings in the problem of counterfeiting because K-drama actresses tend to wear designer clothing, and Chinese women prefer to buy the more affordable versions.

Chinese women easily constitute the largest number of consumers of Korean media products, such as K-dramas and related industries, such as tourism, fashion, and beauty. To demonstrate the gargantuan effect K-dramas have on Chinese female fans, the researcher will examine the two top dramas: *My Love from the Star* (*Byeoreseo on geudae*) and *Descendants of the Sun* (*Taeyangui Huye*). The fan response to these two programs exemplify the K-drama craze in China.

My Love from the Star *(Byeoreseo on geudae): The Search for Cheon Song-yi's Look*

In 2014, *My Love from the Star* was extremely popular in China, attracting more than 2.7 billion viewers on iQiyi (Doland, 2014). According to the storyline, an alien in the form of a man named Do Min-joon (played by Kim Hyun-soo) who has lived on the earth for 400 years falls in love with a Korean actress named Cheon Song-yi (played by Jun Ji-hyun) who looks like a woman he had loved long ago. Their relationship endures despite his physical obstacles, such as his inability to become physical with a human as well as social obstacles such as love rivals.

Cheung et al. (2015) conducted an impressive case study regarding the popularity of this particular K-drama. According to them, "A fandom can grow up cent[er]ed on any area of human interest or activity, and it can be extended more widely than its original interests." They hypothesized that *My Love from the Star* fans could be divided into ones who just care about the storyline or characters or "[t]he other group of fans can be "...described in terms of a wider interest, encompassing the love for the entire drama, as well as the delving into other aspects such as the hobbies and actions of the characters portrayed, or the fashion and products placed in the drama" (Cheung et. al, 2015).

In discussing the latter type of fan, they mentioned the term, "star-nomics," a portmanteau of "star" and "economics" which can be used to describe profits made from stars. This is an appropriate term considering that due to its huge popularity in Asia, this particular drama brought in profits from external fields, such as fashion and cosmetics, food, and tourism. Cheung et al. (2015) referred to a study by Professor Hwang Bae of the Chung-Ang University in Seoul titled "The Effects of Hanryu Culture on Clothing Purchase Behaviour in Chinese Female Consumers." He asserts that "more than 45% of Chinese consumers aware of South Korean brands have high levels of trust in such South Korean products" (qtd. as cited in Cheung et al., 2015).

Therefore, fans became easily obsessed with what the heroine, Cheon Song-yi, wore—her clothing, accessories, and cosmetics despite their luxury prices—were hot-ticket items. When the IOPE lipstick she wore in the drama had sold out, similar lipsticks by Yves Saint Laurent, Chanel, Lancôme, Dior, and Laneige were sold out as well (Tine, 2014; qtd. as cited in Cheung et al., 2015). Fans who purchased the lipstick thought "it looked good on the character and ... wanted to try for themselves the effects of the use of the product" (Cheung et al., 2015). One 26-year-old bank manager in Sichuan stated, "I ordered this hot pink IOPE lipstick online and waited for more than a week for it to come.... I paid 150 yuan ($24.25) for it. Now it is much more expensive on taobao.com, since so many people are going after it" (Chen, 2014).

A particular dress Song-yi wore designed by French designer Isabel Marant, despite its price of $1,975 U.S., sold out within a month. Additionally, 2,500 trench coats in the same Korean brand and tan color she wore were sold in 10 days with another 3,000 waitlisted (Cheung et al., 2015). Fans rushed to buy other accessories, such as "handbags, sunglasses, shoes, [and] jewelry" (Cheung et al., 2015) as well as "...hair sprays and finishing cream ... and IOPE blemishing balms," which were merely seen on the heroine's dressing table. A sneaky thing the showrunners did was subtle product placement—by showing the products without logos—prompting audiences to do research on their own, notes Yang Yang, an analyst for Beijing entertainment group Entgroup (Chen, 2014).

These K-beauty companies' success could arise from the fact that Korean industries understand the importance of the Chinese she-economy. In fact, Innisfree kept them in mind as they "used a blend of aggressive marketing, often making good use of carefully—chosen celebrities—and a wide range of beauty products tailored to Chinese consumers. [Innisfree has] also made use of product placement, dropping references to its products into *My Love [f]rom the Star*. This approach has really helped establish the brand in China" (Translate Media, 2016).

Also, due to the drama's popularity, the Korea Tourism Organization experienced a tourism surge of 42% (Cheung et al., 2015). Naturally, the place where Min-joon and Song-yi kiss, Petite France Town in Ga-Pyeong, outside of Seoul, became a popular tourist attraction. The Visit Korea page (2014) added some new filming locations of the drama. Special exhibitions and museums related to the drama or actors are popular places to visit as well.

Descendants of the Sun *(*Taeyangui huye*):* *The Search for Kang Mo-yeon's Look*

In China, *Descendants of the Sun* was viewed more than 440 million times via iQiyi (Cho, 2016). Released a couple years after *My Love from the Star*, this particular K-drama tells the love story of a military captain named Yoo Shi-jin (played by Song Joong-ki) and a medical doctor named Kang Moyeon (played by Song Hye-kyo) who face a time of war. They face conflicts because he is a soldier and must kill to protect others; she is a doctor who has sworn to save others. They both end up on an island and begin dating. He and another soldier, Seo Dae-young (played by Jin Goo), are presumed dead but manage to find their way back to their lady loves.

Similar to what happened with *My Love from the Star*, female fans were flocking to buy lipstick worn by the heroine of this military romance drama, Dr. Kang Mo-yeon, played by Song Hye-kyo. AmorePacific, one of the largest cosmetics companies in South Korea, which sells a popular brand, Laneige, saw a "360 percent in sales" and lipsticks sold out in the Myeongdong retail district. It is important to acknowledge for the sake of this paper that the majority of shoppers in that particular area are Chinese tourists (Hernandez, 2016). Laneige manager, Doreen Chia, explained, "Riding on the popularity of the show, we can amplify the effect through postings on social media platforms to emphasi[z]e on the featured products, as well as using point of sale materials to highlight the products and the show" (qtd. as cited in Tay, 2016). For example, Laneige's market specialists noticed that "[t]he number of the so-called "Song Hye-kyo" lipstick searched on the Internet surged 11 times after the drama started to air.... The lipstick (Laneige's Two-tone Lip Bar) has become a best seller in March and sold out in some stores" (Cho, 2016). Soon after, "Laneige's blemish balm pact BB Foundation Cushion surged tenfold between March 14 and March 20" (Cho, 2016). Dayacap (2016) a Filipina writer for *Cosmopolitan* noted the majority of the designer pieces worn by the heroine of *Descendants of the Sun*. Female fans went crazy for her accessories, such as the charcoal-colored Eco shoulder bag from Korean company J.estina, a tan leather shoulder bag by French company, Céline, and a white Kelly-style bag by French company Hermès. Regarding Mo-yeon's jewelry, they searched high and low for the J.estina starburst necklace from Captain Yoo Si-jin as well as her moonlight earrings from H. Stern, a Brazilian company. Also, they coveted her shoes, such as her nude-colored Christian Louboutin Bianca pumps, the Junya Watanabe Comme Des Garçons white mesh platform sneakers in the scene where Si-jin ties her rogue shoelace for her. And of course, they wanted her clothes, such as the Victoria Beckham floral dress, her black short-sleeved Equipment blouse, and her Vince double-breasted tweed coat (Dayacap, 2016).

One reason for these surges, according to Yoo Sang-woo of 11st Street's Chinese shopping site, is the fact that "Korean dramas are usually released in China at least several months later and the sales of related products reflect that time lag." Cho (2016) stated that simultaneous airing of the drama in Korea and China lead to instant customer response. According to the *Korea Herald*, not only fans but producers are paying attention to the gargantuan amount of success such dramas are bringing. In fact, "China and Japan have bought broadcasting rights to the drama series for $250,000 and $100,000 per episode, respectively. The show will be aired in an additional 25 countries including the U.S., England, France, Italy, Germany, Russia, Saudi Arabia" (Cho, 2016). During this time, however, fandom grew increasingly serious with the Chinese ministry warning others of "legal troubles" and cited "real-life cases of domestic violence, divorce and plastic surgery, all of which it related to an obsession with Korean dramas and accompanied with photos of similar incidents from various Korean television series" (Tan, 2016).

Some fans are also likely to take their K-dramas a little too seriously. While K-dramas have obviously stimulated the fashion and tourism industries, one possible negative effect of K-dramas is how it influences Chinese women's self-esteem. In 2014, the hottest look in Korean plastic surgery offices was Jun Ji-hyun's. Fifield (2014) lamented that not only did women "covet.... Jun's wardrobe and lifestyle, but her face, too." It is no surprise to Chinese women to hear that Korean actresses or even actors have had something surgically done. DramaFever (2015) listed 13 Korean celebrities who admit to having had plastic surgery—the number continues to grow. "South Korea is notorious for its enthusiastic, and often controversial, approach to plastic surgery" (Buckley, 2017). Reporting for *The Independent*, Buckley (2017) pointed out, "Up to half of women under 30 in Seoul are estimated to have had surgery; graphic advertisements of before and after photos are strewn across the metro system billboards, and the chi-chi Gangnam district, where many clinics are based, is known as the 'Improvement Quarter.'" She also revealed that "more than 500,000 Chinese residents a year are said to make trips abroad for medical tourism" (Buckley, 2017) although the numbers aiming for plastic surgery are well hidden.

Fifield (2014) interviewed young Chinese women to find out their objectives for visiting Korea. A 29-year-old office worker from Tsingtao stated, "Korean dramas definitely had an effect on my decision to come [to Korea]." A 35-year-old not only came to get some plastic surgery done, but also went to check out different tourist sites, bought some things, and dined in nice restaurants—spending a grand total of $8,000, claiming, "I've done a lot to help the Korean economy" (Fifield, 2014). Tai (2015) warned of Chinese tourists who would go to South Korea for new faces but ended up deformed or dead. Sometimes, the plastic surgery is so well done that the patients are no longer recognizable on their passport photos, which leads to detainment at airports. The South Korean government responded to such cases quickly: "It announced a series of measures to prevent illegal medical tourism practices and better ensure the health and safety of foreigners" (Tai, 2015).

Marketing to Chinese Women

However, nobody can really argue that "...Korean beauty brands are now the hottest ticket item in China" (Shadbolt, 2014). According to an unknown writer for Translate Media (2016), "Duty free shopping is a big draw for Chinese visitors to the Korean peninsula [because] shoppers are able to purchase clothing, accessories, and beauty products in shopping centers designed specifically to cater to their needs." The same writer argued, "It's just one of the ways Korea has managed to give Chinese consumers what they need. It's an approach that western brands would do well to learn from" (Translate Media, 2016).

Reuter Communications (2016) provided some criteria for beauty businesses wishing for success with Chinese female consumers: holistic beauty, niche brands, K-beauty, star power, and digital. Holistic beauty involves eco-friendly, healthy, and natural ingredients. Niche brands include smaller unknown brands. K-beauty is more attractive to Chinese women because their products seem to fit their skin types compared to western skin products. Regarding the digital aspect, Chinese females buy more than a third of their beauty products online, so finding the right key opinion leaders (KOLs), starting an online store, finding the right social media platforms, and getting creative are key (2016).

CEO of Parklu, Whaley (2017) provides some insight into the platforms that these Chinese female KOLs can utilize, such as WeChat, Weibo, live-streaming venues, and niche. He referred to a statistic by AdMaster: "63% of brands want to invest more in KOL marketing this year." He explained how WeChat is more of a messenger-type platform, which allows users to add details, photos, gifs, and videos and makes things more private and personal (Whaley, 2017). Next, he told how Weibo is blog format that is appealing due to its ability to spread information faster than WeChat, has a more open design, and less expensive advertising. Shao (2014) elaborated that because WeChat is the app used the most for communication in China, "[a] lot of brands, even luxury brands are leveraging WeChat for their business in China…[U]sers can share their activities, follow the new from the brand account they have subscribed…" This makes it easier for them as clients to ask questions to get more details about their brand. Along this line, companies can "be in touch with their target consumers and to promote in a more efficient way" (Gentleman Marketing Agency, 2018). Shao (2014) provided another site where women can buy makeup, Jumei.com, as well as Alibaba's Tmall and Taobao, which can be compared to eBay.

The Wanghong *Phenomenon*

Much has been studied about Chinese female consumers and their habits, but not much academic research has been done on *wanghong*, which have only been a phenomenon for less than 10 years. Wishcrys (2018) gathered a bibliography on internet celebrities on her WordPress blog. Of the thirteen sources she discovered, only two were on Chinese internet celebrities in particular. Wang (2017) wrote a master's thesis "We are famous on the internet: A study of the Chinese phenomenon of *wanghong*" and studied two females and a male; one of the females was a make-up artist. Meng (2014) wrote a PhD thesis, "Camera girl 2.0: A study of Chinese women's online visual representation in the age of individualization."

Besides being influenced by the K-dramas and related merchandise, Chinese female consumers are highly influenced by *wanghong*. Just like Americans have their YouTube stars, fashion-conscious Chinese turn to their own internet celebrities. According to one source, "They are often popular on Chinese social media and are leading the trend in the beauty industry. They share tips, products, advices or feedbacks to their followers" (Gentleman Marketing Agency, 2018). Another source explained, "Just five years ago, the first generation of KOLs had streams built almost exclusively around aggregating content ad images from the websites of the West. But now, key fashion bloggers have pivoted into lifestyle bloggers, posting healthy recipes and self-help missives alongside designer products" (Marketing Interactive, 2015).

According to Teo (2016) of *Straits Times*, "...[T]hese homegrown celebrities create original content and advertisers want them for being opinion leaders in certain fields—such as make-up, fashion and gaming—or because of the many fans of their videos and livestreams in cyberspace." Park (2016) of the *Korea Times* quantifiably shed light on the *wanghong* influence: "The online stars, who have millions of followers on the internet, exert a strong influence over young Chinese people." Naturally, "The Chinese are already among the most active social media users in the world, but the rise of cloud computing in recent years has allowed more content—particularly videos and livestreams—to be put online than previously, resulting in more channels and self-made celebrities" (Teo, 2016). In fact, Teo pointed out that "Five of Taobao's 10 best-performing shops ... belonged to Internet celebrities who started out as fashion bloggers but subsequently opened their own online fashion stores." According to CBN Data, a commercial data company affiliated with Alibaba, the "Wang[h]ong economy is set to be worth 58 billion yuan ($8.7 billion) in 2016, more than China's box office in 2015" (qtd. as cited in Park, 2016).

Wanghong appeal to the general public because they are more like peers than celebrities. They are not necessarily beautiful, but personable, relatable, and trustworthy. How Chinese female consumers find out about products which they are unable to test is through *wanghong*: "Because, even Chinese people are willing to spend, cosmetics products remain costly and there is a need to do some research before buying something and apply it on their skin" (Gentleman Marketing Agency, 2018). Of course, live-streaming KOLs are more concerned with their appearances and are even willing to undergo plastic surgery to attain the ultimate *wanghong* face. Additionally, they are more than happy to divulge "their cosmetic procedures and personal experiences" (Whaley, 2017).

Tsoi (2016) of the BBC warned, "Others in China worry about the standards of beauty online celebrities are creating for Chinese women.... An attractive appearance seems to have become an indispensable quality for internet celebrities, and 'internet celebrity face,' which refers to the combination of doe eyes, a pointy chin, a high nose and fair skin, is a commonly used shorthand in China." Carr-Engler, Goodman, and Venkatraman (2017) noted in a Medium article, "With one of the highest cosmetic surgery rates in the world, many working people in China see achieving certain beauty standards as a necessary step in employment." In fact, "[c]ertain jobs related to public service … have requirements of specific uniforms, makeup, and body type" (Carr-Engler, Goodman, & Venkatraman, 2017). They revealed, "Since many Chinese people, especially women, have to worry about body image and beauty to find work, plastic surgery procedures are often done to improve chances in the job market rather than for pride and confidence" (Carr-Engler, Goodman, & Venkatraman, 2017).

Redbang founder Ding Chenlin claims that with the help of the mobile and internet sector, a rising *wanghong* does not need much more than 1,000 fans. He advised, "You don't even need to be extremely smart or beautiful to do that. The thing is, you first need to know who you are and what makes you different from the others" (qtd. as cited in Qian, 2016). Moreover, media powerhouse Alibaba recognized their power and plans to seek and train new *wanghong* (Armstrong & Wang, 2017). *Wanghong* have even inspired new businesses, such as Tophot. Tsoi (2016) elaborated, "Incubators like Tophot provide training for budding internet celebrities, with skills in photography, make-up and performance. They also represent internet celebrities and help them find jobs like product endorsements. In return, they take a cut from their earnings." Tsoi referred to Janet Chen, founder of Tophot, who said "internet celebrities had already 'outperformed' showbiz A-listers."

To demonstrate their popularity, these female internet celebrities are raking in close to double or more annually than what actual Chinese actresses make. For example, fashion student/model turned *wanghong*, Zhang Dayi, made around $48 billion on her own online storefront on Taobao named *Wuhuanxide Yichu* or "The Wardrobe I Like," compared to top actress Fan Bingbing who made around $21 million. Tsoi (2016) attributed this to the fact that *wanghong* are more down-to-earth and approachable. Relating back to K-beauty, a China Daily (2016) reporter explained, "…a huge number of Chinese Internet celebrities use their platform to promote skincare and makeup products, behavior they are likely getting paid for." Zhang is trained by Ruhan, who has a 51% stake in Zhang's earning. They assist her with business aspects, such as "supply chain management, fabric purchases, design and pattern-making, manufacturing, and production" (Pan, 2017). *Wanghong* Sophia Yufei Shao, who has around 2.15 million fans on Weibo, prefers to promote K-beauty items due to their high quality and attractive packaging, exhibiting her love and trust for them. She takes advantage of the popularity of lipsticks and various types of masks. Additionally, "She delivered her wish to work with K-beauty industry since she has big affection and interests for Korea" (Lee, 2017).

The K-beauty industry is well-aware of these influential women. "On Oct. 3, Minister of Culture, Sports and Tourism, Cho Yoon-sun said, 'We would like you Wang[h]ongs, who lead the trend in China, to be a bridge between Korea and China'" (qtd. as cited in Park, 2016). Reketan, an agency for cultivating such internet celebrities, brought their top *wanghong* to visit Garosu-Gil in Seoul, which is known for its fashion and cosmetics, and live-streamed it on Weibo (Yoo, 2017). Park (2016) reported for the *Korea Times* that in March and September 2016, AmorePacific invited some *wanghong* to Korea to promote a new shampoo, leading the shampoo sales in China to rise seven times more than before. In May, Aekyung invited ten online stars to promote their cosmetics. One duty free shop invited five to stay overnight in Yongsan while Galleria Duty Free Shop hired two to promote their store in China. Shinsegae utilized a few *wanghong* to broadcast "K-beauty fashion week." LG Household and Health Care invited nine to promote their cosmetics line in September, and The Face Shop invited five to promote their products before that (Park, 2016). In 2018, Korean SNP Cosmetic Brand was proud to report on their accumulated 25 million cumulative views by six live broadcasts through *wanghong* in China. SNP introduced various types of masks: Birds Nest Aqua Ampoule Mask, which are sold over 200 million pieces in China, Aqua Cooling Sun Spray, Aloe Vera 97% Soothing Gel, Snake 99% Soothing Gel, 92% Soothing Gel, Pomegranate 92% Soothing Gel and so on. Chinese consumers were enthusiastic about Wang Hong, saying that "Their products are unique" and "The sheet mask suits great on me and I would like to buy something else from this brand" (SD Biotechnologies, 2018).

Although it is common for *wanghong* to work with Korean companies, they are not cheap. According to Park (2016) of the *Korea Times*, "...it costs at least 30 million won (US $26,350) to invite the A-level Wang[h]ong a day and 10 million won (US $8,783) to invite the C-level Wang[h]ong a day. Under the current circumstances, it is hard for South Korean companies to carry out Wang[h]ong marketing campaigns while paying such costs." Also, Choi (2017) writing for *Business Korea* argued,

> Wang[h]ongs are also limiting their promotions for South Korean cosmetics products due to oppositions from some Chinese consumers. An official from the industry said, "Ahead of the launch of our new brand, we tried to target the Chinese market with a popular Wang[h]ong. But, we are seeking for another plan as followers are now bombarding Wang[h]ongs, which sell South Korean brands, with abusive posts on Weibo.

Another industry official also said, "Wang[h]ongs themselves are also studying the pressure of the Chinese government and consumers and reluctant to promote South Korean brands due to the pressure" (Choi, 2017). With the *wanghong* influence, the Chinese she-economy is growing more than ever.

Wanghong are also inspired to expand their streaming channels into full-fledged companies. Niki Liu started as one in 2013 at the age of 23. By 2016, she became the founder and CEO of UChange and in addition to 30,000 regular employees, she hired 100 *wanghong* whom she personally trains (Yoo, 2016).

In contrast, lesser known *wanghong*, such as 19-year-old Er Xuan, must work long hours for less pay and face poor living conditions, described as a tiny room containing a computer, desk, and light but no bed, which makes resting next to impossible (Jing Daily, 2017). One *wanghong* trainer said that for any girl who wants to earn at least 10,000 RMB a month, she would need to be online for at least eight hours a day and continue this for at least three months, hence she would need to put in 720 hours of initial "hard work." These women are also told how to dress and how to put on makeup. Er Xuan had a good start; she attracted 10,000 followers in less than two months. She also receives daily fan gifts of 700–1,000 RMB a day. Again, she needs to sacrifice her sleep, but she does not mind. Fame seems to be within her reach. Many young women such as Er Xuan are hired by companies that sell fame and fortune.

Readers of this article may be curious about Korean counterparts to *wanghong*. As a matter of fact, Reketan founder, Hyunjoo Lee shared the different between Chinese and Korean online content creators: "Currently, Chinese wanghong are not professional content creators. Chinese wanghong can easily gather a fanbase of 1 million followers, while professional content creators in Korea manage to gather a fanbase of only 20,000. There is a clear difference between wanghong and content creators, who specialize in one vertical like game broadcasting, beauty, or food reviews" (qtd. as cited in Yoo, 2017). Lee advised that Chinese online content creators might do better selling on Taobao where they could "generate up to $46 million U.S. in revenue" (Yoo, 2017). *Wanghong* are capitalizing from profits related to Korean dramas, yet they are not the only reasons for South Korean economic losses.

Implications for the K-Drama Industry: The Problem with Politics

Reporting for *The Telegraph*, Smith (2016) warned, "K-pop and K-dramas are hugely popular in China, but their success in the Chinese market also puts them at risk of economic exploitation during political crises." This happened quite recently, as South Korea and China are not necessarily political allies due to the North Korean situation. However, due to the fact Chinese fans do make up a large portion of K-drama fans, South Korean companies would need to tread lightly in anything they do or suffer drastic losses. Moreover, Li & Shen (2018) noted, due to the popularity and influence of the *wanghong*, "As geopolitical tensions rose, some groups in China staged online campaigns calling upon consumers to boycott South Korean products" due to the South Korean support of the U.S. defense-missile system, "Terminal High Altitude Area Defense," or THAAD.[1] This upset the Chinese government since they are allies of North Korea: they responded by threatening to restrict mainstream Korean media in China. An All KPop (2016) reporter added, "Chinese authorities recently ordered that all Korean dramas, variety shows, and movies be banned from broadcast." The Chinese government also prevented K-pop stars from performing and ceased screenings of Korean films. Not to mention, fans who love K-culture would be unable to meet their favorite stars, and collaborations between Chinese and Korean production companies were halted. Kim (2016) of *South China Morning Post* referred to Chinese daily newspaper *Huanqiu Shibao* who cited that the government's ban "includes Korean product commercials on TV." Yoon (2017) of *South China Morning Post* noted, "According to Yonhap News Agency, Chinese authorities have recently refused to approve imports of 11 [tons] of cosmetics. Beijing announced that 28 cosmetics products failed to win approval for import, and among them 19 were Korean." Due to the THAAD issue, however, Seoul Fashion Week 2017 in April found itself losing half of its usual Chinese buyers and Chinese celebrity cameos (Tai, 2017). On the other hand, a few *wanghong* were not fazed by the ban: "I don't feel the THAAD row has affected too much of my perception towards [South] Korean products," said Grace Yang, a thirty-something entrepreneur who operates an education start-up in Beijing" (qtd. as cited in Li & Shen, 2018). She added, "I choose to use Korean cosmetics because they offer good value for money" (qtd. as cited in Li & Shen, 2018). This shows the power of brand loyalty as well as fandom.

In April 2017, all of the *wanghong* suddenly disappeared. A *Business Korea* journalist seemed shocked by their disappearance despite the fact the Chinese government has the power to control all media outlets. Choi (2017) reported, "Internet and media celebrities, known as Wang[h]ong, who were considered great influencers in marketing to the Chinese market, have disappeared. Beauty product manufacturers, which made every effort to secure Wang[h]ong with thousands of online fans last year, have stopped their marketing campaigns…" On June 8, 2017, it was reported that the South Korean government suspended the idea of going through with THAAD—which was a smart move because November 2017 marked the end of the ban on Korean products. This was fortunate for Korea since, according to a Korea Customs Service report, "South Korean cosmetics exports to China reached US$151 million in January, up from US $81 million in the same period a year earlier" (qtd. as cited in Li & Shen, 2018). The ban made a huge impact upon the Korean economy. In fact, South Korea Assembly's Budget Office reported, "China's decision to boycott South Korea's tourism industry over Seoul's decision to install a US–made anti-missile system cost the economy some 7.5 trillion won ($6.8 billion)" (qtd. as cited in Huang, 2017).

Duan (2018) referred to a Jing Daily report in which "AmorePacific, which owns 33 brands and is the 14th largest cosmetics company in the world, suffered a 76% drop in net profit in the final quarter of 2017. According to the company, the decline resulted directly from a significant drop in the Chinese market." Lee & Jin (2018) added that "Amorepacific … reported revenue fell 10 percent and operating profit slumped by nearly 30 percent in the first three months of 2018 (brands include the top-end Sulwhasoo, mass market Innisfree, and young makeup offering Etude House)." Chinese female consumers also supported *wanghong* and Chinese authorities who did not approve of THAAD. A young Chinese woman stated, "K-beauty brands like to use celebrities who have done a lot of cosmetic surgery that indicates a value proposition about women that I cannot agree with any longer as I am getting older" (Duan, 2018). Naturally, such a drop came from the THAAD issue. All of this allowed Japanese and European brands to get ahead of Korean products. Therefore, what is important to remember is that if South Korean industries are not careful, other countries' industries are not far behind them. However, Song (2018) noted that industry experts are not worried. She referred to analyst Yang Ji-hye who stated, "Despite the diplomatic tension, Chinese preference for Korean beauty products remains intact especially in the luxury segment…"Technology and quality are important but emotional appeal and brand power count more in this market" (Song, 2018).

Despite the recent disagreement between China and South Korea regarding THAAD during which Korean tourism and media products were banned for a short time, South Korean tourism has thrived. Tai (2017) of the *South China Morning Post* wrote about the current political situation: "In March [2017] South Korean media reported that Chinese government officials had given verbal guidance to tour operators in China to stop selling trips to South Korea, while more than 3,000 Chinese tourists refused to leave their cruise ship and set foot on the Korean island of Jeju." In 2016, South Korea welcomed more than 8 million tourists; the year after, due to the ban, Chinese tourism was cut in half, which will take time to rebuild. In December 2017, the tourism ban was lifted. Jennings (2018) of *Forbes* is hopeful since "Individual tourism from China, however, is beginning to recover already…." Besides government control, fans are still staunchly standing by their favorites perhaps due to their vanity. While it would be nice to garner some opinions toward the ban, particularly the *wanghong* themselves, China is still a country that prevents public dissention so much that *wanghong* who do not promote beauty products and espouse their own opinions are often censored.

Therefore, Korean and Chinese companies must learn to work together and come up with compromises. In a March 2016 post from *Dong A Ilbo*, a blogger argues, "The Korean government and Korean companies need to pull wisdom and power to prevent K-beauty, a new driver behind Korea's exports, from being affected by China's non-tariff barrier to imported goods." Spencer (2016) of Cosmetics Design Asia revealed, "Chinese online retailing agent Alibaba and South Korea's largest ODM Cosmax have recently signed a distribution agreement between the two countries in a bid to increase trade, while TonyMoly, a leading K-beauty retailer, has forged ahead with new plans to build a manufacturing plant in Jiaxing, Zhejiang province." TonyMoly already opened its first store in China in Shanghai in 2016. Hence, what they need to do is work with those *wanghong*, the vast amount of Chinese fans, and open their own companies in China.

Conclusion

What all of this has shown is that the Chinese She-Economy is huge and continues to grow. This allows women to empower themselves and within their families despite the fact they cannot take on political roles. The sheer volume of K-drama viewers in China proves that they are the largest consumers and should not be ignored. Moreover, Chinese women connect to their favorite K-dramas emotionally and financially. In fact, they care about the female characters so much that they want to look like them, which largely contributes to the Korean economy if they are buying original products. Fandom, however, has led to buying crazes, addiction, and strange behavior which concerns Chinese authorities.

Two examples of K-dramas—*My Love from the Star* and *Descendants of the Sun*—have demonstrated just how crazy Chinese female consumers become regarding their fandom. Designer items are immediately sold out. However, political differences may create trouble for both the K-drama and K-beauty industries and stifle aspects of freedom of speech, such as marketing. *Wanghong* are great influencers, but the money is going more to them than the Korean economy when they are overly successful; they are also affected politically. Moreover, the quality of products can be affected if there are counterfeit counterparts available.

To bring money back to Korean companies, those companies need to continue to work with *wanghong* to raise their customer base and find ways to bring original products to China by building more Korean factories in China. Another idea is to encourage for co-productions of Chinese and Korean films or dramas.[2] Rhim (2016) of Invest Korea encourages investors from outside of Korea to put their money into this lucrative business. This leads to the question: which aspect would be more lucrative: seeking overseas investors or working with what Korea already has—the K-drama and K-beauty industries?

A question that arises within the discussion is this: "How is the money not making its way back to Korea? Ma Jung-hoon, a K-drama producer, notes that the K-drama industry has 'tripled in size since the early 2000s'" (qtd. as cited in Maybin, 2018). Korean dramas bring in about $239 million as exports with 70% of that money from Asia and 30% from the U.S. (Maybin, 2018). The International Trade Administration (2018) points out that Korean cosmetics rate #8 in the world's cosmetics, which represents just 3% of the global market. This makes up a $13 billion economy. Certainly, the beauty industry brings back any losses incurred. One could argue that in fact, it is a symbiotic relationship between the K-drama and K-beauty industries and the influencers. For example, the money they lose on product is more than made up for by the free advertising or the lower price of advertising. Yet, the THAAD-related ban hurt various industries, especially tourism. All in all, by acknowledging the powerful Chinese she-economy and working in tandem with the *wanghong* in China, South Korean production and cosmetics companies can find ways to reach and keep their large fan bases of Chinese females.

Notes

1. For more on this issue, refer to the essay by Tony Tai-Tung Liu and Phyllis Yeh in this book.
2. For more on this issue, refer to Elaine Chung's article in this book.

References

Bierbower, A. (2015, May 20). The empowered female market in China. [Blog post]. Retrieved from https://www.chinaskinny.com/blog/the-empowered-female-market-in-china/.

Buckley, J. (2017, October 10). Women turned away from flight after plastic surgery means they no longer resemble passport photos. *Independent.uk*. Retrieved from https://www.independent.co.uk/travel/news-and-advice/women-turned-away-flight-south-korea-plastic-surgery-passport-photo-airport-refuse-boarding-a7992106.html.

Carr-Engler, A., Goodman, L., & Venkatraman, L. (2017, May 19). An unattainable ideal: The struggle for beauty in China. *Medium*. Retrieved from https://medium.com/foreign-accent/an-unattainable-ideal-the-struggle-for-beauty-in-china-3086eb9ba71a.

CGTN America. (2015, January 19). More couples taking "superstar" engagement photos in South Korea. *CGTN America*. Retrieved from https://america.cgtn.com/2015/01/19/more-couples-taking-superstar-engagement-photos-in-south-korea.

Chen, T. (2014, March 5). Gotta have it. *Global Times*. Retrieved from http://www.globaltimes.cn/content/846423.shtml.

Cheung, S.M., Lim, D., Kim, J., Kim, L., & Loh, S.Q. (2015, April 13). Popularity of Korean dramas in the region: My love from the Stars-A case study. [Blog post]. Retrieved from http://anie-brainworks.weebly.com/posts/popularity-of-korean-dramas-in-the-region-my-love-from-the-stars-a-case-study.

Cho, C. (2016, March 31). "Descendants of the Sun" buoys Korean economy. *Korean Herald*. Retrieved from http://www.koreaherald.com/view.php?ud=20160331000660.

Choi, M.H. (2017, April 21). Chinese power bloggers "Wang Hong" disappear all at once. *Business Korea*. Retrieved from http://www.businesskorea.co.kr/news/articleView.html?idxno=17908.

Cinebibliophile. (2017, April 14). Wang Hong: A report on China's social media microcelebrities. [Blog post]. Retrieved from https://cinebibliophileblog.wordpress.com/2017/04/14/instafamous-a-report-on-chinas-micro-celebrities/.

Coco. (2017, April 26). 9 K-drama filming locations every fan must visit on their dream trip to Korea. *Drama Fever*. Retrieved from https://www.dramafever.com/news/9-k-drama-filming-locations-every-fan-must-visit-on-their-dream-trip-to-korea/

Cohen, P.M. (2010). What have clothes got to do with it?: Romantic comedy and the female gaze. *Southwest Review*, *95*(1/2), 78–88. Retrieved from https://www.jstor.org/stable/43473039?.

Doland, A. (2014, October 20). How a TV show from Korea sparked a marketing craze in China. *AdAge*. Retrieved from http://adage.com/print/295447.

Duan, N. (2018, March 13). Despite the boom in K-beauty brands, Japan is still Asia's true beauty leader. *QZ*. Retrieved from https://qz.com/quartzy/1226815/despite-the-boom-in-k-beauty-brands-japan-is-still-asias-true-beauty-leader/https://qz.com/quartzy/1226815/despite-the-boom-in-k-beauty-brands-japan-is-still-asias-true-beauty-leader/.

Fifield, A. (2014, August 26). Chinese tourists, with Korean drama stars in mind, flock to Seoul for cosmetic surgery. *Washington Post*. Retrieved from https://www.washingtonpost.com/world/chinese-tourists-with-korean-drama-stars-in-mind-flock-to-seoul-for-cosmetic-surgery/2014/08/26/6f91c23b-cdae-4d27-aff3-d10fd634e2f4_story.html?noredirect=on&utm_term=.f7178e115c56.

Hernandez, V. (2016, April 12). South Korean cosmetic sales up 22%, thanks to "Descendants of the Sun." *Yibada*. Retrieved from http://en.yibada.com/articles/115784/20160412/south-korean-cosmetic-sales-up-22-thanks-to-descendants-of-the-sun.htm.

HML Team. (2018, January 13). The alarming dangers of counterfeit cosmetics. *Verdict Victory*. Retrieved from https://verdictvictory.com/dangers-of-counterfeit-cosmetics/.

Huang, E. (2016, November 29). South Korea says China is retaliating against its missile-defense system by taking aim at Korean dramas. *QZ*. Retrieved from https://qz.com/847900/chinas-retaliating-against-south-koreas-missile-defense-system-by-taking-aim-at-korean-dramas/.

Huang, E. (2017, December 21). China inflicted a world of pain on South Korea in 2017. *QZ*. Retrieved from https://qz.com/1149663/china-south-korea-relations-in-2017-thaad-backlash-and-the-effect-on-tourism/.

International Trade Administration. (2018, October 2). Cosmetics. Exports.gov. Retrieved from https://2016.export.gov/southkorea/doingbusinessinskorea/leadingsectorsforusexportsinvestment/cosmetics/index.asp.

Jennings, R. (2018, March 4). Why it hurts less now as China punishes South Korea with tourism cuts. *Forbes*. Retrieved from https://www.forbes.com/sites/ralphjennings/2018/03/04/china-keeps-punishing-south-korea-with-tourism-cuts-for-now/#6e11d616366c.

Jennywill. (2016, November 20). China to block Korean dramas, movies, and variety shows? *AllKpop*. Retrieved from https://www.allkpop.com/article/2016/11/china-to-block-korean-dramas-movies-and-variety-shows.

Jing Daily. (2017, July 3). The ugly truth behind China's live streaming mills. *Technode*. Retrieved from https://technode.com/2017/07/03/the-ugly-truth-behind-chinas-live-streaming-mills/.

Kane, C. (2016, January 26). What selfies in America vs. China can tell us about beauty standards. *Mic*. Retrieved from https://mic.com/articles/133484/what-selfies-in-america-vs-china-can-tell-us-about-beauty-standards#.6WLQVO5Cl.

Kim, J.H. (2016, November 23). Korean entertainment industry falls victim to Korea-China diplomatic row. *SCMP*. Retrieved from https://www.scmp.com/news/china/policies-politics/article/2048551/korean-entertainment-industry-falls-victim-korea-china.

Korean Economy News. (2016, January 29). South Korean cosmetic makers battle Chinese knockoffs. *Kita*. Retrieved from http://www.kita.org/global/ecoView.do?seq=15907&searchWrd=&result_url=.

Le, C.N. (2014, June 4). The homogenization of Asian beauty. *The Society Pages*. Retrieved from https://thesocietypages.org/papers/homoegenization-of-asian-beauty/

Lee, H.J. (2017, May 19). [bnt pictorial] Chinese popular "Wanghong" Sophia (Shao Yufei) "My charming point is my honesty." *Yahoo Lifestyle*. Retrieved from https://sg.style.yahoo.com/bnt-pictorial-chinese-popular-wanghong-sophia-%E9%82%B5%E7%8E%89%E8%8F%B2-my-074212429.html.

Li, J. & Shen, A. (2018, February 24). South Korean beauty products remain a hot seller in China, even as missile row simmers. *SCMP*. Retrieved from https://www.scmp.com/

business/article/2134510/south-korean-beauty-products-remain-hot-seller-china-even-missile-row.

Liang, O. (2017, March 14). The growing power of women consumers in China. *LinkedIn*. Retrieved from https://www.linkedin.com/pulse/growing-power-women-consumers-china-ophenia-liang/.

Liao, S. (2018, April 30). Amazon still sells counterfeit goods despite efforts to clean up. *The Verge*. Retrieved from https://www.theverge.com/2018/4/30/17301714/amazon-counterfeit-goods-crackdown.

Luna-Cortes, G. (2017). The influence of symbolic consumption on experience value and the use of social networks. *Spanish Journal of Marketing*, 21(1), 39–51.

Luo, C. (2013, July 23). Korean TV dramas attract less educated Chinese fans. *SCMP*. Retrieved from https://www.scmp.com/news/china/article/1289188/korean-tv-dramas-attract-less-educated-chinese-fans.

Marketing Interactive. (2015, February 11). Keeping up with China's young female consumers. *Marketing Interactive*. Retrieved from http://www.marketing-interactive.com/keeping-chinas-young-female-consumers-2/.

Maybin, S. (2018, June 14). The other big Korean drama right now. *BBC News*. Retrieved from https://www.bbc.com/news/business-44453310.

Ni, V. (2012, March 8). Consumption trends and targeting China's female consumers. *China Briefing*. Retrieved from http://www.china-briefing.com/news/2012/03/08/consumption-trends-and-targeting-chinas-female-consumer.html.

Park, J.H. (2016, September 9). Chinese celebs promote "K-beauty." *Korea Times*. Retrieved from https://www.koreatimes.co.kr/www/news/biz/2016/10/123_215667.html.

Parsons, G. & Su, S. (2017). The Chinese and Korean beauty market: Consumer buying behavior. *EPAM*. Retrieved from https://www.epam.com/content/dam/epam/en/free_library/whitepapers/The_Chinese_and_Korea_Beauty_Market.pdf.

Philip. (2012, June 9). Consumption habit of Chinese female cosmetics users. *Marketing To China*. Retrieved from https://www.marketingtochina.com/consumption-habit-chinese-cosmetics/.

Pulse. (2014, April 8). Economic effect of "My Love from the Star" estimated at $2.8bn. *Pulse News*. Retrieved from http://pulsenews.co.kr/view.php?year=2014&no=549150.

Qin, A. (2015, July 20). China's love affair with irresistible Korean TV. *New York Times*. Retrieved from https://www.nytimes.com/2015/07/21/arts/television/chinas-love-affair-with-irresistible-korean-tv.html.

Rahman, A. (2015, October 23). Fueled by fashion, the Korean Wave is taking the world by storm. *SCMP*. Retrieved from https://www.scmp.com/magazines/post-magazine/article/1870798/fuelled-fashion-korean-wave-taking-world-storm.

Rein, S. (2009, August 5). China's new purchasing powerhouse: Women. *Forbes*. Retrieved from https://www.forbes.com/2009/08/05/china-women-marketing-leadership-managing-retail.html#7c84d03a58af.

Reuter, C. (2016, September 7). 5 things brands need to know about winning in China's beauty industry. *Jing Daily*. Retrieved from https://jingdaily.com/op-ed-5-things-brands-need-to-know-about-winning-in-chinas-beauty-industry/.

Rhim, J. (2016, June 2). How Korean dramas are raking in profits for investors. *LinkedIn*. Retrieved from https://www.linkedin.com/pulse/how-korean-dramas-raking-profits-investors-ji-hyun-rhim/.

SD Biotechnologies Co., Ltd. (2018, March 9). SD Biotechnologies! Wang Hong broadcasting cumulative views recorded 25.39 million! *Korea Newswire*. Retrieved from http://www.koreanewswire.co.kr/newsRead.php?no=865769.

Shadbolt, P. (2014, November 6). How South Korea drives Asia's love affair with cosmetics. *CNN*. Retrieved from https://www.cnn.com/2014/11/05/world/asia/virtual-think-tank-china-asia-cosmetics/index.html.

Shao, H. (2014, December 16). Chinese female online shoppers: Not your stereotypical selfless housewives. *Forbes*. Retrieved from https://www.forbes.com/sites/hengshao/2014/12/16/chinese-female-online-shoppers-not-your-stereotypical-selfless-housewives/#1451cc276884.

Sirgy, M.J., Rahtz, D.R., & Portolese, L. (2014). *Consumer behavior today*. Boston: FlatWorld.

Song, J. (2018, January 8). South Korean beauty brands lose a little glamour. *Financial Times*. Retrieved from https://www.ft.com/content/bbddfe82-dbf7-11e7-a039-c64b1c09b482.

Sun, C. (2015, March 25). "Trendy" South Korean cosmetics catch on with Chinese shoppers. *SCMP*. Retrieved from https://www.scmp.com/news/china/article/1746609/trendy-south-korean-cosmetics-catch-chinese-shoppers.

Tai, C. (2015, May 2). Beauty's dark side: Chinese tourists lured by South Korean cosmetic surgery face risks. *SCMP*. Retrieved from https://www.scmp.com/news/china/society/article/1784085/beautys-dark-side-chinese-tourists-lured-south-korean-cosmetic.

Tai, C. (2017, April 21). South Korean fashion industry fears slump from fall-out over rocket system. *SCMP*. Retrieved from https://www.scmp.com/lifestyle/fashion-luxury/article/2089259/south-korean-fashion-industry-fears-hit-fall-out-over-thaad.

Tai, C. (2017, April 27). Big drop in Chinese buyers at Seoul Fashion Week suggests China-South Korea tensions over anti-missile system that has hit Korean retailers, K-pop and tourism could dent K-fashion's popularity. *SCMP*. Retrieved from https://www.scmp.com/lifestyle/fashion-luxury/article/2089259/south-korean-fashion-industry-fears-hit-fall-out-over-thaad.

Tan, H. (2016, March 16). Descendants of the Sun smash hit prompts Beijing to warn on South Korea dramas. *CNBC*. Retrieved from https://www.cnbc.com/2016/03/16/descendants-of-the-sun-smash-hit-prompts-beijing-to-warn-on-south-korean-dramas.html.

Tao, L. (2017, June 9). Want fame and fortune? China's internet celebrity business offers both. *SCMP*. https://www.scmp.com/business/china-business/article/2097688/want-fame-and-fortune-chinas-internet-celebrity-business.

Tay, V. (2016, April 21). Descendants of the Sun shines bright for brands. *Marketing Interactive*. Retrieved from http://www.marketing-interactive.com/descendants-of-the-sun-shines-bright-for-brands/.

Teo, C.W. (2016, May 18). China's internet stars have huge ad value. *Straits Times*. Retrieved from https://www.straitstimes.com/asia/east-asia/chinas-internet-stars-have-huge-ad-value.

Translate Media. (2016, October 10). The Korean brands succeeding in China. *Translate Media*. Retrieved from https://www.translatemedia.com/us/blog-usa/korean-brands-succeeding-china/.

Tsoi, G. (2016, August 1). Wang Hong: China's online stars making real cash. *BBC News*. Retrieved from https://www.bbc.co.uk/news/world-asia-china-36802769.

Wang, Y. (2017, January 26). Superstar influencers: China's internet celebrities at heart of Alibaba's growth. *Forbes*. Retrieved from https://www.forbes.com/sites/ywang/2017/01/26/superstar-influencers-chinas-internet-celebrities-at-heart-of-alibabas-growth/#4a8ee8452c98.

Whaley, E. (2017, May 26). ABCs of Chinese KOLs (key opinion leaders). *Parklu*. Retrieved from https://www.parklu.com/abcs-chinese-kols-key-opinion-leaders/.

Wishcrys. (2018, July 3). MA and PhD theses on cultures of internet celebrity. [Blog post]. Retrieved from https://wishcrys.com/2018/07/03/ma-and-phd-theses-on-cultures-of-internet-celebrity/.

Yoo, E. (2016, December 21). Weishang knows cosmetics: Internet celebrities tap into cosmetics. *Technode*. Retrieved from https://technode.com/2016/12/21/weishang-knows-cosmetics-wang-hongs-tapping-cosmetics-business/.

Yoo, E. (2017, June 4). Lessons from failed influencer campaigns in China. *Technode*. Retrieved from https://technode.com/2017/06/14/wanghong-agencies-failed-campaigns-china/.

Zhang, M. (2015). Chinese couples flocking to South Korea for $4,000 TV set engagement photos. *PetaPixel*. Retrieved from https://petapixel.com/2015/01/22/chinese-couples-flocking-south-korea-4000-tv-set-engagement-photos/.

Zhen, L. Drama series gives boost to Korean economy. *The Epoch Times*. Retrieved from https://www.theepochtimes.com/descendants-of-the-sun-takes-asia-by-storm_2040914.html.

Riding the Drama Waves

Reconsidering Korean Soft Power and Clashing Nationalisms

TONY TAI-TING LIU *and*
PHYLLIS WEI-LIH YEH

Over the past two decades, *hallyu*, otherwise known as the Korean Wave, has taken the world by storm. Not only have Korean drama stars such as Bae Yong-joon, Choi Ji-woo and Lee Young-ae become household names in many parts of Asia, the popularity of K-dramas has also given rise to the development of a craving for anything Korean—from fashion to mobile phones and electronics to music and cuisine. The emergence of a celebrated popular culture in South Korea has led many observers to refer to the phenomenon as "pop nationalism," a term coined by Iwabuchi (2001) to refer to the nationalistic ways in which the export of popular culture is discussed by a nation. Through the lens of political science and cultural studies, many observers also refer to the concept of "soft power" and look into the implications of popular culture on policy making and the construction of a national image or nation branding. In the context of *hallyu*, besides the general reference to an assortment of cultural objects, soft power specifically refers to the South Korean strategy to advance economic and diplomatic interests through cultural attraction, particularly through the display of cultural values and lifestyle as portrayed in television dramas.

Noting the concepts of pop nationalism and soft power, the authors of this article seek to address the often-overlooked lacunae of how non-traditional forces can be challenged by traditional nationalistic sentiments through issue linkage that sometimes suggest ambiguous causal relations. The feud over the installation of the Terminal High Altitude Area Defense (THAAD) system between China and South Korea is such a case—when state security is at stake, cultural and economic exchange may be sacrificed, regardless of whether security is indeed challenged in the first place. In a globalized age when intercultural exchange has become faster, easier, and more widespread, the counterchallenges posed by traditional nationalism and national interests should not be slighted. Corresponding to the foregoing claim, the authors of this article examine the recent episode of China's sanction on the promotional activities of Korean actors and actresses and demonstrate how soft power can be limited in the face of provoked Chinese nationalism. The authors also consider the clash between Korea's pop nationalism and China's traditional nationalism as well as the consequences of the verbal tussle between netizens for the future export of Korean pop culture.

This essay is carried out in six parts. Part one discusses the concepts of pop nationalism and soft power and their application in the analysis of *hallyu*. Parts two and three observe the development of the second and third Korean drama wave in China, headed by the immensely popular dramas *Jewel in the Palace* (*Dae jang geum*) and *My Love from the Star (Byeoreseo on geudae)*. Part four focuses on the dispute between Korea and China over the establishment of the U.S. Terminal High Altitude Area Defense (THAAD) system in Korea, which has led to Beijing's sanction on the promotional activities of Korean actors and actresses in China despite claims otherwise. Part five follows up on the previous section by examining the discursive faceoff between Korean and Chinese netizens and the potential effects of such phenomena for Korea and China. Part six concludes by considering the potential political challenges to Korea's soft power and possible strategies Korea may adopt to enhance its cultural diplomacy in the near future.

Revisiting Soft Power and Pop Nationalism

Two concepts come to mind when thinking about the emergence of the Korean wave in the new century—soft power and pop nationalism. In the discipline of political science and international relations, over the past two decades, "soft power" has become one of the main ideas used to understand culture related topics, or anything non-political. Meanwhile, in the discipline of cultural and media studies, besides soft power, in the new century "pop nationalism" has emerged as a common way of thinking about the development of popular culture. In many ways, both concepts are useful for understanding the Korean wave.

As proposed by Nye (2004), in contrast with hard power, soft power is the ability to attract, or "to induce others to voluntarily pursue the wishes of the powerful through the use of attraction" (p. 86). Hard power uses inducements and threats, or a "carrot and stick," to directly force others to change their mentality or behavior; soft power induces others to voluntarily adopt rules of the system through an appeal to attractive concepts and ideas (Nye, 2004). In the most basic sense, democratic and liberal ideals and the rule of law are good examples of soft power. Since its first appearance, however, the scope of soft power has expanded to include categories as wide apart as the (U.S.) education system, technological advancement and popular culture.

On the other hand, "pop nationalism" is another concept associated with *hallyu*. The term was introduced by Iwabuchi (2001) to refer to the nationalistic ways in which the export of Japanese popular culture is discussed in Japan (Joo, 2011). With Japanese popular culture partially giving way to the Korean wave in the new century, increased attention has shifted towards the consideration of Korean popular culture and nationalism.[1] Pop nationalism is a concept used to describe discourse that emerges as a result of a strong stream of cultural exports that generates national pride. While the establishment of discourse is within the realm of soft power as well, discourse related to pop nationalism generally originates with the ordinary populace as opposed to the state. In such sense, one may say that pop nationalism is a bottom-up concept.

Soft power and pop nationalism, together, effectively describe *hallyu* or the export of Korean popular culture. Following the re-emergence of Korean soft power near the turn of the new century, as a nation, South Korea became more confident in its industries and recommenced on the path of economic growth. In addition to economic benefits, in the past decade, popular culture has become a tool used to advance Korea's diplomatic interests. Some notable examples include the broadcasting of pop music as propaganda against North Korea and the inclusion of large scale cultural events featuring Korean popular culture in Park Geun-hye's summit diplomacy (Onyanga-Omara, 2016; Faure, 2016). Meanwhile, as this essay seeks to describe, television dramas also play a major role in spreading Korean culture beyond the peninsula. After the mid–1990s—noting the huge blow on the South Korean economy by the Asian Financial Crisis—dramas including *Winter Sonata* (*Gyeoul yeonga*) and *Jewel in the Palace* among others helped to reboot the engine of the Korean economy and once again boost the confidence of its people.

Acknowledging the significance of *Winter Sonata* as the landmark drama that drove the development of the Korean Wave, the following sections center on the subsequent success of *Jewel in the Palace* and *My Love from the Star* and their contribution to the sustainment of *hallyu*, especially in terms of the advancements in Korea-China relations. The popularity of Korean drama in China and its spillover effects that caught the attention of China's top leadership demonstrate just how effective television dramas can be as a vehicle of soft power. Korea's pop nationalism, or the national confidence that grows from possessing such soft power, is to a certain extent an inevitable outgrowth.

Jewel in the Palace *and Rise of the Second Korean Wave*

As one of the hardest hit countries in the Asian Financial Crisis, South Korea went through a period that could be called an "economic dark age." The crisis forever changed Korea in recent memory: as inflation and unemployment increased, families broke up and social problems increased. According to a study by Choi and Chung (2002), by 1999, about 1.7 million South Koreans were unemployed and almost 25% of unemployed households suffered serious marital crisis. As the Korean economy drowned, the International Monetary Fund (IMF) stepped in to bail out Seoul on the condition of domestic structural reforms. The fact that foreigners once again cast their will on the peninsula could not be more demoralizing for South Korea. It is against such backdrop that the global expansion of *hallyu* is meaningful.

According to a comprehensive study by Yan (2015), the term *hanliu* or *hallyu* came from two possible origins. A popular explanation is that the *Beijing Youth Daily* first coined the term in a report on November 19, 1999, and the term remained the popular one used to describe the general flow of Korean popular culture into China. Another explanation is that also in 1999, the Korean Ministry of Culture and Tourism freely distributed CDs with Korean popular music to radio stations, universities and Korean representative offices oversea to promote Korean music. The title of the initiative was "Song from Korea," which was translated into Chinese as *han liu*. Since then, *hallyu* has become a set term connected with Korean popular culture (Yan, 2015).

Regardless of how the term *hallyu* came about, China clearly played a major role in the phenomenon. As Han (2012, p. 16) plausibly points out, the rising middle class in China had an increasing desire for quality cultural content, and *hallyu* filled the vacuum with fortuitous timing. The sheer size of the Chinese middle class—estimated at more than 400 million people as of 2018—deems China as a market force that will inevitably influence the development of the Korean wave. On the other hand, although Japanese popular culture also enjoyed widespread popularity in East Asia in the 1990s, the fact that China and Japan shared historical tensions and memories of war dating back to the 1930s means that Japanese culture would have a hard time gaining ground in China. The comfort woman issue and atrocities during the fourteen-year Japanese invasion of China (1931–1945) made "Japan" a politically-sensitive term in China and inevitably curbed its demand among Chinese audiences. Meanwhile, Taiwanese popular culture had yet to mature and internationalize in the same period, and in some sense, cultural similarity between China and Taiwan makes the latter less attractive, especially in terms of TV dramas. The combined effect of Japan and Taiwan's lackluster cultures in China effectively set the stage for *hallyu* to shine.

While *Winter Sonata* in a sense re-invited the world back to Korea, one could argue that *Jewel in the Palace* was the drama that rekindled the world's interest in Korea and established the *hallyu* phenomenon in the new century. Set in the Joseon Dynasty, *Jewel in the Palace* is a historical drama that portrayed the story of an orphaned kitchen cook who went on to become the first royal female physician in Korea. In addition to the plot, the drama showcased traditional Korean culture, putting the spotlight on aspects such as cuisine, medicine, and attire.

The unexpected global success of *Jewel in the Palace* is telling through numbers. The drama was broadcasted in more than 60 countries worldwide, including countries as far apart as China, Japan, Australia, and Israel, and boasted a peak rating of 57% in South Korea and 47% in Hong Kong. In one of the least expected locations, Iran, *Jewel in the Palace* attracted over 90% of audience attention in Tehran when it aired in 2006. In three years since its broadcast, *Jewel in the Palace* grossed over 10 million USD from broadcasting rights and DVD sales (Shim, 2008, p. 225). The lead actress, Lee Young-ae, became an international pop icon in a short time and a household name on the peninsula.

In China, *Jewel in the Palace* was first broadcasted by Hunan Satellite TV in September 2004 after the station acquired the rights to broadcast from Taiwan's TV8. After its initial broadcast, according to Leung (2008, p.60), ratings peaked at 180 million viewers or 14% of viewership in China and generated over 35 million yuan for Hunan Satellite TV, including 150 million yuan in advertising for the first quarter of 2005 alone.

Following the success of *Jewel in the Palace*, observers noticed the widespread effect of the drama on Korea's foreign relations, especially with China, where the drama found unrivalled success. The immense popularity of the drama was evidenced on the occasion of Chinese President Hu Jintao's meeting with the visiting head of the Yeollin Uri Party in 2005, when the former stated that he regrets for not being able to watch the drama everyday due to his busy schedule (Cai, 2008). In August 2008, on his official visit to Korea, Hu met Lee Young-ae at the welcome dinner; the Blue House confirmed that Lee was invited to the dinner because Hu Jintao was known to be a fan of the hit drama ("Hu Jintao," 2012). It was clear that beyond its entertainment value, *Jewel in the Palace* fulfilled the function of cultural diplomacy by establishing goodwill between South Korea and China. The lasting impact of the drama can be seen even in 2014, when the first lady of China, Peng Liyuan, noted how she felt like walking into the world of *Jewel in the Palace* when she and Xi Jinping visited Changdeok Palace whilst their official visit to South Korea (Zhang, 2014).

Noting soft power as the ability to attract others to one's culture and values, through *Jewel in the Palace*, South Korea had Chinese observers reflecting on many issues. As Jang (2012, p. 101) points out, "Korean drama series gave [Chinese viewers] a glimpse into Korean family life and society, history and culture, in a more vivid and emotionally charged way than through news reports focusing on facts." As such, Chinese viewers have come to appreciate various cultural characteristics and similarities displayed or expressed through Korean dramas, especially traditional moral values such as respect for the elderly, family bonds and loyalty between friends. In addition, some viewers are also attracted to Korean fashion, cuisine and the attractiveness of actors and actresses. In the case of *Jewel in the Palace*, as a Chinese observer Wu (2005, p.62) notes, the wisdom and strong determination that the protagonist, Jang-geum, possesses is something the Chinese can learn from.

Complementing cultural reflections, *Jewel in the Palace* served as a watershed for visible progress in Korea-China relations. In 2004, Korea's Munhwa Broadcasting Corporation (MBC) established the first K-drama theme park, the Dae Jang Geum (Jewel in the Palace) Theme Park, in Gyeonggi-do. The park became a new attraction for Chinese tourists visiting Korea, which increased from a meager 264,910 in 2004 to over 4.7 million by 2015—or more than tenfold in a decade—according to the Korea Tourism Organization (2018). In the same period, Korean tourist agencies that specialize in Chinese tourist groups expanded from 70 in 2003 to 180 by 2012 (China News, 2013). Meanwhile, perhaps catching on to the new Korean wave, in 2004, Korean conglomerate Lotte began expanding its retailing service in China with Lotte Mart while China and South Korea agreed to commence studies on the possibility of establishing a free trade area between the two countries. In terms of drama entertainment, the success of *Jewel in the Palace* established a bar for comparison for Chinese historical dramas that were released afterwards, including *Legend of Lu Zhen* (*Lu Zhen Chuanqi*) and *Nothing Gold Can Stay (Na Nian Hua Kai Yüe Zheng Yuan)*. In such sense the Chinese and Korean drama industries began to compete while the former tried to reproduce the success of *Jewel in the Palace*.

Despite its popularity, *Jewel in the Palace* nonetheless invited critics in China who were displeased with the emergence of a new Korean wave in the country that fed into a developing feud between China and Korea over cultural objects. Such objection was clearly pronounced by renowned Chinese actor Zhang Guoli at a meeting on cultural development at the annual Boao Forum in 2005. As Zhang vehemently noted:

> This is the first time for me to accept media interview on the topic of Korean drama. I watched an episode of Dae Jang Geum (Jewel in the Palace) and I was not touched. Rather, I was quite frustrated. In the series, acupuncture, a Chinese invention, was allegedly invented by the Koreans. Media acclaims are widespread despite such a big

> hole in the plot. I think we are too strict towards homemade dramas and too easy towards Korean dramas. If the rhythm of the plot of domestic dramas are as slow as Korean dramas, they will surely be heavily criticized. Although China had been invaded before in history, it had never been enslaved culturally. If our broadcasting companies and our media are only keen on airing Korean dramas all day long, are they not simply traitors? [Jiang, 2005].

Criticism and wariness towards the cultural invasion of Korea caused China's State Administration of Radio, Film and Television (SARFT, the predecessor of the State Administration of Press, Publication, Radio, Film and Television) to issue a quota on the number of Korean movies and TV dramas that can be imported into the country in 2005. Coupled with nationalistic disputes over the origin of historical figures and cultural inventions (such as the Ming Emperor Zhu Yuanzhang and the compass) that grew in the same period between China and Korea, the Korean fever began to cool down. Although dramas such as *Princess Hours* (*Goong*) (2006) and *IRIS* (2009) somehow sustained the Korean wave following the restrictions put in place by China, it was clear that none of the succeeding dramas had as much impact as *Jewel in the Palace* and another influential drama was needed to keep the Korean wave going.

Meanwhile, Korea-China relations continued to grow. In November 2004, China established its first overseas language training center—the Confucius Institute—and the first Chinese cultural center in Asia in Seoul. Perhaps due to the favorable atmosphere partially generated by the Korean wave, for good or bad, South Korea became the first location for Chinese reciprocity in cultural export. Besides tourism, political leaders from both China and Korea carried out exchange visits and in 2007, Chinese Prime Minister Wen Jiabao and Korean President Roh Moo-hyun agreed to set the year as a year of friendship and exchange between the two countries. Since 2003, China had consistently served as South Korea's biggest export destination while bilateral trade greatly increased from less than one hundred billion USD before 2005 to just below 2,400 billion USD in 2007 (Ministry of Commerce PRC, 2018).

My Love from the Star (Byeoreseo on geudae) *and the Third Korean Wave*

Amidst growing relations between China and South Korea, the release of *My Love from the Star* in December 2013—almost a decade since the initial airing of *Jewel in the Palace*—proved to be the drama that was needed to revitalize the Korean wave. Starring Jun Ji-hyun and Kim Soo-hyun, *My Love from the Star* was a romantic comedy that portrayed the love story between a man from the future and a woman from modern day Korea. The drama belongs to a genre so called "time travel," as it features the protagonist, Do Min-joon (played by Kim Soo-hyun), traveling to a world before his time and falling in love with Cheon Song-yi (played by Jun Ji-hyun).

Just like hit dramas before, *My Love from the Star* struck a chord with Chinese viewers and became a major success. Although *My Love from the Star* was not broadcasted on TV until 2016, online video platforms in China—iQiyi and PPS–acquired the rights from Korea to stream the drama series simultaneously in China. In the first week of broadcast through the platforms, more than 10 million viewers tuned in to the hit drama. By episode 15, *My Love from the Star* caught the attention of more than five hundred million viewers online (Xiang, 2014).

The popularity of the drama generated a number of interesting developments that carried over from the plot to the real world. Nongshim, one of Korea's biggest producer of instant noodles, claimed that, thanks to a scene in the drama that featured Cheon Song-yi and Do Min-joon enjoying a cup of instant noodles, its sales reached a record high in China while the drama aired (Lee, 2014). Furthermore, a casual rhetorical comment by Cheon Song-yi noting that one cannot do without fried chicken and beer on the first snowy night of the season created a trend of eating Korean fried chicken with beer, or so called "chimaek" in China. Noting the market potential of China, in May 2014—merely months after the streaming of *My Love from the Star* online–Pelicana, a major fried chicken restaurant chain in Korea opened its first restaurant in China in Guangzhou. Since then, Pelicana (2018) has opened more than 60 locations in China, spanning 14 provinces and the direct-controlled municipalities of Beijing and Shanghai.

The Chinese craving for Korean fried chicken and beer subsequently carried over to tourism. As reported by the *Joongang Daily*, on March 29, 2016, a group of 5,400 employees from Guangzhou based cosmetic company Aurance gathered in Wolmido, Incheon, to celebrate their annual convention with chicken and beer (Lee and Choi, 2016). The group is the largest single tourist group to arrive in Incheon. Furthermore, according to statistics released by the Korean Ministry of Agriculture, Food and Rural Affairs in April 2014, beer exports to China increased threefold or 200% in one month (Sammi, 2015). China's *chimaek* fever was so widespread that in 2015, at the annual China-South Korea business forum, Korean President Park Geun-hye noted that the Chinese taste for fried chicken and beer—stemming from the airing of Korean drama (*My Love from the Star*)—is a sign of cultural and economic integration between the two countries ("Pujinhui," 2015).

It was clear that *My Love from the Star* regenerated the attractiveness of Korean culture. In terms of soft power, however, the appeal of *My Love from the Star* is somewhat different from *Jewel in the Palace*. Rather than evoking sentiment for cultural similarities and appreciation for the qualities and values exemplified by the protagonist, *My Love from the Star* perhaps borders more on the superficial due to the plot's modern setting. In contrast with *Jewel in the Palace*—which portrayed traditional Korean culture and values—the attraction of *My Love from the Star* comes from the unique storyline, lifestyle, fashion and good looks of the protagonists. In other words, in terms of soft power, the appeal of Korea keeled from the traditional to the modern—Korean culture is not only ancient and historical like the courtyards in *Jewel in the Palace*, it is also cool, sexy and beautiful like Cheon Song-yi and Do Min-joon in *My Love from the Star*. Until the release of *My Love from the Star*, a drama that revolved around the love story of an earthling and a time traveling outer space being was almost unheard of. Since then, one could note the growing popularity of Korean dramas that featured time travel, including *Legend of the Blue Sea (Pureun bada-ui jeonseol)* (2016, starring Jun Ji-hyun) and *Guardian: The Lonely and Great God* (*Sseulsseulhago challanhasin—Dokkaebi*) (2016) among others.

On the other hand, not shy to hint at the good looks of lead actor Kim Soo-hyun, China's First Lady Peng Liyuan allegedly claimed that Kim looks like Xi Jinping in his younger days (Wan, 2014). Also, *The Miraculous Journey of Edward Tulane*, a children's book by Kate DiCamillo, became a hot seller because in the drama, the title is read by Do Min-joon (played by Kim Soo-hyun) before he retires to bed. Chinese media reported that an online retailer sold 3,443 copies of the title in one month with customers leaving review comments such as "I bought this because of *My Love from the Star*" or "I bought the book because it was what Professor Do reads before he sleeps" ("Laizi Xingxing," 2014). Lead actress Jun Ji-hyun enjoyed her share of the spotlight through the drama by becoming an instant fashion icon, particularly in China. Online discussions not only carried out total tallies of the brand name cosmetics Cheon Song-yi used in the drama ("Laizi Xingxing," 2016), but also earrings, sunglasses, dresses, whatever Cheon Song-yi put on increased discussions and viewers' cravings. The "Cheon Song-yi phenomenon" reportedly boosted the sale of luxury goods such as brand name handbags and cloaks in China while the lead actors Jun Ji-hyun and Kim Soo-hyun were featured in fifty commercials combined in the span of three months following the airing of the drama.

In some sense, *My Love from the Star* can be considered as the driver behind a renewed Korean wave, particularly in China, where *hallyu* entered into a lull after the success of *Jewel in the Palace* caused China to tighten restrictions on the broadcasting of Korean dramas domestically. While observers have proposed different ways of accounting for the successive Korean waves, in terms of TV drama alone, one can perhaps argue that *My Love from the Star* followed the success of *Winter Sonata* and *Jewel in the Palace* in becoming a cornerstone in the waves of Korean cultural dissemination across the world in the past two decades. If *Winter Sonata* represents so called *Hallyu* 1.0 and *Jewel in the Palace* represents *Hallyu* 2.0, *My Love from the Star* deserves the title of representing *Hallyu* 3.0.

As a result, national pride naturally grew from the huge success of *My Love from the Star*. According to a 2013 survey conducted by the Korean Culture, Sports and Tourism Ministry on the mindset and values of Koreans, more than 90% of the respondents took pride in the country's cultural heritage, 81.5% were proud of Korean pop culture, and 54.5% thought the level of the country's culture was higher than the level of its economy (Bae, 2013). Korea's pop nationalism could be examined from reports and studies that followed. For example, Korean media widely reported on a *Washington Post* front page article titled "Chinese officials debate why China can't make a soap opera as good as South Korea's," which elaborated on the Korean wave that took over China following the airing of *My Love from the Star* (Sohn, 2014). Meanwhile, Korean observers provided their own interpretations. As Park Seong-hyeon pointed out, "people in China… achieved rapid economic development and they want to see the improved life of economic development [and] Korean drama shows it visually" (qtd. as cited in Lim, 2014).

In a study on the consumption preference of Chinese viewers on TV dramas, Kang Myung-koo concluded that corresponding with the level of education and income, individuals with a high level of education and income prefer to watch Japanese and Western dramas while those with a lower level of education and income prefer Taiwanese and Korean dramas (Luo, 2013). Regardless of whether Kang's conclusion was neutral or not, the study generated an outrage among fans of *My Love from the Star*, who issued a full page advertisement in the *Chosun Ilbo* in defense of their status. The incident suggests the level of confidence Korea has built up through the Korean wave. Such confidence proved to be significant as Korean-China relations began to deteriorate in a fast-changing regional environment.

Curbing the Korean Wave: THAAD and China's "Half-Open" Sanctions

Since the election of Park Geun-hye as president of South Korea in 2012, Korea-China relations have warmed rapidly. Historical tensions with Japan naturally encouraged cooperation between South Korea and China while the latter's economic boom in the new century added to the attractiveness of closer relations between the two countries. Not long after taking office, in 2013, President Park made an official visit to China and expressed the wish to improve bilateral relations amidst the U.S. rebalance to Asia. Besides agreeing on issues such as denuclearization of the Korean Peninsula and support for the China-Japan-Korea Trilateral Summit, Park also brought along a business entourage of 71 representatives from major Korean enterprises, which demonstrated the expectation and importance Seoul put on relations with China. South Korea's turn toward China reflected a logical decision to hedge between China and the U.S. while seeking support from Beijing in an effort to reign in the threat from Pyongyang.

Korea-China relations culminated in 2014, when both sides reached a consensus on the establishment of a bilateral free-trade agreement (FTA), which was signed and entered into force the following year. Aside from Southeast Asia, South Korea became the first country in the region to conclude a FTA with China, providing it with trade advantages over regional competitors such as Japan and Taiwan. Not only did Korea expect the FTA to boost exports toward China, spillovers into cultural and entertainment products were also anticipated. In addition, South Korea has welcomed a steady growth in the stream of incoming Chinese visitors, which makes up almost half of all foreign visitors to the country by the end of 2016 (Korean Tourism Organization, 2018). *Hallyu* remained central in the developments as Kim Soo-hyun and Jun Ji-hyun among others became ambassadors for Korean tourism. Clearly, Korean popular culture played an important role in sustaining warm relations between South Korea and China. In such context, the quick dwindling of Korea-China relations in 2016 was both unexpected and difficult to imagine.

The crux of the issue between South Korea and China centered on the installation of the Terminal High Altitude Area Defense system also known as THAAD. THAAD is a U.S.–developed anti-ballistic missile defense system designed to shoot down short, medium, and intermediate range ballistic missiles in their terminal or descent phase. Under Kim Jong-Un, North Korea's continued security threat—particularly the development of nuclear weapons—encouraged South Korea to consider the adoption of THAAD as an effective countermeasure against North Korea. Such a thought, however, unnerved Beijing, which considered South Korea's adoption of THAAD as a highly disruptive action that would challenge regional stability. While Seoul considered THAAD as a means to check Pyongyang from resorting to the use of missiles against it, Beijing thought the defense system was capable of being transformed into an offensive system. In addition, noting both South Korea and Japan's security treaty with the U.S., China feared that THAAD would effectively unite the three countries into a "mini Asian version of NATO" on its border. As stated by Chinese Foreign Minister Wang Yi, "THAAD exceeds the defense need of the Korean Peninsula… we absolutely have the reason and right to suspect the true motive behind the move" ("Wang Yi claims," 2016). Regardless of whether Beijing's claim is persuasive or not, THAAD became a breaking point in Korea-China relations and bilateral relations deteriorated rapidly after South Korea and the U.S. jointly announced the establishment of the THAAD system on the peninsula on July 13, 2016.

While South Korea and China did not engage in open conflict in the aftermath of the former's decision to adopt THAAD, Beijing's displeasure soon played out in the realm of Korean entertainment exports to China, particularly in terms of television drama series and related promotional activities.

Rumors about a potential ban on Korean entertainment in China emerged on the internet in the weeks following Korea's decision to establish THAAD. In a report released online on July 31, 2016, the State Administration of Press, Publication, Radio, Film and Television (SAPPRFT)—China's main censorship agency—was claimed to have ordered a ban on all television and public appearance of Korean entertainers in various forms, including television dramas, movies, concerts, entertainment programs, and advertisements ("Goodbye Oppa," 2016). Soon after the report was released, a leaked blacklist including 42 Korean entertainers and 53 drama series began circulating online, and discussions went viral (see table 1) ("Suspected Blacklist," 2016). The ban was confirmed to have set in when Beijing Television (BTV) issued an emergency statement on November 18, 2016, that called for self-censorship by all advertisement companies: beginning November 19, 2016, all commercials related to South Korean enterprises, brands and imports, or those that contain endorsement by South Korean celebrities or South Korean elements (including commercial scenes, slogans and iconic buildings) were terminated ("Restriction against Korea," 2016).

Interestingly, since the rumors surfaced in July 2016, Chinese authorities have not come out with any official statements confirming the truth of the ban. Rather, as Geng Shuang, a spokesman at the Ministry of Foreign Affairs (MOFA) (2016), put it, "I have never heard about any restrictions on South Korea, and the Chinese side is always positive to people-to-people and cultural exchanges with the country." Yet, according to a report by the *Dong-a Ilbo*, one of the biggest news agencies in Korea, "The [Chinese] ban is put implicitly without an official document" (Koh, 2016). Regardless of the "neutral" claim by MOFA that neither admits nor denies the rumors, various reports have suggested otherwise, and the ban's impact on South Korea and Korea-China relations was clear. Besides the blacklist mentioned above, some notable examples of the ban in-effect include the following:

According to a *Yonhap News* report dated November 23, 2016, based on data collected from the Korean Film Council, since the opening of the South-Korean movie, *Assassination*, in China in September 2015, no Korean movies have been shown publicly in China. In previous years, up to four Korean movies were released annually in the Chinese market. *Train to Busan*, a widely acclaimed box office hit released in July 2016, never made its way into Chinese cinemas (Woo, 2016). According to another source, *Saimdang, Mem-*

oir of Colors, a drama series starring Lee Young-ae and Song Seung-heon, was originally scheduled for simultaneous broadcast in China, Japan, and Korea in October 2016. The drama was highly anticipated as it was Lee Young-ae's first drama appearance since *Jewel in the Palace*. Nonetheless, *Saimdang* never acquired the approval of Chinese authorities and the series aired in Korea in January 2017 (Im, 2016).

Besides films not being released, Korean actors lost advertising opportunities in China. Song Joong-ki, the lead actor for the drama series *Descendants of the Sun* (co-starring Song Hye-kyo), allegedly lost his endorsement opportunity with Chinese smartphone company Vivo due to Beijing's clamp down. Song's role was replaced by Taiwanese actor Eddie Peng (Tee, 2016). Similarly, Jun Ji-hyun, one of the most renowned Korean actresses in China, lost her endorsement opportunity with smartphone company Oppo as well following Song's replacement. Jun's role was replaced by Chinese actress, Angelababy. Even though public statements concerning the changes were never released, it was clear that a sense of uneasiness surrounded Korean celebrities who largely represent Korea's presence in China at this time. Such changing of tide signaled a stop to the hitherto influx of Korean dramas into the Chinese market and profits to be earned from the potential sale of products featured in the dramas and tourist revenue. The Korean drama industry suddenly lost its biggest market.

A quick search on the internet reveals that two terms, *jinhanling* and *xianhanling*, were used interchangeably to describe the Chinese sanction against Korean cultural imports. While different in merely one character, the terms vary in meaning. *Jinhanling* or literally "ban against Korea" suggests a complete ban while *xianhanling* or "restriction against Korea" suggests partial restrictions, or in other words, select Korean entertainment imports are allowed. Which particular media products were not specified since the Chinese government believes such disclosure may be harmful to the populace. Indeed, as claimed by some sources, when the rumored ban was put in place, in the early stage, things did not come to an immediate halt. Programs and events that received official approval continued as scheduled. One may describe that "restrictions" rather than a complete ban against Korean entertainment have taken their toll against Korean celebrities active in China since August 2016. Thereafter or since MOFA China released the statement denying any knowledge of a ban against Korea, the State Administration of Press, Publication, Radio, Film and Television likely upgraded its ban. By 2017, most online discussions have described China's action against Korea as an outright ban.

Regardless of the controversy surrounding THAAD and China's possible retaliation, the economic impact of the ban on Korea has been real. In the three days since rumors were first floated online, the stock price of Korea's top entertainment companies—SM, YG, CJ and JYP—all plummeted, with

YG Entertainment falling nearly 12% and both SM and JYP dropping about 5% respectively ("China set to place restrictions," 2016). AmorePacific, Korea's largest cosmetic company that earned a third of its revenues from the Chinese market in 2016, had its profit slashed by more than 50% since the ban became effective (Hancock and Wang, 2017). In addition, in September 2017, Korean conglomerate Lotte announced the sale of its retail operation in China, Lotte Mart, in response to heavy losses incurred as a result of boycotts following the THAAD incident. The Lotte Group provided a golf course that served as the initial site for the deployment of THAAD. On the other hand, in March 2017, a cruise ship carrying 3,400 Chinese passengers made headlines around the world by refusing to set foot on Jeju Island, a popular Korean tourist destination, which left some 80 charter buses and tour guides standing by in vain (Oh, 2017). In short, China's retaliation worked, and Korea has suffered because of it.

Clashing Nationalisms and Implications for Korea and China

In a sense, China's ban on Korean entertainment is a good case study on the limits of soft power, a concept that has often been used to highlight South Korea's achievements in the new century. Perhaps South Korea was so successful in maintaining the attractiveness of its popular culture that few heads sat on the possibility of Korean soft power or the tide of the Korean wave subsiding any time soon. However, as the current case shows, soft power has its limits and gives way to the state, especially an authoritarian state, at the end of the day. While viewers in China can access the latest Korean drama series, movies and music through the internet regardless of the state clamp down, fans are, no doubt, dismayed to learn that they cannot have the chance to be closer with their favorite idols.

For South Korea, the fact that China makes up an excessively large share of its cultural export suggests dependency on the latter, which makes Korea economically vulnerable should China decides to cut off imports. Issue linkage is at work in the Chinese ban on Korean entertainment that suggests a limit to soft power. The curse for soft power is that dependence may make a state vulnerable. Once locked into a dependent relationship, perhaps the only viable way to break loose is to search for alternative trade partners and gradually divert away from dependency. Diversion weakens the leverage the dominant state has over the dependent state and the effectiveness of issue linkage.

In an alternative light, the Chinese ban is also a case of clashing nationalisms—between Korea's pop nationalism and Chinese nationalism. Soon after rumors about China's ban surfaced on the internet, so called "netizens" from both Korea and China engaged in a heated debate on the issue, which quickly escalated into a shouting match based on national pride. Unlike arguments in the past that centered on the cultural origin of figures and objects, the fight among netizens, this time, seemed to be founded on pride and anger alone, and the verbal crossfire seemed to betray the true nature of Korea-China relations.

Both Korean and Chinese netizens employed ridicule and greatly hostile language against one another. Regarding the ban, netizen afds**** left the comment: we should use the opportunity to weaken China's influence; we should sink more Chinese fishing boats. For netizen nuke****, "as imagined, China is still a closed country." Netizen dhcr**** expressed that "if they (China) want it like that, we should also begin to develop nuclear weapons." Netizen awk8**** suggested that "if Xiaomi TV is imported, we should give it a 200% tariff" ("After China issued the ban," 2016). Netizen good**** thought that "if we (Korea) always need to please China, we will become slaves one day; therefore, we should develop our capabilities and strengthen our economic development" ("SAPPRFT rumored," 2016). In short, the exasperation of Korean netizens was clear.

In contrast with the anger of Korean netizens, Chinese netizens seemed to be ecstatic over SAPPRFT's hard hand on Korean entertainment. In fact, "No idols before the state" became a common refrain circulated in China's online community. According to a survey on China's microblog, Weibo, concerning the state restriction on Korean popular culture, among approximately 320,000 respondents, 87% were in favor of the clamp down ("Do you support SAFFRFT's ban?" n.d.). In another survey carried out by *Global Times*, a mouthpiece of the Chinese Communist Party, among 280,000 respondents, a staggering 86% supported the government's action (Pu, 2016). Comments from Chinese netizens echoed the numbers. For example, in response to the government ban, netizen ZhaoH_nnnn left the comment, "Well done! [The ban] keeps us away from those who despise China and can only say 'hello' in Chinese from hanging around in China to make money" ("SAPPRFT finally puts restriction," 2016). Another netizen noted that she rejects large amount of entertainment imports from Korea, and SAPPRFT's ban is "an opportunity to clean up the Koreans" ("SAPPRFT bans Korean stars?" 2016). Finally, in a curt statement, one netizen simply wrote, "Get out of China, and go eat your kimchi" (Qin and Choe, 2016). In short, *hallyu* was demonized and anything less than purifying the television screens in China of Korean content was not acceptable for furious netizens.

Even though it is rather doubtful whether internet communities or netizens are significant actors worth studying in international politics, as exposed by the THAAD incident and its repercussions, the implications of heightened nationalism for domestic politics and foreign relations warrant attention. Noting the double-edged nature of Chinese nationalism—the fact that popular sentiments can be exploited to advance national interests or can generate a backlash if mismanaged—in terms of China, while its hard hand on Korean popular culture seems to keep Seoul on a leash effectively, online discourse of Chinese netizens and other boycotts against Korea nonetheless go against the peaceful international image that Beijing is trying to establish. On the other hand, regarding Korea, nationalism gets in the way of politics, as policymakers find themselves in the difficult position of trying to satisfy the demands of popular sentiments while realpolitik in the international arena dictates otherwise.

First, despite the seeming success of the ban, the case of China suggests consequences to the contrary. While Beijing seems to have taught Korea a lesson in power politics and once again showed the world its strong economic leverage, the THAAD incident adds another line to the notorious record of Chinese economic statecraft. It is not the first time China has dealt a blow to other economies through policy adjustments; Taiwan is a good example of China's carrot-and-stick strategy in practice. Nonetheless, the tradeoff of the strategy is that China loses its credibility as a peaceful and benevolent great power, or what it would like to be recognized as since the mid–2000s. Although popular sentiment—either exuded as online discourse or real boycotts—may not be powerful enough to influence policymakers, it could indirectly bear on the state by affecting the outer image of the latter. In turn, policymakers may need to make adjustments to policy accordingly, particularly if the state image is at stake and tied to national interests.

In a sense, the irony of the THAAD issue is that South Korea has continued with the establishment of the defense system in spite of the Chinese ban, and rather than being shaken by China's action, Korean nationalism seemed to be hardened in turn. In a study on domestic public opinion concerning the THAAD incident carried out by the Asan Institute for Policy Studies, more than half of the Korean population consistently supports the establishment of THAAD (see Figure 1).

The study shows that support for THAAD peaked in February 2016, right after North Korea's fourth nuclear test, and steadily declined over the succeeding six months. Interestingly, support for THAAD increased again in the one month interval from August to September 2016, or when rumors of a Chinese ban on Korea were first circulated, before dropping to 46.3% in November 2016. In the months since then, until the study ended in March 2017, support for the adoption of THAAD increased to over 50% again. On the other hand, disapproval for the installation of THAAD never amounted to half the population (Asan Institute for Policy Studies, 2017).

While support for THAAD was partly the result of general frustration against Park Geun-hye, who was impeached in 2017 due to a political scandal, the numbers may also suggest that there was a strong sense of insecurity towards North Korea, and the China factor was not enough to displace the fear. Clearly, a perception gap existed between China and Korea; the former felt threatened while the latter thought the threat came from elsewhere. The ensuing ban and boycott effectively damaged China-Korea relations, as according to a survey done by the Asan Institute for Policy Studies, in March 2017, China replaced Japan as the second least favorable country for the Korean public—an unprecedented development (see Figure 2).

In other words, even though China seemed to have the upper hand on the issue of THAAD in light of the Korean economy falling, from a wider perspective, it is also true that China's international image has further deteriorated as a result of its move. The boycott against Korea was the latest action by China in recent memory that demonstrated pure might and realpolitik at the expense of its image. The THAAD incident recalled memories of the Chinese boycott against Japan in the aftermath of the latter's nationalization of the disputed Senkaku/Diaoyu Islands in 2012. Nationwide demonstrations broke out in major cities in China while the sales of Japanese goods suffered as a result of boycott. On the other hand, the THAAD incident occurred in the aftermath of disputes concerning the establishment of Confucius Institutes around the world. The Confucius Institute, or language institutes set up in higher education institutions abroad by the Chinese government, began to raise suspicions in 2014 as renowned institutions such as the University of Chicago and Stockholm University terminated cooperation with the Institutes due to reports on interference in administrative appointment and ex-

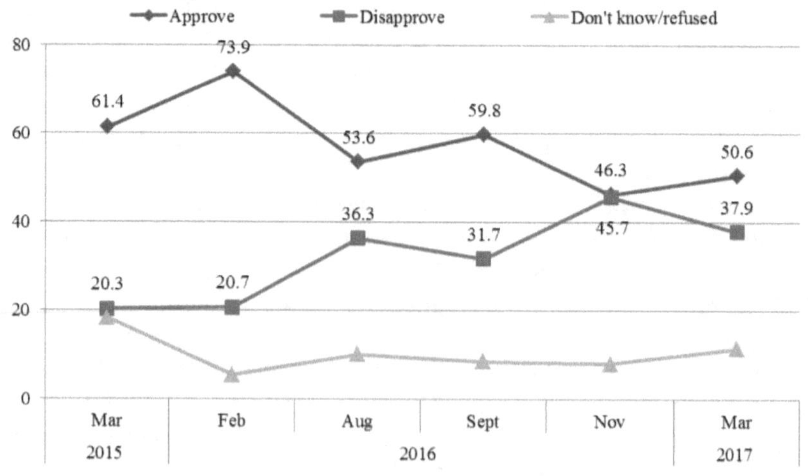

Figure 1: South Korean public opinion (%) on THAAD (Kim, Lee, & Kang, 2017).

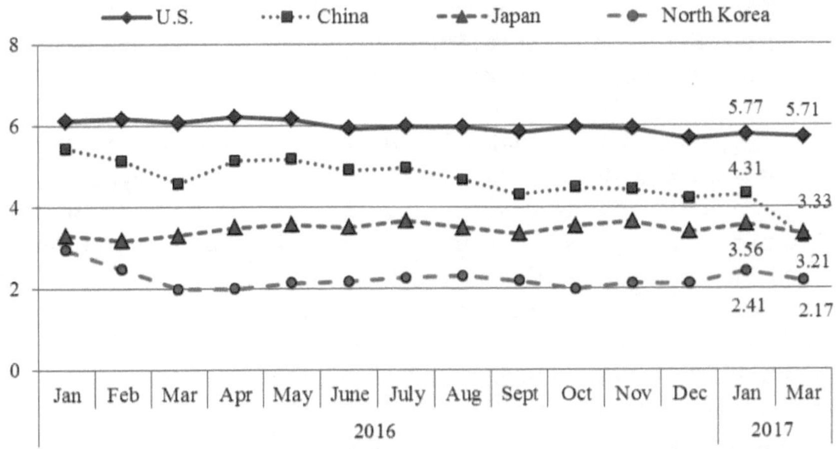

Figure 2: South Korean country favorability rating (Kim, Lee, & Kang, 2017) (0=least favorable, 10=most favorable).

cessive ideological preaching in class. China's hard hand on Korea in a sense merely reaffirmed the belief of China threat supporters who harbor strong doubts over the intention of China as it continues to rise.

Meanwhile, Korean nationalism did not bend but took up another form. According to the *Joong-ang Ilbo*, noting the tense relationship between China and Korea, Korean gamers began chanting phrases such as "Taiwan no. 1, China no. 19," "THAAD no. 1," "Tibet independence," and "Hong Kong independence" during multiplayer online games in order to mock and anger their Chinese counterparts (Luo, 2017). Mr. Kim, a regular gamer interviewed for the report, noted that making fun of the Chinese was a way for Korean gamers to relieve their negative feelings concerning China's ban, and the gamers did not think their actions could have serious diplomatic repercussions (Luo, 2017). Regardless of the gaming strategy involved, the preceding phenomenon hints at Korea's antagonism towards China that was clearly intensified by the Chinese boycott on Korea following the decision to implement THAAD.

In the case of Korea, on the other hand, nationalism brought Korea's dilemma in Northeast Asia to the forefront: North Korea is an internationalized issue that involves great power politics, which unfortunately limits South Korea's policy options on the issue. However, public opinion—presenting itself as nationalism in this case—is an influential factor in a democratic state that cannot be easily neglected by policymakers, and oftentimes the public does not agree with the government. THAAD is a typical case that demonstrates the disagreement between the populace and the state. As the Asan Institute for Policy Studies poll in Figure 1 shows, more than half of the Korean population supported the installation THAAD. In other words, security against

North Korea was prioritized over relations with China. Yet, such rationale went against the Moon Jae-in government's position of rebuilding relations with China, which entails the hope for restoration of economic relations as well.

While THAAD is an undeniably difficult issue for policymakers in Korea, it is worth noting that the impeachment of Park Geun-hye occurred alongside domestic discussions over THAAD. The Park Geun-hye scandal stoked public fury against government—an emotion that built up through the Sewolho incident and Korea's imbalanced wealth distribution—which generated further pressure and expectations for the succeeding government to perform and meet the demands of the people.[2] The Moon Jae-in government was clearly between a rock and a hard place, as it tried to save relations with China while the Korean public had other thoughts. Besides re-energizing trade, for South Korea, a less-discussed benefit of improving relations with China is the latter's potential ability to curb the North Korean threat. Yet, whether China could be counted on to hold back Pyongyang remains a mystery; the strong support for THAAD provides a hint at the weak confidence the South Korean public has in China.

As Easley (2017) insightfully points out, the deterioration of Korea-China relations may not be easy to heal at the public level, and "state leaders cannot just turn nationalist sentiments on and off like a switch." Indeed, as a poll by the *Hankook Ilbo* showed, South Korean public opinions of China reached a new low in 2017, with 81 percent of respondents perceiving relations as bad and only 19 percent saying they trust China (Easley, 2017). Meanwhile, since the Chinese ban on Korean entertainment took its toll in 2016, the Korean wave has begun to turn south, with a number of pop singers performing in Southeast Asian countries such as Thailand and Vietnam. Such a turn coincidentally corresponded with the Moon Jae-in government's initiation of the New Southern Policy that emphasizes the strengthening of political and economic relations with Southeast Asia.[3] Noting the damage of China's boycott on the Korean economy, the Moon government seemed keen to divert away from China and relieve Korea of its over dependence on the Chinese market. In such a sense, Korean nationalism has provided momentum for the government to search for alternatives other than China.

Since the revelation of the New Southern Policy in November 2017, Korea has made steady progress in expanding its ties with Southeast Asian countries and India. Ahead of his visit to China, President Moon Jae-in embarked on an eight day tour in Southeast Asia, visiting Indonesia, Vietnam and the Philippines while attending important regional forums such as APEC and the East Asia Summit. In July 2018, Moon called on India and Singapore, reaffirming his new focus on Southeast Asia. The policy culminated in the elimination of tariffs on a dozen number of traded goods between Korea and

India, the conclusion of defense cooperation between Korea and Indonesia and Brunei, and the decision to establish the New Southern Economic Committee. It remains to be observed whether the Korean wave can be revived in Southeast Asia.

Conclusion: Reflections on THAAD and Soft Power

Tracing the development of the Korean wave in the new century, following the spark provided by *Winter Sonata*, *Jewel in the Palace*, and *My Love from the Star* produced succeeding waves that sustained the Korean fever and pushed South Korea's soft power to a new height. Through the successful promotion of its culture through TV drama, Korea seemed to have introduced a development model that helped it to move out from the woe of the Asian Financial Crisis and transform the country into one that boasts a highly competitive entertainment industry. However, as the THAAD incident demonstrates, the expansion of soft power can be effectively cut short by the implementation of bans and boycotts, especially in the case of excessive or overwhelming dependence on a specific market. Such condition corresponds to what Keohane and Nye (2011) describe as "vulnerability."

As exposed by the THAAD incident, a major barrier for the continued growth of soft power is the authoritarian state, or a state that has the ability to censor information and control what comes through its border regardless of internet technology and the virtual world. In the case of THAAD, China was the authoritarian state that South Korea had to deal with. Korea's heavy dependence on the Chinese market for the export of its dramas and related products suggest that China sits in a more advantageous position vis-à-vis Korea in terms of bilateral relations. By using boycott as a leverage against Korea, China practiced a form of economic statecraft that effectively hurt its counterpart. A similar tactic has been employed by China against its other neighbors including Taiwan and Japan, both known for their soft power. It is suffice to say that as long as the world cannot avoid trading with China—the world's biggest market—cultural exports will be constantly under challenge. In a world where inter-state wars have become nearly obsolete, an authoritarian state as big and economically strong as China holds immense power.

Correspondingly, South Korea clearly needs to reconsider its relationship with China, especially in terms of soft power. As the THAAD incident reveals, the entertainment industry is a vulnerable point for Korea. Such development exposes the fact that the Korean wave is largely built on popular culture, which in turn attracts mass attention to Korean cosmetics, cars, and other goods. This brings up some questions: Is this a sustainable strategy?

Can popular culture serve as an effective tool for advancing Korea's economic interests? Perhaps even sustaining the international relations of Korea?

With the exit of Park Geun-hye and arrival of Moon Jae-in in office in 2017, Korea-China relations seemed to have rebounded and Korean dramas were once again accepted in China. Nonetheless, China's ban left a mark in bilateral relations, which in turn encouraged both the Korean government and the entertainment industry to diversify away from China. Such a strategy, however, is not a proposition to give up on China but to take into account other markets and groups yet to be fully tapped into. Besides Southeast Asia, for example, Taiwan has yet to reach its full potential. Noting similarities between the Korean and Taiwanese economy, observers have chronically regarded the two countries as global competitors. Yet the entry of Korean drama has dampened the competition between South Korea and Taiwan somewhat, and effectively fostered the latter into an important locale for the Korean wave to flourish. It is therefore easy to see that besides China, there are many other choices for expanding the market of Korean dramas.

In short, this essay seeks to record and reflect on the development of the Korean wave in the new century pertaining to TV dramas. This essay contributes to the existing literature on the subject by noting the THAAD incident and how matters concerning international politics can adversely affect Korea and dilute its soft power. The event of THAAD is interesting in that it showcased the intertwining of different forces that seemed unlikely to cross paths in the first place. How China wields its market power against others, or so called "economic statecraft," remains an understudied topic that demands further research. On the other hand, reflections provided in this essay are invariably limited by the availability of open official material for research and hindered by the accuracy and honesty of related descriptions. Beyond the measurement of power—the traditional concern of political science—another important concern to note from the THAAD incident is the methodology that is required to examine instances of state intervention or censorship of media content. It remains to be explored in the near future as the Chinese economy continues to develop.

Notes

1. See: Rowan Pease, "Korean Pop Music in China: Nationalism, Authenticity, and Gender," in Chris Berry, Nicola Liscutin and Jonathon Mackintosh eds., *Cultural Studies and Cultural Industries in Northeast Asia: What a Difference a Region Makes* (Hong Kong: Hong Kong University Press, 2009).

2. Lisa Collins also points this out. See Lisa Collins, "National Commentaries: A South Korean Perspective," http://www.theasanforum.org/a-south-korean-perspective-5/.

3. See: Moon Jae-in, "Toward a People Centered ASEAN Community," Project Syndicate, November 10, 2017, https://www.project-syndicate.org/commentary/korea-asean-cooperation-at-50-by-jae-in-moon-2017–11?barrier=accesspaylog.

References

Bae, J. (2013, December 19). South Koreans are really proud of their culture and K-pop. *The Star Online*. Retrieved from https://www.thestar.com.my/lifestyle/features/2013/12/19/south-koreans-are-really-proud-of-their-culture-and-kpop/.

Cai, J. (2008). China's first taste of the Korean Wave. In The Korean Herald (Ed.), *Korean Wave*. Gyeonggi: Jimoondang.

Choi, Y., & Chung, C. (2002). Social impact of the Korean economic crisis. *EADN Regional Project on the Social Impact of the Asian Financial Crisis*. Retrieved from http://citeseerx.ist.psu.edu/viewdoc/download?doi=10.1.1.545.3768&rep=rep1&type=pdf.

Chuan Guandianzongju yao banbu xianhanling, Hanguoren zheyang fanying [SAPPRFT rumored to order restrictions on Korea, Koreans react thusly]. (2016, August 2). *KKNews*. Retrieved from https://kknews.cc/zh-tw/entertainment/qq3yvxr.html.

Collins, L. (2018, January 2). National commentaries: A South Korean perspective. *The Asan Forum*. Retrieved from http://www.theasanforum.org/a-south-korean-perspective-5/.

Easley, L. (2017, November 13). China's charm offensive on South Korea is starting to work. *Foreign Policy*. Retrieved from https://foreignpolicy.com/2017/11/13/chinas-charm-offensive-on-south-korea-is-starting-to-work/.

Faure, A. (2016, May 10). K-culture diplomacy: From Sao Paulo to Tehran. *The Diplomat*. Retrieved from https://thediplomat.com/2016/05/k-culture-diplomacy-from-sao-paulo-to-tehran.

Guangdianzhongju fengsha Hanxing? Wangyou: guojia mianqian wu ouxiang [SAPPRFT bans Korean stars? Netizens: no idols before the state]. (2016, August 3). *Taiwan Read*. Retrieved from https://read01.com/AEdj5R.html#.W9tdKNJKg4I.

Guangdianzongju zhongyu xianzhi Hanxing le wangyou: guojia mianqian wu ouxiang [SAPPRFT finally puts restriction on Korean stars, Netizens: No idols before the state]. (2016, August 1). Retrieved from *KKNews*. https://kknews.cc/zh-tw/entertainment/meoze6.html.

Han, C.M. (2012). The new Korean Wave catches a tailwind of popularity in China. *POSRI Chindia Quarterly*, 7, 15–20. Retrieved from https://www.posri.re.kr/files/file_pdf/71/275/2918/71_275_2918_file_pdf_1456386606.pdf.

Hancock, T., & Wang, X. (2017, August 20). South Korean consumer groups bear brunt of China's THAAD ire. *Financial Times*. Retrieved from https://www.ft.com/content/f3c78afe-821d-11e7-94e2-c5b903247afd.

Hanguo zhuanmen chengban Zhongguo tuanti youke luxingshe juzeng, yida 179 jia [Korean travel agencies specializing in Chinese group tours see explosive increase, reaching 179 agencies]. (2013, May 9). *China News*. Retrieved from http://www.chinanews.com/hr/2013/05-09/4800271.shtml.

Hu Jintao gongzuo shiyu aikan hanju, shi Dachangjin jumi [Hu Jintao loves watching Korean drama in time off work, a fan of Dae Jung Geum]. (2012, December 6). *Sina*. Retrieved from http://news.sina.com.cn/c/2012-12-06/131625746302.shtml.

Im, H.Y. (2016, September 29). Airing of drama featuring "Lee Young-ae" delayed till January due to THAAD conflict. *Dong-a Ilbo*. Retrieved from http://english.donga.com/List/3/08/26/750931/1.

Iwabuchi, K. (2001). Uses of Japanese popular culture: Trans/nationalism and postcolonial desire for "Asia." *Emergence*, *11*(2), 199–222.

Jang, S.H. (2012). The Korean Wave and its implications for the Korea-China relationship. *Journal of International and Area Studies*, *19*(2), 97–113.

Jiang, X. (2005, October 23). Xin Hanliu vs. Fan Hanliu wenhua liguo fengyunqi [New Korean Wave vs. Anti-Korean Wave culture]. *Yazhou Zhoukan* (Asia Weekly), 19(43). Retrieved from http://www.yzzk.com/cfm/content_archive.cfm?id=1367810820055&docissue=2005-43.

Joo, J. (2011). Transnationalization of Korean popular culture and the rise of "pop nationalism" in Korea. *The Journal of Popular Culture*, *44*(3), 489–504.

Keohane, R., & Nye, J. (2011). *Power & interdependence* (4th ed.) New York: Pearson.

Kim, J., Lee, J.J., & Kang, C. (2017, March 20). Changing tides: THAAD and shifting Korean public opinion toward the United States and China. The Asan Institute for Policy Studies. Retrieved from http://en.asaninst.org/contents/changing-tides-thaad-and-shifting-korean-public-opinion-toward-the-united-states-and-china/.

Koh, M.S. (2016, November 22). China's ban on Korean culture. *Dong-a Ilbo*. Retrieved from http://english.donga.com/List/3/all/26/786409/1.

Korea Tourism Organization (2018). Statistics of arrivals and departures by item. *Korea Tourism Organization*. Retrieved from https://kto.visitkorea.or.kr/eng/tourismStatics/keyFacts/KoreaMonthlyStatistics/eng/.

"Laizi Xingxing de Ni" Qiansongyi tongkuan huazhuangpin dasouluo [Cosmetic collection of My Love from the Star Cheon Song-yi]. (2016, November 3). *Zai Seoul*. Retrieved from http://www.zaiseoul.com/article/view/137.

"Laizi Xingxing de Ni" yinbao fensi jingji jiasu waiguo pinpai ruhua [My Love from the Star sparks fan economy and facilitate the entry of foreign brands into China]. (2014, February 19). *Phoenix Finance*. Retrieved from http://finance.ifeng.com/a/20140219/11693151_0.shtml.

Lee, S.E. & Choi M.R. (2016, March 29). Incheon welcome Chinese tour group of 5400. *Korea Joongang Daily*. Retrieved from http://koreajoongangdaily.joins.com/news/article/article.aspx?aid=3016787.

Lee, S.Y. (2014, March 10). [Newsmaker] "My Love" signals K-drama revival. *Korean Herald*. Retrieved from http://www.koreaherald.com/view.php?ud=20140310001393.

Leung, L. (2008). Mediating nationalism and modernity: The transnationalization of Korean dramas on Chinese (satellite) TV. In B.H. Chua & K. Iwabuchi (Eds.), *East Asia pop culture: Analysing the Korean Wave* (pp.53–69). Hong Kong: Hong Kong University Press.

Lim, H.K. (2014, April 7). "My Love from the Star," how did it penetrate the bamboo curtain? *Kookmin Review*. Retrieved from https://english.kookmin.ac.kr/kookmin/special/189.

Luo, C. (2013, July 23). Korean TV dramas attract less educated Chinese fans. *South China Morning Post*. Retrieved from https://www.scmp.com/news/china/article/1289188/korean-tv-dramas-attract-less-educated-chinese-fans.

Luo, Y.C. (2017, October 27). Hanguo nianqingren de liuxingyu jingshi Taiwan no.1! Zhongguo jinhanling hou yueyanyuelie de Hanguo fanzhong qingan ["Taiwan No.1" the popular phrase among Korean youngsters! Rising Korean anti–Chinese sentiments after the Chinese ban on Korea]. *Business Weekly*. Retrieved from https://www.businessweekly.com.tw/article.aspx?id=21067&type=Blog.

Ministry of Commerce-People's Republic of China. (2018). *Mofcom*. Retrieved from http://english.mofcom.gov.cn/.

Ministry of Foreign Affairs of the PRC. (2016, November 21). Erlinyiliu nian shiyi yue ershiyi ri waijiaobu fayanren gengshuang zhuchi lixing jizhehui [November 21, 2016, MOFA spokesman Geng Shuang hosts regular press conference]. *FMPRC*. Retrieved from https://www.fmprc.gov.cn/web/fyrbt_673021/t1417148.shtml.

Moon, J.I. (2017, November 10). Toward a people centered ASEAN community. *Project Syndicate*. Retrieved from https://www.project-syndicate.org/commentary/korea-asean-cooperation-at-50-by-jae-in-moon-2017-11?barrier=accessreg.

Ni zhibuzhichi Guangdian fengsha Hanxing? [Do you support SAPPRFT's ban on Korean stars?] (n.d.). *Weibo*. Retrieved from http://vote.weibo.com/poll/137378462?display=0&retcode=6102.

Nye, J. (2004). Soft power: The means to success in world politics. New York: Public Affairs.

Oh, J.Y. (2017, March 13). Chinese cruise passengers refuse to go ashore in Jeju. *The Chosun-Ilbo*. Retrieved from http://english.chosun.com/site/data/html_dir/2017/03/13/2017031301286.html.

Onyanga-Omara, J. (2016, January 8). Seoul hits North Korea with barrage of K-pop. *USA Today*. Retrieved from https://www.usatoday.com/story/news/world/2016/01/08/seoul-propaganda-barrage/78453602/.

Ouba zaijian? Jingchuan Guangdianzongju jiangyao chedi fengsha Hanguo mingxing [Goodbye Oppa? The SAPPRFT will allegedly ban all Korean stars]. (2016, July 31). *Toutiao*. Retrieved from https://www.toutiao.com/i6313501807196766722.

Pease, R. (2009). Korean pop music in China: Nationalism, authenticity, and gender. In C.

Berry, N. Liscutin & J. Mackintosh (Eds.), *Cultural studies and cultural industries in Northeast Asia: What a difference a region makes* (pp.151–167). Hong Kong: Hong Kong University Press.

Pelicana Overseas Store. (2018). *Pelicana*. Retrieved from http://www.pelicana.co.kr/cn/store/overseas.html.

Pu, S.Y. (2016, August 17). Baofu sade, Zhongguo bangda Nanhan Ouba [Avenging THAAD, China clamps down on South Korean Oppa]. *The Initium*. Retrieved from https://theinitium.com/article/20160817-international-SKpopstar/.

Pujinhui: Zhongguoren xihuan pijiu zhaji, hanguoren ye xihuan yangrouchuan [Park Geun-hye: Chinese likes chimaek, Koreans also like roasted lamb skewers]. (2015, September 6). *Huanqiu Wang*. Retrieved from http://world.huanqiu.com/hot/2015–09/7418289.html.

Qin, A. & Choe, S.H. (2016, August 7). South Korean missile defense deal appears to sour China's taste for K-Pop. *New York Times*. Retrieved from https://www.nytimes.com/2016/08/08/world/asia/china-korea-thaad. html?_ga= 2.54742312.2027410220.1518243381–225454762.1518243381.

Sammi. (2015, March 3). Hanju zai Zhongguo rebo de wenhua fenxi yu fansi [The success of Korean TV drama in China: A cultural analysis and reconsideration]. *Sina*. Retrieved from http://ent.sina.com.cn/zl/discuss/blog/2015–03-03/17363063/1634954595/61736d630102vg0v.shtml.

Shim, S.G. (2008). Behind the Korean broadcasting boom. *NHK Broadcasting Studies*, 6, 205–232. Retrieved from http://cgi2.nhk.or.jp/bunken/english/reports/pdf/08_no6_10.pdf.

Sohn, J.A. (2014, March 18). Alien love story goes viral in China. *Korea.net*. Retrieved from http://www.korea.net/NewsFocus/Culture/view?articleId=118197.

Tee, A. (2016, November 28). Descendants of the Sun's Song Joong Ki loses endorsements in China due to THAAD. *Yibada*. Retrieved from http://en.yibada.com/articles/175734/20161128/descendants-sun-song-joong-ki-loses-endorsements-china-due-thaad.html.

Wan, W. (2014, March 7). Chinese officials debate why China can't make a soap opera as good as South Korea's. *The Washington Post*. Retrieved from https://www.washingtonpost.com/world/asia_pacific/chinese-officials-debate-why-china-cant-make-a-soap-opera-as-good-as-south-koreas/2014/03/07/94b86678-a5f3–11e3–84d4-e59b1709222c_story.html?utm_term=.4f6fca269a78.

Wang Yi cheng sade yuanchao fangwei xuqiu Zhongguo youquan zhiyi beihou tumou [Wang Yi claims that THAAD far exceeds defense need, China has the right to question its ulterior motive]. (2016, July 11). *Sohu*. Retrieved from http://mil.sohu.com/20160711/n458697768.shtml.

Woo, J.Y. (2016, November 23). No S. Korean films released in China this year, industry suspects THAAD fallout. *Yonhap News*. Retrieved from http://english.yonhapnews.co.kr/national/2016/11/23/87/0301000000AEN20161123009900315F.html.

Wu, Z.L. (2005). Dachangjin: Hanguo wenhua de yici chenggong denglu [Dae Jang Geum: a successful landing of Korean culture]. *Shangye Wenhua* (Business Culture), 11, 60–62.

Xiang, M. (2014, February 20). Laizi Xingxing de Ni rebo: Iqiyi ruhe shixian minglishuangshou [My Love from the Star a Success: How iQiyi gained both name and profit]. *DO News*. Retrieved from http://www.donews.com/net/201402/2708948.shtm.

Xianhanling shengji pinpai ciaociao huanxia daiyanren [Restriction against Korea upgraded, brand names quietly replace spokespeople]. (2016, November 21). *Taiwan Read*. Retrieved from https://read01.com/85moBG.html#.W9tnOdJKg4l.

Yan, M. (2015) Sekai ni mukeru taishuu bunka—Hanryu [To the world of popular culture—the Korean Wave]. *Jinbun Kenkyuu* (Journal of Humanities), 187, 89–137.

Yi jinhanling mingdan wailiu 42 ming Hanguo yiren 53 bu ju zao fengsha [Suspected blacklist of Chinese ban leaked, 42 Korean stars and 53 dramas banned]. (2016, August 8). *Sohu*. Retrieved from http://www.sohu.com/a/109587554_120055.

Zhang, C. (2014, July 7). Hanmei zan Peng Liyuan jingyan, diyi furen ye mi hanju [Korean media report on an amazed Peng Liyuan, First lady also a Korean drama fan]. *Fenghuanwang Henan* (Phoenix News Henan). Retrieved from http://hn.ifeng.com/shishangnvren/detail_2014_07/07/2547641_0.shtml.

Zhongguo fale jinhanling zhihou, Hanguo wangyou de fanying shi zheyangde [After China issued the ban on Korea, this is the reaction of Korean netizens]. (2016, August 3). *Weibo.* Retrieved from https://weibo.com/ttarticle/p/show?id=2309351000084004434182016010.
Zhongguo yao chu xianhanling? Hanguo yuleye jingkong yipian [China set to place restrictions on Korea? Mass panic in the Korean entertainment industry]. (2016, August 4). *Sohu.* Retrieved from http://www.sohu.com/a/109082540_453791.

Part 2

Identity Formation, Transformation and Gender Relations

Gender, Aging and Disability in *Dear My Friends* (2016)

JaeYoon Park

"It's not over. We're still alive." This is the tagline for a particular Korean drama, *Dear My Friends* (*Dieo mai prenjeu*, 2016), which echoes the prevalent feelings of loss and isolation felt by many senior citizens in the midst of a growing generational gap in contemporary Korean society. Penned by a critically-acclaimed writer, Noh Hee-kyung, *Dear My Friends* centers around a group of elderly women in their sixties and seventies as they cope with the social, psychological, and biological aspects of aging. The series also features two male characters with physical disabilities that ultimately function to reveal the social stigma of limitation and inability. Such portrayals of characters with aged or disabled bodies differ markedly from most contemporary Korean dramas' thematic concerns and audience reception. The discourses surrounding K-dramas and *hallyu*, the Korean wave, lean towards young adults' and middle-aged women's desires and aspirations, encompassing various topics such as transnational media culture, fandom and consumerism, star and celebrity studies, and representations of femininity and masculinity (Kim, 2013; Kim & Choe, 2014; Kim 2014; Choi & Maliangkay 2017; Kim, 2018). Therefore, the issues of ageism and ableism portrayed in *Dear My Friends* are worth investigating considering the series' examination of the often-ignored topics of aging and disability in K-dramas, as well as its effort to connect these marginalized issues to the notion of a socially-constructed identity. With its own strength and limitation, *Dear My Friends* dramatizes marginalized individuals' struggles in relation to the wider context of social stigma and misperception while simultaneously fostering intergenerational and intercultural understanding.

A number of scholars in the gerontology and disability studies fields note that earlier discussions about aging and disability primarily focus on biological or bodily differences that serve to define ourselves in terms of the "us versus them" binary (Andrews, 1999; Calasanti & Slevin, 2001; Twigg, 2004; Calasanti & Slevin, 2006; Cox, 2015; Barnes, 2016; Goodley, 2016; Morgan & Kunkel, 2016; Sasser & Moody, 2018). Morgan and Kunkel (2016) explain that categorizing people in terms of age relies on the concept of an *other*, and this *othering* process frequently leads to ageism, "a systematic stereotyping of and discrimination against people because they are old" (p. 10). Our persisting obsession with youth (or looking young and fit) and the growing popularity of antiaging industries hence privilege the values of the young. Consequently, the older people become associated with disease and physical decline, which reinforces the widespread "fear of and disgust with growing old" (Calasanti & Slevin, 2006, p. 3). Likewise, the body has been central to the discussion of disabilities. As Goodley (2016) observes, the biomedical model has prevailed since the mid–1800s, contributing to the idea of disability as "a defect in or a failure of a bodily system that is inherently abnormal and pathological" (p. 7). This tendency to frame people with disabilities as flawed, deficient individuals inevitably promote and perpetuate ableism, an oppressive ideology and discriminatory practice that normalizes prejudicial and stigmatizing behavior directed against the persons with disabilities (Barnes, 2016).

The aforementioned scholars also argue that aging- or disable-bodiedness is not a direct result from physical changes or impairments, but it relates to the workings of multiple factors and variables stemming from the dominant social values and norms, power relations, and individuals' life experiences. More specifically, bio-social-psychological dimensions of aging processes, the ways in which aging intersects with other socially-constructed categories such as gender, race, class, and sexuality, and a life course perspective on aging that emphasizes cumulative and varying life experiences all combine to construct the experiences of aging and old age (Calasanti & Slevin , 2001; Calasanti & Slevin, 2006; Morgan & Kunkel, 2016; Sasser & Moody, 2018). Similarly, disability studies scholars recognize social, cultural, historical, economic, and relational factors, which turn physical or mental impairment into disability. Therefore, the focus is on the structural barriers that dictate how such impairment is interpreted in a given society (Sherry, 2007; Thomas, 2007; Goodley, 2016). In short, physical changes or impairments cannot be a deciding factor that naturally leads to ageist or ableist practices. The systemic inequalities and oppression arise from hegemonic relations of power that prioritize particular social values and usefulness over others.

Throughout its sixteen episodes, the Korean drama, *Dear My Friends*, proposes visions of the elderly as an oppressed minority, thereby taking the focus away from this group's biological or pathological conditions to social structures and human rights struggles. However, the ways in which the series constructs differences in relation to people with disabilities are closer to the conventional portrayal of these populations as isolated individuals disconnected to one another. In other words, while this Korean drama successfully dramatizes how old age can be a time of change and new possibilities for individuals and families, it falls short on acknowledging the social barriers and exclusions that people with disabilities experience. Although *Dear My Friends* is perhaps the most inclusive television series produced in Korea thus far, with the rarely seen on-screen images of aged and disabled bodies (Choi, 2016; Hahn, 2016; Hwang, 2016; J.H. Lee, 2016; Lim, 2016), the series primarily functions to facilitate intercultural dialogue and reconciliation between the young and the old.

Gendered and Aged Bodies: A Gaze of the Young

In this particular K-drama, at the center of such intercultural communication is Park Wan, a writer/translator in her late thirties (portrayed by Go Hyung-jung). Wan's mother, Nan-hee (portrayed by Go Doo-shim), and Nan-hee's friends are the main characters of the series. The story unfolds through Wan's voice-over narration as she tries to write a book about her mother's friends and their families. Relating to ageism in the drama, *kkondae* is the term often heard in *Dear My Friends* to describe stuffy old people that Wan is at first hesitant to write about. A degrading, slang word *kkondae* has become part of South Korea's popular lexicon in recent years, referring to old fogies with a sense of entitlement for respect and authority. Besides being entitled, *kkondae*s like to meddle with others' lives, giving unsolicited advice and forcing their outdated views on others with no regard for changing social values and economic conditions (Kim, 2015; C.H. Lee, 2016; Park, 2017). Wan's mother, Nan-hee, keeps pushing her writer daughter to stop doing translation jobs and instead write a book, entitled *My Mother's Elderly Friends*.

Wan rejects Nan-hee's book idea, saying that she does not want to get involved at all in *kkondae*'s business. In episode two, Choong-nam (one of Nan-hee's friends) says to Wan, "You're OUR daughter," to which Wan responds, "I take a pass. It's too much to deal with my mother alone." Wan's mother, Nan-hee, is a strong woman in her sixties, who lost her husband (i.e., Wan's father) five years ago and now runs a Chinese noodle restaurant. Wan, regardless of her resistance, becomes caught up in the web of her mother's "old" friends' various dramas while serving as their driver, server, helper, caretaker, but most importantly, as a surrogate for the viewers. The series invites us the viewers to experience what Wan goes through, while bearing witness to Wan's transformation from a younger individual who finds the elderly gross and grotesque to their true friend and supporter. In a nutshell, the narrative structure of *Dear My Friends* follows the process of Wan's coming to terms with *kkondae-ism*. Wan's young and able body positions herself completely outside of the elderly group at the beginning of the series, but at the series' finale, she narrates that her new book, *My Elderly Friends*, will soon be published. The title change *My Mother's Elderly Friends* to *My Elderly Friends* signifies Wan's acceptance of the elderly as her own friends in spite of the age difference and *kkondae-ism*.

Calasanti and Slevin (2006) note in their edited book, *Age Matters: Realigning Feminist Thinking* that, too often, inequalities associated with aging are seen to be a natural part of life and thus beyond dispute (p. 6). The four general ways that older people experience inequalities, which these authors discuss, are all portrayed in *Dear My Friends*: loss of power, workplace issues and marginalization, wealth and income, and finally cultural devaluation. While Wan observes, contemplates, and narrates what it means to become older, the elderly encounter varying types and degrees of inequalities in both private and public spheres throughout the series. All the older characters in their sixties and seventies in *Dear My Friends* find themselves in a position of diminished authority and autonomy. Yet, the narrative arc and images of Hee-ja (portrayed by Kim Hye-ja) shows the most drastic loss of power due to an early-stage dementia diagnosis. Disoriented, confused, and even disillusioned at times, Hee-ja frequently loses her dignity and independence. Strangers in the streets as well as her own children often yell at her out of frustration and worry. Recently widowed Hee-ja wishes to live an independent life. Trying not to become a burden on her family, due to her mental state, she still ends up in need of others' help despite her repeated self-confirmation, "I can live by myself."

Wan's voice-over narration at the beginning of the series describes Hee-ja as a childish and reckless oddball. In episode two, whereas Wan is having difficulty understanding and sympathizing with Hee-ja, the audiences share Hee-ja's audio-visual perspectives, albeit briefly. The point-of-view shots that describe Hee-ja's hallucination offer a literal identification with her perception of a reality. Another intriguing scene takes place at the end of episode two, in which Hee-ja watches a recording of herself after her son, Min-ho, installs a surveillance camera in her house in order to monitor his mother's delusion and memory loss. Audiences watch Hee-ja watching herself acting reckless and bizzare, and then in the following episode, the audiences see Hee-ja's suicide attempts, first as she stands in the middle of the street, and then, as she is tries to jump off of a bridge. However, the loss of her authority and autonomy even prevents Hee-ja from making decisions about her own life and even death. Seen through the eyes of the young, in this case, a truck driver's and police officer's, Hee-ja is merely a "crazy" old woman that needs to be stopped. The weakening of physical and mental health relegates Hee-ja's body to something to be monitored, contained, and intervened for her own safety. The brief moment of identification with Hee-ja's reality in episode two is a double-edged sword in this sense: whereas some audiences may emotionally feel close to her, the point-of-view shots serve as a justification for the need to watch and control her behavior. Hee-ja cannot be trusted, as evidenced by the objective footage of video recording. The recently-widowed, delusional old woman does not attempt to end her life out of despair, however. While it is a common misconception that those who commit suicide disregard their loved ones, Hee-ja does keep her children in mind because she is afraid of being a burden on them. Such selflessness reemerges even at the moment of contemplating on suicide. "I shouldn't cause any inconvenience to the public," Hee-ja says to herself.

Dear My Friends' storyline also problematizes the workplace marginalization and the dwindling income that threaten the elderly's economic independence and social worthiness. In a capitalist society that values productivity above anything else, a decrease in income and lack of participation in the labor market results in low self-esteem among senior citizens. As paternalistic views that associate older persons with impairments continue to be pervasive, the elderly are subject to further dependency (on family or welfare) and, as a result, their human rights are at stake (Cox, 2015). Choi (2018) maintains that the approach to resolving older persons' issues primarily through welfare programs is no longer suited to face multifaceted issues posed by fast-growing aging populations in society as these issues are intrinsically related to their human rights, self-worth, and dignity (p. 145).

Jung-ah's fight for independence and dignity in *Dear My Friends* is emblematic of the shared feelings and struggles that older housewives experience in contemporary Korean society. At first, Jung-ah's penny-pinching husband seems to be the main cause for her second-class citizen status. Her husband is patriarchal, verbally abusive, controlling, and misogynistic. Jung-ah (portrayed by Na Moon-hee) plots to divorce him, dreaming of "emancipation" and "freedom" at last. However, the viewers soon learn that she is not only dependent on her husband, but also financially dependent upon her three daughters as she makes money as their domestic help. As in any family, a mother's job never ends, but for Jung-ah, tedious domestic labor sprawls outside of her own home. With no discernible skills valued by a capitalist patriarchy, Jung-ah ends up taking care of four households.

Although Jung-ah's three daughters pay for her labor (about $10 per hour), they pay little attention to their mother's struggle for independence and dignity. They are preoccupied with their own problems—family, children, and work. Perhaps, Wan's voice-over-narration sums up the unappreciative daughters' outlook best: "I want my mother to be happy, irrespective of me" (episode two). A sentiment of self-interest like this contrasts with a selfless and devoted image that Jung-ah portrays in the series. The money Jung-ah earns as her daughters' domestic help is to cover the expenses of her mother's nursing home. Jung-ah, too, is a daughter. As a self-sacrificing wife, mother, grandmother, and daughter, Jung-ah serves as a caretaker of many while being unpaid and underpaid. After her mother dies in episode seven, Jung-ah begins to carry out her "emancipation" plan. In episode ten, she finally leaves her husband, becomes a "liberated" woman in her own place, and sleeps like a baby.

Jung-ah's husband, Suk-kyun, transforms into a more sympathetic character over the course of the series, especially after Jung-ah leaves him. As a retired factory worker, Suk-kyun currently works as a janitor at an apartment complex. According to HelpAge International (2015), a global NGO that promotes older people's rights, ageism exacerbates when it intersects with other forms of discrimination such as racism, sexism, and ableism. In the case of Suk-kyun, the other form of discrimination that he faces in the workplace is based on class. To the eyes of the young residents of the apartment complex, Suk-kyun is a powerless, working-class older man who has little to contribute to the community and society. The responsibilities of his thankless job include delivering heavy boxes on behalf of the residents and tolerating verbal abuse by someone much younger than he is. Furthermore, at different points of the series narrative, the audiences learn that Suk-kyun is ashamed of his middle-school level education. Overall, Suk-kyun is an uneducated, working-class, older man; however, his character arc shows the most changes in *Dear My Friends* as the later episodes depict him having heart-felt regrets and guilt for not having been a good father and husband. In the end, Suk-kyun realizes that his personal worth is at risk in addition to the erosion of his social worth. Therefore, he tries to make amends with Jung-ah.

Another character that harbors a feeling of shame about their education is Choong-nam (portrayed by Yoon Yuh-jung). Sixty-five-year-old, never-been-married Choong-nam runs a café in the suburbs of Seoul. She likes to mingle with younger men who are professors, intellectuals, and artists. Although no romantic feelings are involved, Choong-nam's relationship with these younger men is a one-directional and unreciprocated one as she repeatedly feeds them at her café for free and buys their expensive artwork. Yet, her pursuit of "friendship" with these men is not simply motivated by her aspiration for higher education. In fact, it stems from her internalizing the cultural devaluation of older persons. The association of old age with disease and physical and mental decline gives rise to the cultural denigration of senior citizens. Some people even view old age as "a social contagion" by co-opting such a stereotypical notion to the extreme, and seek the company of younger groups while avoiding older persons (Calasanti and Slevin, 2006). Choong-nam's fear of and disgust with old age is evident throughout the series. She not only talks about her disgust, but she makes a conscious effort to not associate with the older people. In other words, she has adopted the gaze of the young that links old age to a social contagion and is not shy about vocalizing it. By acting as a patron of starving artists and intellectuals, Choong-nam is both self-fulfilling and self-conflicting: she is self-fulfilling because she enjoys the company of those younger than herself; she is self-conflicting because she belongs in the demographic group that she detests.

The obsession with youth is not limited to older persons' yearning for youthful appearances in contemporary South Korean society. Shangri-La syndrome is a relatively new phenomenon in Korea, which describes its senior citizens' deliberate attempt to act or behave like younger individuals. Originating from James Hilton's 1933 novel *Lost Horizon*, Shangri-La refers to a mythical place that is believed to be an earthly paradise in which people enjoy youthful, immortal lives (Park & Yoo, 2011; Lee & Yoo, 2011). A socio-cultural pattern developed from the equation of youth with wealth and power encourages the elderly in Korea to not only look young and fit but to impersonate youth as well (Kim & Kim, 2018). Choong-nam in *Dear My Friends* clearly lives with Shangri-La syndrome. As clothing is the most effective tool for young appearances (Park & Yoo, 2011), Choong-nam's attire resembles that of high-school students, especially when she attends GED preparation classes. With a backpack and casual clothing, Choong-nam visually blends in well with her teenage classmates. In addition, she lacks *kkondae-ism*, which Wan, the series narrator, abhors, and as such, there is little difference between Choong-nam and her classmates in terms of behavior. Despite her age, she has not lost the common touch with the young. However, Choong-nam is the most conflicted character in the series. Upon realizing that her friendship with the professors, intellectuals, and artists will never be reciprocated, Choong-nam plots revenge while acting like an entitled, stuffy old person (i.e., *kkondae*). Furthermore, she cherishes her female friendship with Nan-hee and her friends (i.e., older women), and is even proud of her old age. In episode three, for instance, when the main characters of the series take individual portrait photos in preparation for their own funeral in the future, Choong-nam says to the photographer, "I am sixty-five years old. In Korea, aging is something you should be proud of." As a younger woman compared to the other older women in their seventies in the series, Choong-nam occupies a liminal space between denial and resistance, oscillating between *kkondae-ism* and Shangri-La syndrome as well as between aversion and pride in response to old age.

Women's Issues and Female Friendships: The Power of Growing Older Together

Dear My Friends is ultimately a feminist TV series, written by a female writer and featuring a predominantly female cast. While the series underscores ageism as a form of social injustice, it foremost foregrounds various women's issues, that is, unique life events that women may encounter in the course of their lives. The women's issues explored in the series include the following: domestic violence, sexual assault, miscarriage, abusive husbands and in-laws, financial dependence due to a capitalist patriarchy, the spouse's adultery, widowhood, ovarian/breast/liver cancer, and the multiple, simultaneous roles older women often take up as house managers and caretakers of their children, grandchildren, husbands, siblings, husband's siblings, relatives, and their own mothers.

As the only married woman among the elderly women of *Dear My Friends*, Jung-ah's life is frequently complicated in familial relationships. Her heartaches and traumatic experiences are gendered ones and still unhealed. She experienced two miscarriages at the beginning of her marriage due to strenuous domestic labor and her abusive in-laws and husband before adopting their first child. Jung-ah's adopted daughter, Soon-young, was then sexually assaulted by Suk-kyun's co-worker when she was in elementary school. Now middle-aged, Soon-young is a battered wife, married to a college professor and living a double-life behind the beautiful façade of financial stability and social respect. Jung-ah is unaware of the repeated domestic violence that Soon-young has to endure until it becomes so severe that Soon-young is not able to hide it anymore. The viewers can infer that Soon-young's unwillingness to disclose the domestic violence is due to her own traumatic experience from the past. When she told Suk-kyun about the sexual assault, the only response she received from him was victim blaming. As Soon-young plots to leave her violent husband, she encounters the obstacle of financial reliance on her husband just like many Korean housewives including her mother, Jung-ah, are subject to. However, Jung-ah is not free from the blame, either. Before finally leaving Korea, Soon-young says to Jung-ah that growing up, she felt that Jung-ah favored her biological daughters, i.e., Soon-young's two younger sisters. Just like Jung-ah's deep emotional wounds still affect many aspects of her life, Soon-young's traumatic memory and experience shape her relationships with the loved ones around her.

Furthermore, the spouse's infidelity is a recurring theme in the series. Hee-ja's husband before his death was a known, frequent adulterer. Nan-hee actually caught the cheating scene in her own bedroom between her husband and her friend, Sook-hee, and still cannot seem to let go. She repeatedly unleashes her anger toward Young-won (portrayed by Park Won-sook), a popular actress and a twice-divorcee. Nan-hee cannot understand why Young-won is still a good friend with Sook-hee, the cheater. As for Nan-hee's father, he was not only a multiple offender in terms of infidelity when he was young, but he was also a violent and abusive husband although Nan-hee's mother did not seem to hold grudge. She still takes care of her oxygen-tank bound, limping husband who has lost speech after a stroke. Health issues, cancer in particular, are also addressed. The feud between Nan-hee, Sook-hee, and Young-won comes to an end when Nan-hee finds out about Sook-hee's final-stage cancer and actually sees Young-won's bare body tormented by cancer. Toward the end of the series, Nan-hee is also diagnosed with cancer. In a strange, twisted way, cancer creates a sense of camaraderie among these three women through their common suffering and changing bodies.

In the series' sixteen episodes, the elderly women present themselves as a socially-marginalized group, rejecting the idea of being simply observed by an outsider as isolated individuals undergoing their own personal tragedy. Through their awareness about the pervasive ageism that deny them opportunities and disable their autonomy, these older women emerge as active, vocal members of the disenfranchised community. Such a strong sense of membership gives rise to their ultimate empowerment as a group engineered by shared life experiences and mutual support. Feminist gerontologist Holstein (2006) offers an insight to how older women can resist the oppressions (both internal and external) that shape their daily experiences as they age. Citing Ferguson, Holstein proposes "oppositional communities" (Ferguson, 1995)—microcommunities of resistance, in which older women treat one another "with respect, affection, and attentiveness" while caring and bringing attention to their nonnormative bodies and also acknowledging together their "pain, suffering, and loss" (Furman, 1997). Holstein further suggests that these microworlds offer a secret space where the "age peers" share their fears, sorrows, and joys, and ultimately empower themselves (pp. 328–329). The group of elderly women in *Dear My Friends* epitomizes a Holsteinian micro-community of resistance. With heightened consciousness, women of older age can "give one another the strength to assert the dignity" (Holstein, 2006) by being there for one another in times of personal crises. The women of *Dear My Friends* are one another's emergency contact and support system. They are not in denial of various bio-social-psychological changes old age brings. They, instead, take charge in affirming their identities and demanding fair treatments. In the process, their sorrows, joys, and intimate fears are shared. Indeed, the personal aging process is political.

Needless to say, female friendships contribute to a strong sense of group identity for these older women. Although they often suffer from the lack of support, whether from their families or from their own society, they often find themselves as caretakers of one another. Throughout their lives, the women of *Dear My Friends* have served as caretakers of everyone else in their respective, extended families. For instance, Nan-hee frequently visits her parents' house in the countryside in order to attend to her aging mother, stroke-stricken father, and younger brother with a physical disability. As previously discussed, Jung-ah takes care of her three daughters' households, grandchildren, and her own mother in a nursing home. Moreover, Jung-ah has been a caretaker of her husband's eight siblings and their families. Choong-nam financially supports her siblings while also covering all of her nieces and nephews' college tuitions. Whether widowed, married, or unmarried, all the elderly women in *Dear My Friends* play a maternal role in one way or another. After decades of self-sacrificial service to their families, these women have created an alternative family of their own in the later stage of their lives. For better, for worse, for richer, for poorer, in sickness and in health, they comfort and support one another. Therefore, this Korean drama, *Dear My Friends*, makes a conscious effort in portraying how aging is a gendered process and how these women in their sixties and seventies form a resistance movement of sort by sharing their life experiences and growing older together. However, it would be remiss not to point out that this microcommunity does not constitute a utopian world where every member lives in harmony all the time. There are conflicts, fights, disagreements, and misunderstanding, some of which dates to some thirty years ago. Nevertheless, this group of women persist, through numerous sleep-overs, get-togethers, and group travels. As the series narrative unfolds, they make up, forgive, and make amends among broken ties and burned bridges.

Individualized and Romanticized Disabilities: A Gaze of the Ableist

The theme of female friendship is evident in *Dear My Friends*' narrative structure, which grants that older women's experiences are worthy of social and cultural inquiries. However, another intersecting identity focusing on the people with disabilities remains rather unexplored as previously mentioned. In episode three, we learn that Wan's (ex-)boyfriend, Yeon-ha, is in a wheelchair, and she has run away even though she seems to be very much in love with him. Wan's inability or rather difficulty in dealing with Yeon-ha's sudden injury—a car accident that paralyzed his legs—and subsequent disability results, in part, from her family history. The fact that her uncle also has a physical disability, and her mother's vehement objection, "I would accept any man in the world, but no married man or disabled person like your uncle, whatsoever" (episode two), may have spurred and intensified Wan's fear of disability. Nan-hee is a controlling mother, and she likes to delineate and prohibit boyfriend materials that are unacceptable for Wan, her grown daughter. In fact, Nan-hee does not know about Yeon-ha's disability when she makes that unequivocal statement, and it is ironic that she pinpoints the exact two types of men with which Wan is currently involved. Wan is dating a married man in order to forget Yeon-ha, her true love. Nan-hee is opposed to the idea of Wan dating a disabled man because she has witnessed all the stigma, disadvantage, and inequalities that her younger brother (Wan's uncle) has to go through. Growing up under a strong, controlling single-mother, Wan has developed a love-hate relationship with her mother, Nan-hee. Although it is unclear what truly makes Wan hesitant to fully commit to her courtship with Yeon-ha, Wan continues to talk with Yeon-ha via video chats while dating a married man.

Unlike the elderly women who have established a great support system and a group identity, the two male characters with physical disabilities are seen isolated in their own domestic space and insulated within family relations. For instance, we do not get to see Yeon-ha and Wan's uncle in a social setting outside of their home or private sphere. The lack of social interactions associated with these two men functions to individualize disabilities. Mogk (2013) maintains that we do not see disability because we "perceive it as the isolated condition of a particular person." Citing Lennard J. Davis (1995), Mogk elaborates that "one tends to sentimentalize it [an impairment] and link it to the bourgeois sensibility of individualism and the drama of an individual story" (pp. 1–2). However, one must understand how experiences of disability are produced by the social environment. According to Goodley (2017),

> Impairments never appear outside of society; impairments are always understood in the register of the social. And impairments are not biological phenomena untouched by the social. A discursive approach reveals the socio-historical origins of impairment. Disability might be defined, then, as a phenomenon that occurs when impairment is understood, lived, measured, felt, thought and enacted in the social world [p. 125].

Media representations of disability often fail to construct experiences of disability as stories of a society unlike the stories that dramatize other recognized forms of social exclusion such as sexism, racism, and classism (Mitchell & Snyder, 1997; Mogk, 2013). As discussed above, *Dear My Friends* tackles ageism as a form of social injustice that marginalizes a group of people based on age. Yet, this K-drama reinforces the conventional idea that disabilities are of a personal problem that each individual should overcome. Interestingly, the series associates Hee-ja's early-stage dementia with aging rather than a type of mental disability. As the older people's hardships and group identity are at the center of the narrative, this feminist show even portrays a misogynistic male character, Suk-kyun, in a sympathetic light while emphasizing the social oppression and inequalities that he experiences due to his old age. Meanwhile, the series makes the two, younger male characters with physical disabilities rather voiceless and marginalized.

Yeon-ha lives in a beautiful town in Slovenia. Wan and Yeon-ha fell in love while Wan was studying abroad. Therefore, the plot segments that depict

Wan and Yeon-ha's relationship in flashbacks utilize the backdrop of an exotic, European setting. The beautiful, exotic, yet "different" Slovenia parallels Yeon-ha's now "different" body. The ways in which *Dear My Friends* renders Yeon-ha's difference are close to the medical model or personal tragedy approach to disability. His paralysis poses a "problem" for himself and for the non-disabled to be cured or cared for, as the focus is on the rehabilitation and treatment of that impairment. Wan, now in Korea, frequently encourages Yeon-ha to do physical exercise when she is video chatting with him. Overcoming the problem of disability through a workout is still on Wan's mind when she flies to Slovenia in episode ten to finally see him three years after the accident.

The personal tragedy theory of the biomedical model is also evident in the portrayal of Wan's uncle. His body with limping legs is often framed through the gazes of Nan-hee and her mother as they look at him with pity and worry about his future. Disability is essentially linked to deficiency, abnormality, and lack of autonomy and self-sufficiency. Thus, *Dear My Friends* focuses more on foregrounding the desires and fears of the non-disabled (e.g. Wan, Nan-hee, and Nan-hee's mother) than exploring the social reality of disability that Yeon-ha and Wan's uncle actually experience. Interestingly, Wan's uncle becomes fond of a Filipino woman in town although their romance does not make visible on-screen. The series' association of foreign-ness with Yeon-ha and Wan's uncle recalls the familiar practices of *othering* bodily difference. In a symbolic sense, disability is an exotic and different *other*. Otherwise, the different body evokes foreign and exotic feelings.

Moreover, the series falls into the conventional category of films and television programs that employ a star with an able body in a disabled role. Regarding the recent controversy surrounding whitewashing in Hollywood—the casting of white actors for minority roles—media producers, actors, and media/cultural critics point out that such a racist practice not only demonstrates disregard for culture-specific stories, but it also perpetuates the implicit bias that only white people can play the lead characters. As a century-old practice, whitewashing has resulted in the erasure of minorities and their experiences in media representations, equating whiteness with the American experience (Gilmore, 2016; Sun & Ford, 2016; Ehrlich & Nguyen, 2017; Fang, 2018). In a similar vein, there is a pattern of media representations when it comes to disability: an actor with a non-disabled body portraying a disabled character. Even though actors, media scholars, and disability advocates alike have criticized this pattern of representation for being offensive, the casting trend is too common in films: *Rain Man* (1988), *My Left Foot* (1989), *Forrest Gump* (1994), *I Am Sam* (2001), *Frida* (2002), *Ray* (2004), *The King's Speech* (2010), and *The Theory of Everything* (2014), to name a few. With their inspirational stories and life-affirming messages, these films frequently receive the best-film-of-the-year nominations at the Academy Awards, and the non-disabled actors in disabled roles are often considered strong awards contenders for their "acting" skills (Siebers, 2008; Mogk, 2013; Ryan, 2017; Stewart, 2018; Enable Magazine, 2018).

In *Dear My Friends*, an A-list star Jo In-sung plays Yeon-ha, an animator living in Slovenia. As one of the most popular and bankable stars currently working in the Korean film and television industries, Jo is known for his flawless face and long legs with exceptionally tall height. Compound with an exotic setting of Slovenia, the casting of Jo In-sung makes it difficult to perceive *Dear My Friends*' story of disability as offering its own valuable perspectives on society. The viewers are well aware that Jo In-sung is not disabled, and therefore, the romance between Wan and Yeon-ha becomes an imaginary story of catastrophic and tragic disability, which intensifies Wan's conflict with her mother. *Dear My Friends*' central narrative thread weaves through decades-old misunderstanding and love-hate relationship between Wan and Nan-hee. Wan's love interest, Yeon-ha, and his disability function as a narrative device that raises the stake in that complicated mother-daughter relationship. In the process, the two supporting characters with disabilities are marginalized in the series narrative, individualized and isolated in their personal stories of struggles, and romanticized in their association with the foreign.

Conclusion

Dear My Friends depicts various women's issues focusing on a group of elderly women in their sixties and seventies. The series explores often-neglected topics such as gendered aging processes, female friendship, and ageism as a form of social oppression. The perspective of a thirty-something year old narrator and her transformation allow the series to engage the viewers with the social approaches to aging and age relations. The thematic concerns center around reconciliation, intergenerational understanding, and intercultural conversation. In the face of the loss of power, workplace marginalization, diminished income, and cultural devaluation, the elderly women of *Dear My Friends* demonstrate how older women can create their own, alternative family for themselves. Domestic violence, miscarriage, adultery, widowhood, and health issues only make their group identity stronger as these women share intimate fears, sorrows, and joys in the course of their lives.

Yet, the issues of disabilities are little explored in relation to a socially-constructed, minority identity while the series foregrounds the emotional process through which Wan makes amends with *kkondae-ism*, and ultimately with her mother. As the desires and fears of the non-disabled are at the center of its narrative, the series leaves out the social dimension of disability with its two male characters with disabilities lacking their own voices or perspectives. This K-drama also continues with the ableist practice of casting a non-disabled actor for a disabled role. The careful attentiveness to the marginalized individuals with gendered and aged bodies is lost when it comes to the representation of disabled bodies. Is it because aging discriminates against no one? Perhaps, aging gets more attention and weight in the series because everyone gets old? As one adage in the series says, "we all have a time limit."

References

Andrews, M. (1999). The seductiveness of agelessness. *Ageing & Society*, 19, 301–18.

Barnes, E. (2016). *The minority body: A theory of disability*. Oxford: Oxford University Press.

Calasanti, T.M., & Slevin, K.F. (Eds.). (2001). *Gender, social inequalities, and aging*. Walnut Creek, CA: AltaMira Press.

Calasanti, T.M., & Slevin, K.F. (Eds.). (2006). *Age matters: Realigning feminist thinking*. New York: Routledge.

Choi, J.B., & Maliangkay, R. (Eds.). (2017). *K-pop—The international rise of the Korean music industry*. New York: Routledge.

Choi, M.Y. (2016, May 24). *Dear my friends*, not a conventional family drama. *Etnews*. Retrieved from http://www.etnews.com/20160524000243.

Choi, S.J. (2018). International trend and issues in protecting and promoting the rights of older persons. *Journal of the Korean Gerontological Society*, *38*(1), 143–168.

Cox, C.B. (2015). *Social policy for an aging society*. New York: Springer Publishing Company.

Davis, L.J. (1995). Enforcing normalcy: Disability deafness and the body. New York: Verso.

Ehrlich, D., & Nguyen, H. (2017, August 31). Why 'Death Note' is guilty of whitewashing, and what we can do to prevent more movies like it. *Indiewire*. Retrieved from https://www.indiewire.com/2017/08/death-note-whitewashing-conversation-1201871811/?fbclid=IwAR2aPSg_zYov2JFcy7iRt6DrjrOZj4-G6yx589U_2XIXVyxrkljYZrN66bE.

Enable Magazine (2018, January 19). Why won't Hollywood cast disabled actors in disabled roles? *Enable Magazine*. Retrieved from http://enablemagazine.co.uk/why-wont-hollywood-cast-disabled-actors-in-disabled-roles/.

Fang, J. (2018, August 8). Yellowface, whitewashing, and the history of white people playing Asian characters. *Teen Vogue*. Retrieved from https://www.teenvogue.com/story/yellowface-whitewashing-history?mbid=social_cp_fb_tny&fbclid=IwARlmvnqeUgOmSkGBMOhraNHTcmeHPDLWceMYLYABVesEk69sSODBrgKoEl8.

Ferguson, A. (1995). Feminist communities and moral revolution. In P. Wiess & M. Friedman (Eds.), *Feminism and community* (pp. 367–398). Philadelphia: Temple University Press.

Furman, F. (1997). Facing the mirror: Older woman and beauty shop culture. New York: Routledge.

Gilmore, C. (2016, April 29). Hollywood's Asian whitewashing: Why it happens so often, and why it must be stopped. *Indiewire*. Retrieved from https://www.indiewire.com/2016/04/hollywoods-asian-whitewashing-why-it-happens-so-often-and-why-it-must-be-stopped-291587/.

Goodley, D. (2016). *Disability studies: An interdisciplinary introduction* (2nd ed.). Los Angeles: SAGE Publications Ltd.

Hahn, H.R. (2016, May 13). *Dear my friends*, the real story of the elderly begins. *10Star: K-wave Magazine*. Retrieved from http://tenasia.hankyung.com/archives/935367.

HelpAge International (2015). A new convention on the rights of older people: A concrete proposal. Retrieved from https://social.un.org/ageing-working-group/documents/sixth/HelpAgeInternational.pdf.

Holstein, M.B. (2006). On being an aging woman. In T.M. Calasanti & K.F. Slevin (Eds.), *Age matters: Realigning feminist thinking* (pp. 313–334). New York: Routledge.

Hwang, J.M. (2016, June 2). Empathy with the elderly and the women. *The Hankyoreh*. Retrieved from http://www.hani.co.kr/arti/culture/entertainment/746578.html.

Kim, I.S., & Kim, G.R. (2018). The meta-analysis on variables related to aging anxiety of middle and old aged in Korea. *Journal of the Korean Gerontological Society*, *38*(2), 309–327.

Kim, J. (Ed.). (2014). Reading Asian television drama: Crossing borders and breaking boundaries. New York: I.B.Tauris.

Kim, J.H. (2015, January 21). Kkondae vs. senior. *NewsTapa*. Retrieved from https://newstapa.org/23015.

Kim, K.H., & Choe, Y. (Eds.). (2014). *The Korean popular culture reader*. Durham, NC: Duke University Press.

Kim, S.Y. (2018). *K-pop live: Fans, idols, and multimedia performance*. Stanford, CA: Stanford University Press.

Kim, Y. (Ed.). (2013). *The Korean Wave: The Korean media go global*. New York: Routledge.

Lee, C.H. (2016, January 24). The 6 tips on how not to be a kkondae. *Huffingtonpost Korea*. Retrieved from https://www.huffingtonpost.kr/2016/01/25/story_n_9066530.html.

Lee, J.H. (2016, May 30). *Dear my friends*, hatred and violence repeat themselves. *Oh My News*. Retrieved from http://star.ohmynews.com/NWS_Web/OhmyStar/at_pg.aspx?CNTN_CD=A0002213468.

Lee, M.H., & Yoo, H.S. (2011). A study of appearance management and Shangri-La syndrome. *Korea Fashion & Textile Research Journal*, *13*(2), 194–204.

Lim, U.Y. (2016, May 26). The harmony of kkondaes. *Woman Chosun*. Retrieved from https://woman.chosun.com/client/news/viw.asp?cate=C01&nNewsNumb=20160558462.

Mitchell, D.T., & Snyder, S.L. (Eds.). (1997). *The body and physical difference: Discourses of disability*. Ann Arbor: University of Michigan Press.

Mogk, M.E. (Ed.). (2013). Different bodies: Essays on disability in film and television. Jefferson, NC: McFarland.

Morgan, L.A., & Kunkel, S.R. (2016). *Aging, society, and the life course*. New York: Springer Publishing Company.

Park, S.H. (2017, February 22). The three ways to tell if you are a kkondae. *Chosun Ilbo*. Retrieved from http://news.chosun.com/site/data/html_dir/2017/02/21/2017022102028.html.

Park, S.J., & Yoo, H.S. (2011). A study of Shangri-La syndrome. *Korea Fashion & Textile Research Journal*, *13*(1), 55–65.

Ryan, P. (2017, October 22). Hollywood is talking about inclusion more than ever, but not for disabled actors. *USA Today*. Retrieved from https://www.usatoday.com/story/life/movies/2017/10/22/hollywood-is-talking-inclusion-more-than-ever-but-not-disabled-actors/771814001/.

Sasser, J.R., & Moody, H.R. (2018). *Gerontology: The basics*. New York: Routledge.

Sherry, M. (2007). (Post)Colonising disability. Special Issue of Wagadu: Journal of Transnational Women's and Gender Studies, 4, 10–22.

Siebers, T. (2008). *Disability theory*. Ann Arbor: University of Michigan Press.

Stewart, S. (2018). The Oscars love movies about disability, not disabled actors. *Film School Rejects*. Retrieved from https://filmschoolrejects.com/oscars-love-movies-disability-not-disabled-actors/.

Sun, R., & Ford R. (2016, May 9). Where are the Asian-American movie stars? *Hollywood Reporter*. Retrieved from https://www.hollywoodreporter.com/features/are-asian-american-movie-stars-890755?fbclid=IwAR1--2t8_BpDj475e9-Cy_aigihcDhLKIHoNJ4gNKvLpQGRmpR7GaoSybgM.

Thomas, C. (2007). Sociologies of disability, 'impairment,' and chronic illness: Ideas in disability studies and medical sociology. London, UK: Continuum.

Twigg, J. (2004). The body, gender, and age: Feminist insights in social gerontology. *Journal of Aging Studies*, *18*(1): 59–73.

A Postsecular Analysis of Two Ghost-Infested Dramas

MARY A. SOBHANI

A heightened interest in Korean dramas began in the 1990s and increased significantly in the first decades of the twenty-first century in the United States with the establishment of such streaming video providers as Netflix, Hulu, and DramaFever established in 1997, 2007, and 2009, respectively. As recent studies have indicated (McGuire & Buchbinder, 2010; Levina & Bui, 2013), during this same time period in the United States, there is also an upswing in the production and popularity of television series that focus on elements of the paranormal, ghostly, or monstrous. This essay positions itself at the point of juncture of these two cultural trends.

Two Korean dramas, *Oh My Ghost!* (*O naui gwisinnim*) from 2015 and *The Master's Sun* (*Jugunui taeyang*) from 2013, form the focal point of this study. Specifically, this essay analyzes these two K-dramas in light of their reception by western audiences and by means of a postsecular theory of analysis. Both of these K-dramas are hybrids of the romantic comedy and horror genres; both are highly-acclaimed television series in Korea, nominees and winners of the APAN Star Awards[1] and the DramaFever Awards[2]; and both depict a reality in which the metaphysical and the mundane co-exist. The argument herein is as follows: without an exploration of the juxtaposition of the supernatural and the "normal" in these two K-dramas—with particular attention to the insights which postsecular theory affords us—a true understanding of their appeal to audiences in the United States has barely a ghost of a chance.

Kim (2013) argues that K-dramas's popularity resides in its focus on universal human themes, where good and evil exist, good triumphs, and beauty, "both visual and *spiritual*" (emphasis mine, p. 140), are emphasized. If the spiritual refers to matters pertaining to the qualities of the soul and the practices of belief, we can understand that the description above alludes to attributes impossible to be measured, such as altruism, faith, and self-sacrifice. As such, Kim's (2013) argument points to a postsecular reading of these K-dramas. After all, in these works, material wealth, fame, and success may have their place, but the happy ending necessitates the actualization of the latent energies, powers, and possibilities inherent in the characters themselves—aspects that are as vital as they are scientifically unquantifiable. Socio-economic upgrades certainly happen—in the case of both of the females leads studied herein, both Bong-sun and Gong-shil arrive at the end of the series in much better financial shape than when they began. However, these upgrades are presented as positive consequences of attaining an integrated life, where the supernatural and the mundane are not relegated to separate spheres of existence.[3]

At the time of this publication, there has been no study of K-drama reception in the U.S. from a postsecular perspective. A postsecular perspective, as Habermas (2001, 2005) defines it, offers a reconceptualization of the secular and spiritual as intricately connected and co-existent. At the same time, postsecular theory seeks to foster a re-engagement with religious or spiritual thought and discourse, while emphatically rejecting religious rigidity or fundamentalism of any sort (Habermas, 2005). It is important to acknowledge at the outset that, although the secular/spiritual divide characteristic of secularist ideologies pervades Western culture in the twentieth century, this dichotomous view of the scientific and the scientifically-unquantifiable is not the dominant mode of thought in either traditional or present-day Korean society. One need only read such works as those by Yu and Yu (2010), Winfield (2011), Laurel (2011) or Lee (2015) to verify that extranormal energies and shamanistic traditions are part and parcel of Korean cultural expressions, whether folktales, fiction, drama, television or film. However, as this essay focuses on the analysis of K-dramas in light of an American viewership, this study proposes that examining the monster narratives of these two series through a postsecular perspective can illumine an important facet of K-dramas' transnational appeal.

Levina and Bui's (2013) essays dovetail interestingly with Habermas' argument that western society is undergoing a significant cultural shift (2008). As indicated by Levina and Bui in their introduction to this work, films and television series which present a "monster narrative" provide a space in which 21st-century society can deal with the anxieties that come from living in a world vastly different from what it was just three decades ago. Specifically, these scholars posit that representations of the supernatural in film and television "have become omnipresent" and they have done so because "they represent collective social anxieties over resisting and embracing change in the twenty-first century. They can be read as a response to a rapidly changing cultural, social, political, economic and moral landscape" (p. 1–2).

From Secularism to Postsecular Theory: An Overview

Kaufmann (2007) writes that the secular metanarrative is "a triumph of empiricism over superstition, reason over faith, and the emancipation of all spheres—science, knowledge, the market, the state—from the oppressive and authoritarian 'yoke of religion'" (p. 607). Indeed, this description of the secularist modality should sound familiar. The notion of science and knowledge as the purveyors of freedom from the "yoke of religion" and the idea that reason and faith are diametrically opposed to each other are not unfamiliar concepts in western academic thought in general or in theories of western analysis in particular.

There is ample reason for this. Prosman (2011) offers a history of secularity in the West from a postmodern framework. Historicizing the concept of the secular, Prosman rightly observes that "in the nineteenth and early twentieth centuries, secularism is a standard assumption for virtually every intellectual" (p. 5). To illustrate, he references Casanova (1994), who analyzed the history of the secularization thesis in the social sciences. Casanova argued that assumptions, whether stated or not, of virtually all the founding fathers of the Western social sciences adhere to the theory of secularization, and listed them as follows: Karl Marx to John Stuart Mill, from Auguste Compte to Herbert Spencer, from E. B. Tylor to James Frazer, from Ferdinand Toennies to Georg Simmel, from Émile Durkheim to Max Weber, from Wilhelm Wundt to Sigmund Freud, from Lester Ward to William G. Sumner, from Robert Park to George H. Mead (p. 17). The secularization thesis, in other words, is largely uncontested in Western thought throughout the last two centuries.

Casanova (1994) explained this lack of critical attention thusly: "as long as there is consensus within the community of practitioners that they already possess a coherent, consistent, and convincing explanation of the phenomena in question, there is no reason why one should look for alternative explanations when the available ones seem to work" (p. 29). This is not to say that there were no scientific minds which felt something was lacking in the secular ideologies of the time. As early as 1933, Jung had the perspicuity of vision to question this state of affairs, lamenting the "modern preference for physical grounds of explanation" for all things, including the soul or "psyche" (p. 179); he bemoaned the fact that "[t]o grant the substantiality of the soul… is repugnant to the spirit of the age" (p. 176). Still, the secularization thesis itself was not collectively contested until, as Casanova indicated, the second half of the twentieth century:

> The decade of the 1960 saw, for the first time, the separation of the theory of secularization from its ideological origins in the Enlightenment critique of religion and to

> distinguish the theory of secularization, as a theory of the modern autonomous differentiation of the secular and the religious spheres, from the thesis that the end result of the process of modern differentiation would be the progressive erosion, decline and eventual disappearance of religion [p. 19].

This new thesis of secularization that develops—which Casanova (1994) calls "functionalist" and attributes to Luckman (1967)—postulates religion's loss of its "traditional societal and public functions" as well as the "privatization and marginalization of religion" (p. 19).

This reformulated thesis of secularization holds sway until the 1980s, after which the dramatic increase of the public role of religion makes obvious the fallacy of the new formulation (Casanova, 1994, p. 19), a state of affairs which Habermas addresses seven years after the publication of Casanova's work, in his 2001 acceptance speech. It is in this address that Habermas coins the term *postsecular*[4] and expands upon it (2005). In this article, Habermas defines the characteristics of a newly-emerging postsecular Western society as one in which the spheres of the sacred and the secular are no longer as rigidly separate as in previous decades.

Notwithstanding this present-day moment of cultural transition from secular to postsecular culture, a postsecular focus even now risks the danger—except perhaps in Religious Studies or Anthropology departments—of raising flags in the academy, since a suspicion of religious discourse is still extant in some arenas of academic study. Levitt (2009) confronts this state of affairs: "[I]n literary studies there is a great deal of suspicion surrounding engagement with any expression of religion whatsoever. Religion continues to carry the taint of abjection. It is primitive, outmoded, and dangerous" (p. 110–111). Certainly, there is a set of understandable reasons for this, one of which is, as Taylor (1996) identified it, the "God question":

> "God" is the place in the discourse when scholarly neutrality slips into something else, negative, positive, evasive. It is the place where historical scholarships meets major issue [i.e., ontological belief in an Omnipotent Creator], and steps back so that the historical structure will not be endangered (often a good move). It is the place where the critic ... is most embarrassed, most exposed, most naked. It demands talk about ultimate questions, indeed the ultimate question. Yet if such talk is excluded, we miss the pith and core and "Ahnung" [idea/ notion] of the literary drive in many cases.

Taylor posited that, in missing the "pith and core" of a text by ignoring the God issue, we become "poor readers"; and this is so because the God question itself is part of the works we study.

It would be anachronistic to identify Taylor as a postsecularist—his article, after all, was not published until 1996, five years before Habermas coins the term—however, his arguments seem to foreshadow the thoughts articulated in postsecular theory. Taylor's "God question" points to the impasse which postsecular inquiry seeks to solve: the lack of a discourse with which to more fully and richly address the sacred or spiritual in a field of study which, as well it should, honors reason and logic.

Taylor made the argument for a "great critical need" in contemporary western criticism for a discourse by which spirituality in literature—and as this essay would add, by which other forms of multimedia text—can be addressed with all its intricacies. He identified the 1996 lay of the land in literary studies as one in which religious critical discourse is not yet one of the major discourses in academia, something he notes does a disservice to texts that "cry out for sophisticated critical treatment" from a perspective of religious critical theory (he provides examples from the works of Sandra Cisneros, William Butler Yeats, and Flannery O'Connor):

> We live in an age of critical discourses that are expert in discussing the dimensions of class, gender, textuality, and historical context. Yet an important part of the literature we read goes untouched by our discourses, or is deconstructed, historicized, sexualized, or made symptomatic of covert power relationships.... There is a need in our time for religious interpretations that are substantial enough to enter into a productive and competitive relation with the reigning critical discourses.

Although this essay does not presume to develop the sort of wide-ranging critical religious discourse that Taylor calls for, it does offer postsecular criticism as a possible answer to the need, a position which Neuman (2008) also offers.

Neuman (2008) provides an explanation of how postsecular thought differs from contemporary modes of thought embodied in postcolonialism and postmodernism. He begins by tracing the history of religious discourse in Western criticism: "Religion has so long wielded the sword of empire—or been appropriated by colonial adventures—that postcolonial criticism is anathema to hegemonic religiosity in general, and to Christianity in particular" (p. 20). Indeed, Edward Said's *The world, the text and the critic* (1979) is exemplary of this logic. In *The world*, as cited in Neuman, Said's take on religious discourse is anything but favorable, for according to Said, Orientalism and religious discourse share the nefarious attributes of "serv[ing] as agents of closure, shutting off human investigation, criticism, and effort in deference to the authority of the more-than-human, the supernatural, the other-worldly" (p. 290). Neuman, (2008) however, argues that Said's position fundamentally misrepresents religious discourse as the antithesis of secular criticism, a key point in postsecular thought.

> Said's argument, and those like it, offers a poignant call for ethical politics and inquiry, but is a reductive and ultimately dangerous restriction of religiosity, one that fundamentally misrepresents "religion," artificially posits it as the antithesis of a "secular" critical methodology, and contributes to the occlusion by which "religion"—and with it concepts like belief, faith, and universality—have become sites of exclusion from critical consciousness [p. 22].

To put it simply, false dichotomies are fortified.

Neuman goes on to cite a number of consequences to this exclusion: "By deploying religion as a negative limit against which liberal critique constitutes itself, critical theory unintentionally perpetuates the myth of secularization" (p. 22). Reminiscent of Taylor's (1996) position, Neuman notes a further consequence: "the critical community abdicates its role in contesting the terms, texts, and ideologies of religious debate" (p. 22). To be sure, this is not to say that discussions on religion or spirituality in literature and cinema are inexistent. There are many journals—*Literature and Theology, Religion and Arts, The Journal of Bahá'í Studies, Christianity and Literature, Bahá'í Studies Online, Religion and Literature*—in whose pages are found precisely such discussions. What a postsecular perspective has to offer western theories of analysis, however, and what critics such as Kaufmann (2005), Neuman (2008), McClure (2007), and Habermas (2005) argue, is a reframing of the spiritual and the secular as complementary and porous, rather than inherently oppositional and relegated strictly to private/public spaces, respectively.

Postsecularism questions the notion that to be modern means to be secular. As such, it offers a reconceptualization of the secular/spiritual binary against a 200-year tradition of—to use Jung's expression—a "spirit of the age" (p. 176) in which the notions of "spirit" are better left unaddressed or, if broached, best done so from the Sunday pulpit. Indeed, Ratti's (2013) critique of secularism centers on the ideologies that result from it, such as "the ideology that people should confine their beliefs to what they can observe in the material world, or that to have a secular outlook, including the belief that state and religion should be separate, is to be modern, progressive and rational" (p.5). In this sense, he echoes Neuman, who argues that a postsecular perspective is nothing less than "a response to the inadequacies of binary understandings of secularism and religion" (2008, p. 33).

From the above overview of postsecular thought, then, it can be argued that a postsecular analysis of K-dramas and their reception in the West offers a theoretical framework that presents the scientifically inexplicable not as a supersession of quotidian reality but in an integral partnership with it. The author of this essay argues that the popularity of K-dramas such as *Oh My Ghost!* and *The Master's Sun* in the United States springs from an appreciation for the imbrication of the spiritual and the secular, of the magical and the mundane, representative of a postsecular culture-shift in Western society.

Ghosts and the Women Who See Them

To analyze the paranormal plot lines of *Oh My Ghost!* and *The Master's Sun* and how they transcend the secular/spiritual dichotomy, the author will look first at the female protagonists of each series. Both *Oh My Ghost!*

and *The Master's Sun* center on women with the ability to see ghosts; it is through the female protagonists' supernatural abilities that secular ideologies are problematized. The female protagonists must learn to accept and confront their reality as a space containing both the mystical and mundane to become stronger, wiser, and have their own happily-ever-afters.

In *Oh My Ghost!*, the female lead, Na Bong-sun, is a shy and mortifyingly unassuming cook. "Weak-spirited," as she herself admits in the first episode, she is vulnerable to having her body invaded by ghosts, precisely the event that precipitates the dramatic unfolding of the story when the thoroughly extroverted ghost of amnesiac murder-victim, Shin Soon-ae, jumps into her body. In *The Master's Sun*, the protagonist Tae Gong-shil is a woman whose life is limited by fear of what she and no one else can see, and indeed, the green spirits that appear to her are gruesome and terrifying. Denial and avoidance of the inexplicable do not suffice in the case of either of these women. The female protagonists, Na Bong-sun and Tae Gong-shil, must come to grips with their unwanted spirit-seeing talents, develop the skills necessary to deal with paranormal entities, and do so as they also navigate the mundane world of labor and love affairs. It is only by doing so that they become fully-realized individuals, capable of standing on their own.

As mentioned above, although this essay does not mean to impose an original postsecular intent upon the writers or producers of *Oh My Ghost!* or *The Master's Sun*, a postsecular analysis of their dramas results in some surprising points of juncture between their works and postsecular thought—or perhaps not so surprising, considering these television series have been so well-received transnationally in societies which cohere with the characteristics that Habermas (2008) has proposed as illustrative of postsecular society. As Habermas has argued, postsecular society manifests a change of consciousness attributed to the understanding that modernization is not "indisputably linked" to the inevitable fading-away of the religious, mystical, or non-scientifically based aspects of reality (p. 20). This feature is certainly in harmony with the K-dramas studied here, as the creators of these television series do not fail to offer their audiences worlds where the dividing lines between the mystical and the mundane blur.

The first words of *Oh My Ghost!* foreshadow the reframing of reality which McClure (2007) identified in his pioneering work of postsecular literary criticism as central to postsecular works: the co-existence of the secular and the spiritual. As the camera pans over a cityscape, a radio host's voice fades in: "Oh, did you know.... Usually people think of a ghost in a white gown, with long black hair, only appearing in deserted houses... the truth is, they exist in our daily lives. Right now. Next to us" (Episode 1). Indeed, mere moments afterward, the audience is introduced to the ghost of Shin Soon-ae, the amnesiac murder victim who cannot remember the circumstances of her demise.

She appears wandering through the city streets, among the skyscrapers and the businessmen. From the onset, the audience is given a visual representation of the overlapping nature of the spiritual and the mundane in a thoroughly modern setting. This is significant, as it problematizes the secularist position that modernity has no space for anything that cannot be identified with the five senses. Although the viewer is unaware at first that Soon-ae is a spirit, this purposeful blindsiding of the viewing audience underscores the very intercalation of the mystical into the every-day. This positioning underlies the entire series and echoes the notion of the blurred dividing-lines between the secular and the metaphysical which is so prevalent in postsecularism.

As with *Oh My Ghost!*, *The Master's Sun* presents a protagonist whose life is defined by her ability to see ghosts. Unlike Bong-sun in *Oh My Ghost!*, however, protagonist Gong-shil is already speaking to ghosts and browbeaten into doing so by their incessant presence in her life, fulfilling their requests as the only way to be rid of them. Because of the constant bombardment of horrific apparitions, Gong-shil's life is in disarray. Like Na Bong-sun in *Oh My Ghost!*, Tae Gong-shil can hardly be said to be living up to her potential. Although nicknamed "Big Sun" at school due to her intelligence and popularity, after the accident that gives her the ability to see ghosts, she is unable to hold a job, make friends, or date successfully. Gong-shil's desire to divorce herself from her ghost-seeing skills draws her to leading man, Joo Joong-won. The protagonist seeks out Joong-won's acerbic company—not because she's a "golddigger," as she is accused of being in Episode 2—but rather because when Gong-shil and Joong-won touch, the ghosts around her burst spectacularly into clouds of dust. This turn of events is striking, as the most secular-minded character in the series–Joo Joong-won—is shown to possess a supernatural power of his own, and ironically, one of which he is unaware of.

In the first episode, Gong-shil narrates the reason behind her life's disarray: "Because I never know when I'll see them, or when they'll start following me, I'm always living in a state of fear." This fear is exacerbated by Gong-shil's sense of being constantly vulnerable. The first episode establishes this clearly. When she is sent to clean one of the apartments that has been vacated, she encounters a grim apparition. She runs, chased by the phantom whose ghostly energy short-circuits the wiring as they pass. Although Gong-shil's terrified run takes her to the roof of her apartment building, and although she closes her door and locks it, mere physical barriers are no obstacle to a ghost. She has done all that is possible, but still the ghost enters her apartment. Running and hiding have no effect. Thus, Gong-shil's life is one of constant vulnerability.

Asma (2009), writes that "[w]herever we find monsters, there, too, we also find heroes" (p.22). This is certainly the rule for both of these K-dramas. With his unwitting ghost-dispersing ability, Joong-won seems, at first, like the hero that Gong-shil needs—both to her and to the viewing audience. After all, as she herself exclaims, Joong-won is a safe harbor, "such a comfort" (Episode 4), and envisions many moments with him, moments of respite from black-jawed, hollow-eyed spirits who give her no peace until she fulfills their demands.

The plot twists, however. Once Gong-shil has her "emergency shelter"—the description Joong-won gives himself at the end of Episode 4—she realizes that she is incapable of ignoring the pain of others, even if they are dead. Episode 6 crystalizes this realization: even though Gong-shil could touch Joong-won to disperse the growling, red-eyed ghost of an army dog, she refuses to do so. Her refusal to ignore the dog-ghost is her first step in discovering that she can find her own path through ghost-sightings, working towards a terror-free life and being her own hero. Indeed, as the final episode underscores, Gong-shil's happily-ever-after comes only when she succeeds in learning how to deal with the specters that she encounters and not upon winning Joong-won's heart and the ghost-annihilating touch he offers with it.

Love, Skepticism and the Leading Men

Love is certainly at the heart of K-drama romantic comedies, even those that are horror hybrids. Like Joong-won, *Oh My Ghost!*'s leading man, star-chef Kung Sun-woo, is the epitome of skeptical and secular. Indeed, it is wonderfully ironic that the recipient of Bong-sun and ghost Soon-ae's romantic interest be a man who, when warned that "there's a ghost in your fortune… attached to you," scoffs and responds with "I don't believe in ghosts" (Episode 1). Who could be a better foil to a leading woman who sees ghosts and to another who *is* one?

Sun-woo berates his mother, an academic, for believing in supernatural things: "You're a professor. Why are you into this superstitious stuff? Do your students know you're like this?" (Episode 1). Sun-woo's questions reflect the dichotomy established by the ideologies of secularism: in a modern-day context, to be intelligent means to be secular, and believing in things unseen is a sign of a lesser intellect, gullibility and lack of sound reason. To be sure, Sun-woo's question implies that his mother, as a professor, should know better and would be ridiculed if her students knew of her belief in ghosts. This scene in particular seems to reflect a Korean academic sphere which coincides with western secularist ideas, as per Levitt (2009), so in a sense perhaps the ideologies of secularism can be said to have infiltrated certain parts of Korean culture. Be that as it may, because the character of Sun-woo is so unapologetically and explicitly grounded in material reality, his eventual realization of the existence of the ephemeral is that much more satisfying to the viewer who, from the start, has been "in the know" about the existence of ghosts.

The central setting of the actions of *Oh My Ghost!* is chef Sun-woo's epicurean Sun Restaurant, including the living space above it. From a postsecular perspective, the choice of a restaurant as the K-drama's principal setting is particularly delicious. A restaurant is an establishment for the nourishment of the material body, but in this series, it also becomes the space in which the scientifically unquantifiable is ascendant. The very space in which the dramatic action unfolds, then, is a multilayered one, a space in which the mystical and the material co-mingle in the form of ghost-possession and the inexplicable and unmeasurable energies of true love.

This very co-mingling of that which cannot be measured in pints, pounds or teaspoons (although, pecks, one could argue) and of the mundane world of food preparation, on the other, is reflected in the opening credits of *Oh My Ghost!* The title sequence offers rich, sensorial images of food and food preparation: the fire of a gas stove, two set of hands slicing apples, cloves of garlic, jars of noodles, bread and olives, rosemary and red peppers. Yet, intermingled with these empirical items are sparkle-effects accompanied by the sound of tinkling bells, an auditory representation of ethereal or magical elements. An animated white chalk-ghost hovers over the names of the cast members as the picture of each appears. Chalk-drawn animations in the same style as the chalk-ghost overlay the pictures: a chef's hat on Bong-sun, stars around Sun-woo, a wedding veil and crown on Soon-ae. These symbols represent an aspect of each character's reality which a mere physical photograph cannot adequately describe. To be sure, via the ghost-chalk animation, the sparkle-effect and the fairy-sound of tinkling bells, the opening credits offer us a world where physical reality is enhanced and overlaid by the ethereal.

The subversion of a strict material/spiritual divide is likewise evident in *The Master's Sun,* in which ghostly apparitions are not relegated to the private spaces of haunted houses, dank basements, family mausoleums, or dust-enveloped attics. Ghosts are everywhere in this urban setting but particularly in the public environs of Kingdom Mall, a bastion of materialist mercantilism. Certainly, in a symbolic sense, the purveyance of other-worldly entities in a shopping center can be understood as a delightful visual representation of Neuman's (2008) more academic description of the secularist modality in which postmodernity is "align[ed]… with a culture of simulacra, vertiginous secular pluralism, and capitalism, while relegating religiosity to the status of anachronisitc metanarrative" (p. 13). And why shouldn't it? There are mysteries in the world that the human intellect has yet to comprehend, and it is the legitimate role of film to show different ways of looking at the real world.

Kingdom Mall is the domain of skeptical leading man, Joong-won, who wanders the corridors of the mall as might a sovereign in the lands he rules. The Kingdom Mall's shoe shops, restaurants, clothing stores, and boutiques for women's apparel– material reality at its most modern and ruled, one could say, by the CEO of skeptics himself—form the backdrop to otherworldly phenomena. It is here, for instance, where the ghost of the murdered wife loses her shoe and chases Gong-shil (Episode 3), where famous model Yi-ryung picks up a demonically red-lipped ghost (Episode 4), where Coffee Ghost takes his coffee (Episode 5) and where the Trashcan Ghost haunts the trash-can where he tossed his winning lottery ticket" (Episode 10).

Asma (2009) notes that the horror genre, with its emphasis on "human vulnerability," is a critique of "rationalist Enlightenment-based modernity" (p.186). This dovetails nicely with postsecular perspectives which also seek, as Ratti (2013) indicates, to subvert the 20th century secular ideology that "people should confine their beliefs to what they can observe in the material world" (p. 5). In *The Master's Sun*, Joong-won is initially presented as an adherent *par excellence* of secularist ideology. He refuses to believe in anything supernatural. He declares that he plans to live his life "intelligently and successfully, like I currently do, while ignoring the things I can't see" (Episode 1). In his view, anyone who assumes there is something supernatural permeating the real world is neither sensible nor sane. He ridicules the widower unwilling to sell his house due to his dead wife's opposition to the real estate deal (Episode 1). The unapologetically self-centered and secular-minded Joong-won is thus set-up as the character whose life will be most disrupted by the ghost-seeing, ghost-hearing Gong-shil.

It is delightfully ironic to note, furthermore, that Joong-won's ability to disperse ghosts is, to be sure, a supernatural ability. This condition in none other than the most material and skeptical of this K-drama's characters can be read as a reflection of what postsecularism itself proposes: there is more to reality than a purely material existence whether individuals recognize it or not. The audience is thus guided towards sitting back and enjoying the forthcoming awareness that will soon be Joong-won's: the re-enchantment of Joong-won's world.

Re-enchantment is a term McClure (2007) uses to explain postsecularism. According to him, postsecular characters "are transformed and steadied, as it were, by the sense that the world is seamed with mystery and benignity, by awakened impulses to reverence, wonder, self-forgetfulness and care, and by coming into company with others" (p. 6). The leading men in these two K-dramas, Joong-won and Sun-woo, are certainly both transformed by the recognition that the world is seamed with the inexplicable. In Joong-won, the audience sees a burgeoning of impulses of "self-forgetfulness and care," particularly startling and satisfying due to his initial crass self-centeredness and thoughtlessness. We also witness Sun-woo awaken to impulses of wonder and reverence as he discovers his love for Bong-sun, a wonder and reverence conveyed extraordinarily well in their first kiss in the Sun Restaurant kitchen (Episode 8).

At the same time that material reality—whether it be a mall or a restaurant kitchen—is presented as an enchanted space, postsecular analyses shed light on the "stubborn spiritual obscurity" (McClure, 2007, p. 6) of the depicted reality. In other words, spiritual or supernatural mysteries are not wrapped up in a neat bow, with all becoming evident and explained and easy. A life that is re-enchanted, in this sense, is not automatically a life of ease and rainbows. In *Oh My Ghost!*, Bong-sun may have accepted her supernatural talents by the latter episodes, but she still gets kidnapped by the serial killer who must be brought to justice. In *The Master's Sun*, Gong-shil realizes she wants to help the pained spirits who come to her, yet she must still find a way of loving herself and becoming self-sufficient. There is still hardship to endure; there are still mysteries in the world which will remain unsolved.

This is not to say that the happily-ever-afters of horror rom-coms cannot provide the closure that audiences expect and that contribute to their positive reception and popularity in the West. And they are indeed popular. To be sure, an *Adweek* (2014) report indicates a 440% one-year jump in K-drama viewership, and of this increased viewing-audience, an estimated 80% of DramaFever's 3.5 million viewers was non–Asian. A postsecular framework for analysis sets in bas relief the irony in the conclusion of *The Master's Sun*. Joong-won poses a rhetorical question from the first episode, "What else is there besides money that any living human being could be after?" (Episode 1). For Joong-won, after all, making money is the primary motive, and financial affluence can only be brought about through purely logical thinking and a focus on concrete reality. At the conclusion of the series, however, the audience recalls Joong-won's rhetorical question when Gong-shil offers him the answer. It is an answer that encompasses nothing less than the epitome of that which is scientifically incalculable: love.

The Postsecular Role of Humor

Recalling the element which McClure (2007) identifies as central to postsecular perspectives—specifically, the "dramatic disruptions of secular structures of reality" (p. 3)—it is significant that the humor in these dramas, which is considerable, centers on a metaphysical disruption of mundane reality. In *Oh My Ghost!*, this centers on the change in personality that Bong-sun undergoes when the spirit of the assertive and bubbly Soon-ae possesses her body, the literal imbrication of the spiritual into the material in the form of ghostly possession. Without a doubt, disruptions of normality ensue as soon as Soon-ae takes Bong-sun over.

For example, the restaurant employees are shocked when Bong-sun, possessed by Soon-ae, pitches chef Sun-woo to the ground. She assumes he is taking physical liberties with her when he is merely desperate to find the key to the store room (Episode 1). The scene is more amusing due to the shock it produces in her coworkers, who ask her if she is "crazy," "drunk," or "sick," and then huddle together outside the restaurant to hypothesize about her strange behavior—could it be multiple-personality disorder, an anger control issue, psychopathy, or perhaps she is even a latent murderer?—scaring themselves with their conjectures (Episode 2). This calls to mind Morreall's (2009) work in humor studies in which he explores the role of incongruity in determining what human beings find funny. Undeniably this K-drama is full of wonderful incongruities, not the least of which is four tall, strong men fearing one small knife-wielding woman who has suddenly changed from painfully timid to extraordinarily outgoing with a determined sex-drive.

As Morreall notes, the violation of the expected patterns of behavior cause amusement when that which was initially incongruous is resolved, when the "joyful click" of something which was initially puzzling becomes reasonable in a whole different sense (p. 11). For the audience, there is amusement at seeing what unfolds with Bong-sun's possession, precisely because the viewing audience knows that it is Soon-ae's personality they are observing, not Bong-sun's. For the audience, in other words, the incongruity is resolved. The other characters, however, do not find the situation funny at all. For them, the incongruity is a source of anxiety and fear. This, in turn, increases the humor for the viewing audience in a lovely upward spiral, since they are aware that Soon-ae's spirit may be stubborn, but she is not at all evil.

Likewise, in *The Master's Sun*, the supernatural is both a source of jump-scares and of laughter for the viewing audience. Gong-shil's ability to see ghosts prompts her to disregard Joong-won's acerbic indifference and arrogance. Gong-shil completely disrupts Joong-won's rigidly secular life, circumventing the seemingly impenetrable barrier he has constructed between him and others. Not only does Gong-shil invade his workplace, his home, and his personal space, she also invades his heart—as he himself expresses in appropriately mystical terms towards the end of the series: "I have been totally bewitched" (Episode 12). Thus, the irascible and self-isolating Joong-won is transformed, revealing marshmallow insides; this transformation is as endearing as it is warmly humorous.

Morreall (2009) writes that "amusement … involves cognitive and practical disengagement from what is going on (p. 31). He notes that in order to experience humor, human beings undergo what he calls a "cognitive shift," which involves sudden shifts in the perception or interpretation of a phrase, action, or story (p. 50). This sudden shift, made funnier by greater contrast, is precisely what happens in the example above, and throughout the plot lines of both of these dramas, with the imbrication of the supernatural into the orderly worlds of Sun-woo and Joong-won. Due to this cognitive shift, these horror K-dramas are also wonderfully comedic.

The humorous ways in which some ghosts come to be depicted, or in the way that the characters interact with ghosts and ghostly possession, mitigate the fear of the inexplicable that is commonly associated with the supernatural. We recall Asma's (2009) explanation of why the monstrous *is* monstrous:

> One aspect of the monster concept seems to be the breakdown of intelligibility. An action or a person or a thing is monstrous when it can't be processed by our rationality, and also when we cannot readily relate to the emotional range involved. We know what it's like to hate, for example, but when we designate a monstrous hate, we are acknowledging that it is off our chart [p. 10].

Humor, then, can be said to serve as a tool for "processing" the monstrous as it gives the viewer an emotional handle with which to relate to the unintelligible. If one can find humor in a scary scene, it is no longer necessary to cover our eyes, hunker down, and wait for the scene to be over.

As such, in *Oh My Ghost!* and *The Master's Sun*, humor mitigates the relationship of the viewer with the initially fearful thing being viewed. It is one of the ways in which the illogical, supernatural, and monstrous becomes *un*-monstrous. This can be seen with the Coffee Ghost. In *The Master's Sun*, when the Coffee Ghost first appears outside Gong-shil's rooftop apartment—with his pale face, blacked-out eyes and blackened mouth—he is a frightful figure, invisible one minute and then grinning through blackened lips the next (Episode 2). As the K-drama continues, however, Gong-shil's attitude towards this ghost underscores his harmlessness; as she explains to Kang-woo, her friend and security officer at Kingdom Mall, the ghost is a "kid who always comes around and asks me for coffee" (Episode 14). The existence of a spiritual-entity coffee-addict is another instance of the imbrication the ephemeral and the material. At the same time, the incongruity of a non-physical entity wanting coffee produces humor.

An analysis of the postsecular role of humor in these two ghost-infested K-dramas would be sadly incomplete without a discussion of the moments of "skinship" that arise due to and as a consequence of the supernatural. "Skinship" is a term used by K-drama and *hallyu* fans to describe moments of touching which demonstrate the closeness of two individuals (Touhami and Al-Haq, 2017). On such websites, blogs and K-drama forums as "Kdramabuzz" (2017), "K-What?!?" (2014), "KDramapal" (2017), and "MyDramaList" (2017), skinship is a focal point of reviews, discussions and reflection. Not necessarily sexual in nature, skinship can exist between friends but can also pave the way to more intimate physical contact just as it builds sexual tension.

In *Oh My Ghost!*, moments of skinship increase after Bong-sun has been possessed by the ghost of Soon-ae, who is intent on seducing a man of high vitality. True to the K-drama romance genre, love spurs the protagonist to do the unexpected, but particular to the supernatural elements of *Oh My Ghost!*, the unexpected involves an agreement between Soon-ae and Bong-sun, that Soon-ae can possess her body with the purpose of, as Bong-sun declares, "making Chef mine" (Episode 8). Soon-ae is delighted as she now has free reign to resolve her virginity grudge by means of the seduction of chef Sun-woo. What is fascinating about this premise from a postsecular perspective is how the very epitome of a physical act—sexual intercourse—becomes the means by which a ghostly plot-line progresses.

The ghost Soon-ae's boldness in her machinations to seduce Sun-woo is funny due to the contrast between her ultra-boldness and Bong-sun's exasperating timidity. Bong-sun is self-effacing to the extreme, and in the initial episode, she can barely make eye-contact with Sun-woo. Sun-woo himself, in dealing with Bong-sun's personality change, is baffled by how she would always apologize and never look him in the eye (Episode 4). When Soon-ae realizes that Sun-woo is in no mortal danger of freezing to death due to the inhuman cold of her sexual ghost-touch, she is delighted. Still inhabiting Bong-sun's body, she tries frantically to take his shirt off, insisting that he "[j]ust do it with [her]. Just once" (Episode 4). Sun-woo's horrified reaction serves to further the humor of the situation; the traditional roles of seducing-male and seduced-female are flipped. Her pleas continue as Sun-woo escapes down the stairs and into the restaurant: "Chef, just once! I really have a reason. I don't even expect twice! Just once! Just once!" (Episode 4). Her fervent cajoling—"So close your eyes once… just once! It's not like you'll use up your body by doing it just once.… Can you think of it as a present? Just once, once!"—increases the humor at this flip in expected gender roles. These requests are accompanied by physical touching: she grabs his hand, tugs his arm, pokes his chest, and sneaks into his bed—all actions that the true Bong-sun would never have contemplated. In short, ghostly possession propels the physicality between Bong-sun and Sun-woo.

The traditional stereotype of the modest and seemly leading woman, then, is turned upside down due to the imbrication of the supernatural into the mundane. Furthermore, Soon-ae's single-minded pursuance of Sun-woo is presented as both funny and forgivable for a number of reasons. First Bong-sun is physically small; there is no danger of her physically overpowering Sun-woo and actually making him do something against his will. This removes the sense of danger that might otherwise derail the humor. Sun-woo, at least a full head taller than Bong-sun, is usually confident and poised, collected and cool. However, with her frank requests for sex, he is completely disconcerted. The audience cannot help but be entertained at seeing the normally self-controlled and relaxed leading male taken aback. Further, since it seems to be the only way for Soon-ae's spirit to avoid an eternity as a malignant ghost with an unresolved grudge, the story line allows a justification of Soon-ae's single-minded focus on getting Sun-woo to sleep with her. On Soon-ae's part, at least she is completely honest in her intent. She just wants sex. This, along with her vivacity and energy, align the audience with her. To be sure, the viewer wants her to succeed in getting Sun-woo in bed and roots for her in every moment of hugging, hand-touching, and arm-brushing that ensues. Just as the presence of a ghost blurs the boundaries between the physical and spiritual, skinship blurs the boundaries between the bodies of the protagonist and Sun-woo. Romantic and carnal love are motivating factors for Bong-sun and Soon-ae, but again, it is the metaphysical reality of ghost possession that upsets the norms of reality so thoroughly.

In *The Master's Sun*, skinship plays an even more central role to the humor of the K-drama. Since ghosts vanish when Gong-shil touches Joong-won, skinship in this K-drama is more than a delightful titillation of a developing love-line. Its prevalence is a direct consequence of the infestation of ghosts in Gong-shil's life. It is the very premise—completely non-sexual in nature at the beginning—upon which the relationship builds. Gong-shil's need to touch Joong-won is even more humorous since Joong-won himself is such a blatantly unfriendly and prickly sort. He informs Gong-shil in the first episode when she touches his arm, "There are only two things I hate. One, anyone laying their hand on my money, and two, anyone laying their hand on my body." Gong-shil, of course, is not so easily dissuaded, and the skinship that follows in the rest of the drama—on the street, at the mall, in Joong-won's bed—not only lends itself to the eventual self-actualization of both the leads (Gong-shil discovers she asked for the gift of seeing ghosts, and Joong-won discovers his warmth and humanity), it also becomes a source of delightful double-entendre dialogue with other characters. For instance, Joong-won's aunt and uncle see Gong-shil departing from Joong-won's home. When the uncle makes a sly innuendo regarding Gong-shil at dinner—he and his wife, Joong-woo's aunt, are fishing for information about Joong-won's love-life—Joong-won tells them not to worry, that he is not going to marry her since "[a]ll she wants is my body" (Episode 4). This dialogue is particularly funny precisely because we know Joong-won is telling the absolute truth at the same time that he willfully and gleefully misleads his aunt and uncle regarding his and Gong-shil's physical relationship. In short, the skinship recourse throughout propels the series forward, creating fertile ground for humorous twists, rescues from spectral apparitions, and the blossoming of true love, K-drama style.

Conclusion

In conclusion, a postsecular analysis of these K-dramas underscores the affinity between these storylines and a postsecular shift in world-view extant in the West. Although the author of this essay does not pretend it to be an exhaustive study of *Oh My Ghost!* and *The Master's Sun*, she has presented a postsecular approach to the analysis of these two Korean dramas rich in supernatural dynamism. This analysis underscores what scholars and philosophers identify as a new trend in contemporary culture: an emergence of the reframing of the spiritual as found in postsecularism. Through a postsecular perspective, we have seen that these K-dramas do not present the spiritual and the mundane as oppositional; quite the contrary. Through the imbrication of the spiritual and the material in these series, humor is foregrounded, self-actualization comes to pass, love is discovered, and happily-ever-afters are achieved. Set in the urban spaces of the contemporary world of restaurants and shopping malls, both of these K-dramas offer their western viewing audience a re-enchantment of reality, one where the metaphysical is an integral part of the twenty-first century mundane.

Notes

1. As reported by C. Hong, Park Bo-young (*Oh My Ghost!*) won the Excellent Award for Acting in a Medium Length Drama in APAN Star Awards of 2015. Lee Yoo-bi (*The Master's Sun*) won the Best Rookie Actress Award in APAN Star Award of 2013. See full citation under "2013 APAN Star Awards—Winners List" in the list of references.

2. According to reporter Coco Kdrama from DramaFever's official website (2016), Park Bo-young (*Oh My Ghost!*) won the DramaFever Best Actress Award in 2016, as did Kim Seul-Gi (*Oh My Ghost!*) for Best Supporting Actress the same year. The drama *The Master's Sun* won the "Most Feels" DramaFever Award in 2013, as well as the 2013 award for Best Cinematography. See references for full citations.

3. For example, the protagonist of *The Master's Sun*, Gong-shil makes a fortune in Europe, but she does so only upon mastering, and not being mastered by, her supernatural talents. This allows her to banish the ghosts in the building she purchases and sell it for an impressive profit (Episode 17). She employs her ability to communicate with ghosts to increase her financial stability, yes, but this incident's relative lack of importance is underscored by the fact that the audience does not actually see any of it happen. It is presented verbally, in a few seconds, as part of Gong-shil's recap of her year away from Korea.

4. Habermas (2001) coined the term postsecular in "Faith and Knowledge," his acceptance address for the Peace Prize awarded by the German Bookseller's Association. See references for full citation.

References

Asma, S.T. (2009). *On monsters: An unnatural history of our worst fears*. Oxford: Oxford University Press.

Beatus Corner. (2013). 2013 APAN star awards—Winners list. *Beatus Corner.* Retrieved from http://beatuscorner.com/2013-apan-star-awards-winners-list-2/

Casanova. J. (1994). *Public religions in the modern world*. Chicago: University of Chicago Press.

Chuang, L.M., & Lee, H.E. (2013). Korean Wave: Enjoyment factors of Korean dramas in the U.S. *International Journal of Intercultural Relations*, *37*(5), 594–604. doi:10.1016/j.ijintrel.2013.07.003.

Greenhill, P., & Rudy, J.T. (2014). Fairy tales, television, and intermediality. In P. Greenhill & J.T. Rudy (Eds.), *Channeling wonder: Fairy tales on television*. Detroit: Wayne State University Press.

Habermas, J. (2001). Faith and knowledge. *Habermas Forum*. Retrieved from http://www.habermasforum.dk/.

Habermas, J. (2005). Religion in the public sphere. *Philosophia Africana*, *8*(2), 99–109.

Habermas, J. (2008). Secularism's crisis of faith. *New Perspectives Quarterly* 25(4), 17–29.

Heine, C. (2014). Korean dramas hook millennial viewers who speak Spanish and English. *Adweek*. Retrieved from https://www.adweek.com/digital/korean-dramas-hook-millennial-viewers-who-speak-spanish-and-english-157679/.

Hogarth, H.K. (2013). The Korean Wave: An Asian reaction to western-dominated globalization. *Perspectives on Global Development & Technology*, *12*(1/2), 135–151. doi:10.1163/15691497-12341247.

Hong, C. (2016). Winners announced for the 2016 APAN Star Awards. *Soompi*. Retrieved from https://www.soompi.com/2016/10/02/winners-announced-2016-apan-star-awards/.

Jenkins, H. (2006). *Fans, bloggers, and gamers*. New York: New York University Press.

Jung, C.G. (1933). The basic postulates of analytical psychology. *Modern man in search of a soul*. San Diego: Harcourt Brace Jovanovich.

K.J. (2015). Winners of the 2015 APAN Star Awards. *Soompi*. Retrieved from https://www.soompi.com/2015/11/28/winners-of-the-2015-apan-star-awards/.

Kauffman, M. (2009). Locating the postsecular. *Religion & Literature*, 3, 68–73.

Kdrama, C. (2014). Announcing the winners of the 2013 DramaFever Awards! Retrieved from DramaFever website: https://www.dramafever.com/news/announcing-the-winners-of-the-2013-dramafever-awards/.

Kdrama, C. (2016). Announcing the winners of the fourth annual DramaFever Awards! Retrieved from DramaFever website: https://www.dramafever.com/news/announcing-the-winners-of-the-fourth-annual-dramafever-awards-/.

Laurel, K. (2011). The contraction and expansion of shamanic landscapes in contemporary South Korea. *Crosscurrents*, 3, 328–344.

Lee, H. (2018). A "real" fantasy: Hybridity, Korean drama, and pop cosmopolitans. *Media, Culture & Society*, *40*(3), 365–380. doi:10.1177/0163443717718926.

Lee, S. (2015). Lost in liminal space: Amnesiac and incognizant ghosts in Korean drama. *Mosaic (Winnipeg)*, 3, 125–140.

Levina, M., & Bui, D. (2013). *Monster culture in the 21st century: A reader*. London, UK: Bloomsbury.

Lin, A., & Tong, A. (2008). Re-imagining a cosmopolitan 'Asian us': Korean media flows and imaginaries of Asian modern femininities. In C.B. Huat, K. Iwabuchi (Eds.), *East Asian pop culture: Analysing the Korean Wave* (pp. 91–125). Hong Kong: Hong Kong University Press.

M.S. (2018). 16 Award-winning K-dramas from the past five years. *DramaFever*. Retrieved from https://www.dramafever.com/news/-award-winning-K-dramas-from-the-past-five-years/.

Maczynska, M. (2009). Toward a postsecular literary criticism: Examining ritual gestures in Zadie Smith's "Autograph Man." *Religion & Literature*, *41*(3), 73–82.

McClure, J.A. (2007). Partial faiths: Postsecular fiction in the age of Pynchon and Morrison. Athens: University of Georgia Press.

McGuire, A., & Buchbinder, D. (2010). The forensic gothic: Knowledge, the supernatural, and the psychic detective. *Canadian Review of American Studies*, *40*(3), 289–307.

Megill, A. (2013). History, theoreticism, and the limits of the "the postsecular." *History & Theory*, *52*(1), 110–129. doi:10.1111/hith.10659.

Morreall, J. (2009). *Comic relief: A comprehensive philosophy of humor*. Malden, MA: Wiley-Blackwell.

Neuman, J. (2008). *Faith in fiction: Postsecular critique and the global novel* (Doctoral dissertation). University of Virginia, Charlottesville, VA.

Parc, J., & Hwy-Chang, M. (2013). Korean dramas and films: Key factors for their international competitiveness. *Asian Journal of Social Science*, *41*(2), 126–149. doi:10.1163/15685314-12341295.

Prosman, H.J. (2011). The postmodern condition and the meaning of secularity: A study on the religious dynamics of postmodernity. *OAIster*. Retrieved from http://oaister.worldcat.org/.

Ratti, M. (2013). The postsecular imagination: Postcolonialism, religion, and literature. New York: Routledge.

Said, E. (1979). *Orientalism*. New York: Vintage Books.

Said, E. (1983). *The world, the text, and the critic*. Cambridge, MA: Harvard University Press.

Sobhani, M.A. (2017). "God, too, has His jests": The postsecular role of humor in Luis Alberto Urrea's *The Hummingbird's Daughter*. *Hispanic Studies Review*, *2*(2), 287–301.

Taylor, D. (1996). The need for a religious literary criticism. *Religion and the Arts*, *1*(1). Retrieved from https://www.bc.edu/publications/relarts/supplements/excerpts/v1–1taylor2.html.

Touhami, B., & Al-Haq, F.A. (2017). The influence of the Korean Wave on the language of international fans: Case study of Algerian fans. *Sino-U.S. English Teaching*, *14*(10), 598–626. doi:10.17265/1539-8072/2017.10.004.

Winfield, P.D. (2011). Introduction: Religion in Asia today. *Cross Currents*, *61*(3), 286–289. doi:10.1111/j.1939-3881.2011.00183.x.

Yu, C. (2010). *Korean thought and culture: A new introduction*. Bloomington, IN: Trafford Publishing.

Portrayals of "Soft Beauty"

Analyzing South Korean Soft Masculinities in Media and in Real Life

Sofia Murell

It could be a blue Christmas-like illuminated children's playground by night with a female character sitting on a swing and a male character kneeling down in front of her, confessing his love. Or during another type of confession, the lights of a village setting are all turned on and the female protagonist is flown towards the handsome man/alien who reveals his true emotions to her. These men are endearing and sensitive. They understand women and would do everything for them. Not only are they devoted to their loved ones, but they are also very handsome and embody the ideal features of Korean men (clear skin, "V-shape" chin, "big" eyes, thin or semi-muscular). These protagonists are representations of soft masculinity, regarded as *kkonminam* or "flower boys."

In this study, soft masculinities entail more than just an image or behavior, as the field of gender studies denominates (soft) masculinities as a social construct. The author of this essay understands the concept as an umbrella term for several interpretations of this masculinity, such as *kkonminam*. Here, soft masculinities are as a manner for young Koreans for coping with the current socio-economic situation in South Korea. By analyzing soft masculinities through this perspective, the author of this study argues that *kkonminam* masculinity is multidimensional. In this paper, the focus lies on the *kkonminam* soft masculinity, as this type of masculinity can be considered an iteration of the past whereby modern young Koreans adapt several *kkonminam* characteristics into alternative models of soft masculinities, such as *hunnam* (handsome and kind man). It is therefore fundamental to study Korean dramas (K-dramas) and their depiction of these masculinities. Although the term *kkonminam* and its associated "original"[1] style have declined in popularity, it is the *kkonminam* masculinity image's perseverance and personality/character that remain present today. For instance, a still-present influence of *kkonminam* is that before them, wearing skinny jeans and the color pink were regarded as feminine. Nowadays, it is acceptable for men to wear pink and skinny jeans, and doing so is often considered fashionable when combined with the right accessories and clothing.

Kkonminam could easily be mistaken for the term "metrosexual" which is commonly used in Western societies. However, there is a difference between these concepts. The Cambridge dictionary defines "metrosexual" as "A man who is attracted to women sexually but who is also interested in fashion and his appearance." *Kkonminam*, however, is not simply about looks, but also about their personality traits when portrayed in the media. Moreover, they have specific physical features that appertain to the *kkonminam*.

The word *kkonminam* translates to "flower" (*kkot*) "handsome man" (*minam*)—literally "flower boy"—and may also be spelled *kkotminam*. This evokes the idea of a handsome or beautiful man. Generally, young males who adopt this interpretation of masculinity are particularly attentive to their appearance. They have a well-groomed and fashionable style and even use cosmetic products. Besides being fashionable, *kkonminam* are often stereotyped as having an effeminate attitude (Jung, 2011; Maliangkay, 2010) and may have an androgynous appearance such as in the case of Korean pop dancers and singers (Oh, 2017, 2015; Shin, 2013). Based on this research's data, attitudes towards the image of *kkonminam* vary from the one presented in the dramas and the "real" image in society. During a three-month ethnographic research period in Seoul (see methodology section for more details), the author of this study encountered a varied notion of *kkonminam* masculinity from a media studies perspective. The media portrayal of *kkonminam* is gentle and caring (Jung, 2011), but society is more likely to regard them as "players" or "bad boys." In other words, people only adopt the looks of the portrayed image. As the analysis of the selected dramas demonstrates, these characteristics are evident in the depictions of the following *kkonminam* masculinity protagonists. By examining these fictional characters, the author of this study attempts to understand and illustrate the presentation of male beauty work and soft masculinities. At the same time, she discusses how these images relate to consumerism and beauty, making *kkonminam* multidimensional.

Multidimensionality allows for the appropriation of a few characteristics of *kkonminam* into other models of soft masculinities, such as *hunnam* or the middle-aged *kkonminam* denominated *kkotjungnyeon*. It also enables *kkonminam* masculinities to be regarded as a commodity, which is used and appropriated into alternative models. However, when adapting the media-portrayed *kkonminam* masculinity to "real life," young Koreans encounter certain limitations, for example, negative connotations attributed to *kkonminam* in "real life" (although it is seen as the *crème de la crème* in terms of beauty), youth life trajectories (maturity) and military service (hegemonic ideals).

Moreover, the author of this study attempts to nuance and reconsider definitions of soft masculinities in media studies (Shin, 2013; Jung, 2011; Maliangkay, 2010), as there lies a gap between scholarship in English and Korean masculinities. Most of the available work focuses on hegemonic masculinities and their association with patriarchy and women (Moon, 2005; Kim and Choi, 1998; Abelmann, 2003; Kendall, 2002). However, those in the field of media studies have been investigating a relatively new phenomenon that can be considered an exception to this. Scholars have described this phenomenon through various terminologies, such as "Pan-East Asian Soft Masculinity" (Jung, 2009, 2010, 2011), "effeminate" (Maliangkay, 2010), and "sissy" or "feminized" (Shiau & Chen, 2009; Yang, 2013), which focus on *kkonminam* soft masculinities, their relation with various forms of media, and their portrayal in *hallyu*.

Other articles on soft masculinities, especially *kkonminam*, have analyzed perceptions of these masculinities in various countries, such as Hong Kong, Japan and Taiwan, in relation to cultural products of Korea, including Korean pop (K-pop) and K-dramas as well as the image of "flower boys" in gay culture (Lin & Tong, 2007; Yang, 2012; Yang, 2013; Oh, 2015; Kwon, 2016). Articles related to the adaptation of this model of masculinity in society are scarce but available, e.g., an article about Taiwan by Yang (2013) which examines the adaptation and performance of *kkonminam* masculinity. Ainslie (2017) wrote on soft masculinity in Malaysia, in which the representation of this type of masculinity in *hallyu* enables restricted groups of Malaysian men to create new modes of masculine identity, as they are marginalized by hegemonic masculinity in the country.

This study was conducted over a three-month period during the winter of 2015 in Seoul, South Korea. This area was selected because it is the city in which the *hallyu* phenomenon emerged. *Hallyu* portrays several interpretations of masculinities, such as *kkonminam* (Louie, 2012; Jung, 2011). The popularity of *hallyu* is increasing and spreading to other countries; for example, Taiwan, China, Japan, Hong Kong, and individuals outside Korea are adapting certain attributes of the model of masculinity, or they are indeed adopting the whole concept as their own (Yang, 2013; Yang, 2012; Louie, 2012; Lin & Tong, 2007). Hence, the *hallyu* phenomenon reveals modes of expression in which individuals can construct new interpretations of masculinities. Seoul is also an interesting site because it contains extensive media forms that range from advertisements in the subway to a giant television promoting plastic surgery in a university cafeteria. Visual representations of idols (Korean celebrities), beauty, and self-improvement are ubiquitous in this city.

The research population consisted of young Koreans (male: 24, and female: 14) born between 1985 and 1995. The average age of interviewees was 24.55 years old (working: 15, studying: 16, other[2]: 7). This age-range was chosen for two reasons. First, participants born in this time frame grew up in a modern and prosperous Korea (Yang, 2007), so they have encountered and continue to experience the *hallyu* phenomenon and the representation of *kkonminam* masculinities. This type of soft masculinity is notably popular in K-dramas, such as *Flower Boy Next Door* (*Yeopjip kkonminam*, 2013), and among K-pop idol groups, e.g., EXO and Shinee. At the same time, these young Koreans must contend with the aftermath of the recovery from the economic crisis of 1997 (*The Economist*, 2011), wherein competition is extremely high—especially when seeking a job—and the level of youth unemployment is consistently rising (Kim and Lee, 2018, *Reuters*). Second, it is more likely that this group of participants would speak English, as a previous visit to Korea indicated that many young university students were able to fluently speak English. The opinions of these young people are relevant to this research as it adds the subjects' voices and views to a topic that has been mostly analyzed from a media perspective.

Through one gatekeeper, the author contacted the first interviewees who are in their early twenties. After a few weeks, social media was used. More than half of the informants volunteered to participate in the interview as a reply to a request on the platform, *CouchSurfing*. The condition for the selection of the interviewees was that they had to have lived their formative years in Korea. *CouchSurfing* provided this study with seventeen respondents in their late twenties who were either students or had just started working. Their English was advanced and easy to follow. The limitations of gaining access to this group through *CouchSurfing* involves a small group (fluent in English) with alternative perspectives compared to "regular" young Koreans who have never been exposed to foreign cultures, as 97% of the respondents did go abroad. Another limitation arises from the author's Korean language level, which restricted her access to certain groups, and that during the interviews, there were non-native English speakers. Besides social media, a host home contributed to the search for interviewees, and the interviewees from that host home introduced the researcher to other interviewees. The host home/student house residence (in Korean *hasukjip*) was located in Sinchon nearby Yonsei University.

This study applied a qualitative research approach that involved 38 semi-structured interviews and six casual interviews. In addition, the study entailed participant observation and textual analysis of visual media (Bryman, 2008). These methods, especially the interviews, are fundamental to understand how *kkonminam* masculinities are produced, consumed, and interpreted in Korean society and therefore help to contextualize the phenomenon of *kkonminam*. The semi-structured interviews were audio-recorded, and notes were also taken.[3] The one-on-one interviews varied in duration from forty minutes to an hour, and the questions addressed topics such as masculinities, military service, beauty, the media, idols, and work in Korea (see appendix for interview questions). These flexible questions were adapted according to each individual's English level and gender; for example, a few male interviewees had firsthand information about military experience while the females did not. In addition to conducting interviews, the author also collected images that respondents had shared when explaining the appearance of *kkonminam* and other interpretations of soft masculinities. Other participants cited the names of celebrities who they thought represented *kkonminam* and other soft masculinities. In short, the semi-structured interviews offered a possibility to understand the point of view and assumptions of young urban Koreans towards soft masculinities in Korea.

Looking at Soft Masculinities in Media and "Real Life"

Teenagers, especially girls and women in their mid–30s, prefer and admire the *kkonminam* figure. They are actually considered to be the "driving force behind" the *kkonminam* "media phenomenon" (Jung, 2010). According to one 25-year-old male interviewee (JW,[4] male, 25 years old), young women admire the beauty of *kkonminam* because they have not matured yet, and they will eventually realize other priorities. Boys who adopt the "*kkonminam* look" are usually between adolescence and 25 years of age because according to interviewees, most young male Koreans have already completed their compulsory military service by that age, so they tend to change their appearance around that time. The respondents argued that when men surpass 25 years of age, their style usually changes to become more "smart-casual." They also mentioned that the work atmosphere was influential in appearance changes, as men feel pressured to conform to their work environment and to follow certain patterns, which connect them to their peers (for more details on this, see section "The Military Service and the 'Standardization' of Men").

In terms of the feminine aspect of *kkonminam*, many interviewees highlighted that this notion is associated with being "weak." For instance, another 25-year-old male YB (male, 25 years old) explained that if he sees a *kkonminam*, he would like to help him and care for him, for example, by offering him a seat or helping him reach an object that is too heavy or out of reach because, to him, *kkonminam* are beautiful and appear frail. Previously, YB this young man had identified the characteristics that he considered beautiful in *kkonminam* ("big" eyes and a "small" head) which correspond with traits that several informants described as "feminine" attributes, and it is well known that the Korean beauty "standard" for women includes these aspects (Kim, 2013, February 17; FlorCruz, 2015; Shim, 2016). Various female interviewees noted that they would not date *kkonminam* because they also felt a need to take care of them in response to their "weak" appearance. These descriptions suggest that people associate signs of frailness (in relation to *kkonminam*) with feminine beauty characteristics. In this sense, the "effeminate" behavior connotes looking feminine, but not behaving in such a way, contrary to the "effeminate" behavior that media studies scholars have suggested.

As Kim (2003) has explained, "the *kkonminam* syndrome"[5] arises from a consequence of the deconstruction and the hybridization of female/male sexual identities rather than males merely becoming feminized" (p. 104 as cited in Jung, 2011, p. 58). Thus, *kkonminam* present masculine and feminine qualities that appeal to the desires of both men and women, though especially the latter (Jung, 2011, p. 58). Conceptualizing *kkonminam* as a multidimensional model not only addresses the desires of consumers, but also embodies the desires and anxieties of Korean youth in present society in terms of beauty and life trajectories. The next sections explain this further.

In order to understand how Korean media depict and promote these *kkonminam* images and how these models of masculine bodies relate to consumption and beauty, the next section analyzes three key fictive characters who are considered to be soft masculine: Bae Yong-joon in *Winter Sonata* (*Gyeoul yeonga*, 2002), Lee Min-ho in *Boys Over Flowers* (*Kkotboda namja*, 2009) and Kim Soo-hyun in *My Love from the Star* (*Byeoreseo on geudae;* also known as *You Who Came from the Stars*, December 2013—February 2014).

Beauty and Visual Representation of Kkonminam *in the Media*

The selected characters are essential fictional protagonists of Korean dramas that embrace soft masculinities. They were immensely successful not only in Korea but also worldwide, having an initial success in Asia. *Winter Sonata* created a furor in Japan that further increased the popularity of *hallyu* in Asia (Lee, 2011). *Boys Over Flowers* conquered the younger public and was an important representation of *hallyu* throughout multiple continents (Jung, 2009). *My Love from the Star* was not only trendy in its home country, where it sold products related to the protagonist and raised Kim

Soo-hyun to fame, but was also successful in China (MacDonald, 2014; Yonhap News, 2014; Jun 2014). In addition to their popularity, the male protagonists that these dramas portray tend to have a "soft" quality regarding their attitude towards women and their facial features. More than 50% of the interviewees (male and female) mentioned Lee Min-ho, the main actor in *Boys Over Flowers*, as an example of *kkonminam*. It is worth noting that the attitude is intertwined with the appearance of the media *kkonminam*. Key facial features of *kkonminam* include bright and smooth skin, incorporating both androgynous and western physical features (Holliday & Elfving-Hwang, 2012).

In *Winter Sonata*, a young woman named Yoo-jin (Choi Ji-woo) falls in love with Kang Joon-sang (Bae Yong-joon). Unfortunately, Joon-sang is hit by a car. Ten years later, Yoo-jin is an architect dating a childhood friend. However, she still cannot forget her allegedly deceased first love, Joon-sang, whom she sees on her wedding day. She cannot believe it and decides to cancel the wedding. Later, she has to work together with a design firm that is led by Min-hyeong, the person who resembles her deceased first love. Besides his warm and kind attitude towards his loved one, the appearance of Bae Yong-joon also conforms to the idea of *kkonminam* masculinity, with his soft features, such as a round face and "big" eyes, a prominent nose, a tall height, and a slim body.

The characters that Lee Min-ho and Kim Hyun-joong portray in *Boys Over Flowers* and Kim Soo-hyun's character in *My Love from the Star* also exemplify (*kkonminam*) soft masculinities. *Boys Over Flowers* tells the story of Geum Jan-di (Ku Hye-sun), a girl from an ordinary, hardworking family, who falls in love with a rich and handsome boy, Goo Joon-pyo (Lee Min-ho). One day, she saves the life of a student from the privileged Shinhwa High School. In return, she receives a scholarship to attend the school, where she meets the F4, a group of four ultimately handsome and arrogant boys from notable rich families who rule the school and terrorize the students and teachers. However, Jan-di is the only person who dares to step forward and challenge them. Joon-pyo, the leader of the F4, falls in love with her positive attitude, innocence, and charm. Yoon Ji-hoo (Kim Hyun-joong), a member of the F4, befriends Jan-di. After spending some time together, he also falls in love with Jan-di. A love triangle develops in addition to conflicts between family members and friends, which they must confront in order to prove their love. Here, the combination of appearance and behavior again represents the *kkonminam* masculine side of the male protagonists.

My Love from the Star portrays the story of an alien with superpowers, Do Min-joon (Kim Soo-hyun), who falls in love with the number one Korean actress, Cheon Song-yi (Jun Ji-hyun). Four hundred years in the past, during the Joseon Dynasty, he lands on Earth and saves a girl for whom he develops a fondness; however, the circumstances make it difficult to stay with her. In the modern era, he has a vision of the girl being involved in a car accident. He intervenes in the incident, despite swearing to himself to never do that. A few years later, he experiences another vision of her and suddenly realizes that the girl—now a woman—is a top actress who is coincidentally his neighbor. Kim Soo-hyun's appearance and behavior in the drama reflect the idea of soft masculinities, though his physique is less slim than it was in his previous dramas, *Dream High* (2011) and *Moon Embracing the Sun* (2012). Nevertheless, his role in this drama, his other performances, and his typical soft facial features established him as one of the most popular actors in Korea. All of the above-mentioned Korean celebrities, who share similar features, have been praised for their good looks and fashion sense.

These protagonists are considered to be handsome and to embody the ultimate beauty ideal in terms of their appearance, masculinity, and behavior. According to the *Oxford Dictionary* (2018), beauty is "[a] combination of qualities, such as shape, color, or form that pleases the aesthetic senses, especially the sight." This definition positions beauty as simply a sense or a feeling that one acquires through aesthetic pleasure. However, this research assumes a wider perspective of beauty that embraces elements beyond aesthetics. As Edmonds (2010) has suggested, beauty incorporates several components besides aesthetic pleasure or attractiveness, including beauty industries (e.g., fashion stores, media, cosmetic surgery clinics), beauty work (i.e., practices associated with the body which aim to improve the appearance) and beauty cultures (related to history of aesthetics) (p. 257). Beauty work is a relevant consideration here because it is a key aspect of constructing soft masculine images in Korea and discourses that surround beauty work, such as the example in the selected case studies. Having now established that beauty encompasses more than just aesthetics, the next section discusses how the "flower boy" image reaches out to consumers of its products through not only the protagonist's appearance but also through his subtle attitude.

Behavior, Consumption and Features of Kkonminam

It is challenging to define *kkonminam* in media or "real life," since many have different opinions on the features of a *kkonminam*. Consequently, there is no absolute standard for the behavior of *kkonminam* in society. Nevertheless, all the interviewees agreed that *kkonminam* are identifiable primarily through appearance, and they specifically mentioned the qualities of a "high" or prominent nose, a "small" face, a tall and skinny physique, "big" eyes, and pale or white skin. According to Holliday and Elfving-Hwang

(2012), these characteristics are part of the "soft" image that *kkonminam* present (p. 61).

More South Korean men are obtaining plastic surgery today than they were 10 years ago. In an interview for the *South China Morning Post,* Dr. Lee Hyun-taek, the head surgeon and founder of Banobagi Plastic Surgery in Gangnam, commented that the number of male plastic surgeries has multiplied by five to ten times since 2002 (qtd. as cited in Tai, 2017). As this beauty trend continues, it demonstrates that the projected image is not solely fictional but is also taken into consideration for adaptation in society ("real life"), and vice versa.

The images of *kkonminam* in K-dramas seem to be more positive than in the descriptions of respondents about *kkonminam* in "real life." In K-dramas, the main characters share specific qualities that could be classified as soft masculine. For example, in addition to being tall (each has a height of less than six feet with the exception of Lee Min-ho, who is slightly over six feet compared to the average five feet and eight inches height of Korean men (KOSIS, 2018), each is slim and fit and has a "small" face, a prominent or "high" nose, and a fair complexion. Their characters are portrayed as quiet (except in Lee Min-ho's role) and intelligent (they all attend privileged schools). Moreover, they are polite, sensitive, and warm-hearted, as apparent from their care for their loved ones. For example, in Episode 10 of *Winter Sonata,* Min-hyeong prepares breakfast for Yoo-jin. When he returns from buying fish for the breakfast, she sees that he has cut his finger, and she decides to finish cooking. This demonstrates that despite lacking the skills to prepare a meal, the man tries to do so for his lover, thus revealing the "soft" side of the protagonist. However, the patriarchal status quo persists as Yoo-jin makes breakfast instead of him.

In the final episode of *Boys Over Flowers,* Joon-pyo does not remember his love for Jan-di due to an accident. When she falls into a pool and starts drowning, Joon-pyo suddenly regains his memory and saves her. In Episode 12, he gives Jan-di a necklace that represents his love. These actions once again reflect the soft side of the character, who was initially presented as selfish and cruel person before finding love.

In *My Love from the Star,* Do Min-joon rescues and assists Cheon Song-yi, a top actress, on several occasions: saving her from being hit by a car when she was a child, and by offering her overnight refuge at his home when reporters try to break into her house. He also brings her to the hospital and remains there with her. Furthermore, he is concerned with her feelings after the removal of a large billboard in front of their apartment that had Song-yi's portrait on it, as it symbolizes that Song-yi's career is no longer relevant. His concern and actions depict the ideal man: a hero who also understands and empathizes with women. These portrayals of soft masculinities concern behavior and physical features that emphasize the positive characteristics in the good behavior and deeds of the male protagonists. In the television dramas, however, kindness is part of the charm of the protagonists, who are, for instance, not interested in material items.

The male protagonists are also charismatic, decisive, and courageous, as they save the female protagonists and must occasionally combat threats to their relationship. Lee (2012) has argued that these qualities are present in the concept of an ideal Korean masculinity (p. 456) and has additionally stated that fictional male characters combine two types of masculine ideals. The first, *seonbi* (also termed Neo-Confucian masculinity), is the most widespread and concerns the intellect and economic wealth of the man, i.e., the wealth of male protagonists (Park, 2010, p. 5 as cited in Lee, 2012, p. 457). The second type, an emerging ideal, is the aspect related to "sensitive, warm, and gentle masculinity" that women demand (Lee, 2012, p. 457). In these K-dramas, the protagonists combine both kinds of masculine ideals in a hybridization of female and male features that has been referred to as "*kkonminam* syndrome," whereby *kkonminam* can satisfy the longings of both genders, though especially females (Kim, 2003, p. 104 as cited in Jung, 2011, p. 58). In this sense, the *kkonminam* hybridization of masculine ideals (tender and attentive characteristics combined with optimal physical features) target consumption of products related to its image, such as clothing or makeup, as both genders can be affected by the hybrid ideals of the *kkonminam*.

Consuming Kkonminam*: The Commodity*

The selected dramas hugely impacted the sales of products. In the case of *Boys Over Flowers*, the show aroused an obsession with the boys of the F4 among young female viewers (Jung, 2010). Within a few weeks after the premiere of *Boys Over Flowers*, Lee Min-ho received several contracts for product advertisements with leading companies, such as Signature Jeans, LG Telecom, and Dunkin' Donuts, that target both male and female consumers (Jung, 2010). Kim Hyun-joong, from the same drama, also received various advertisement deals, some of which offered up to $4 million (ibid.). Kim Soohyun was no exception to this trend. For example, a sweater that he wore during the filming of *My Love from the Star* was sold out, as were other items, such as the Samsonite leather backpack that he used in several episodes (Binkley, 2014; Son, 2014; Jun, 2014). There are also numerous pages dedicated to his fashion in the drama (see *Crazy9drama.wordpress.com*'s "My Love from the Star: Do Min Joon's Fashion" post). In 2014, he signed 35 endorsement contracts with several companies that focus on global marketing. In addition, he endorses numerous products for domestic companies such as Caffe Bene, FILA, ZIOZIA, The Face Shop, Lotte Duty Free (in Asia) and Jeju Air

(Stanley, 2015; Sung, 2015). By affiliating with marketing companies, they sell not only the brand but also their body image, as companies generate profit through the connotations that their body image ascribes to the product that is for sale. Thus, the affiliation with marketing companies embraces their soft masculine image, beauty and, finally, the commodity, which becomes intertwined with the appearance, body, and character that the advertisement and drama present. This embraces *kkonminam*'s multidimensionality: from image to beauty ideal and commodity, and vice versa.

Besides purchasing merchandise to acquire the *kkonminam*-look, makeup and other technologies related to beauty work enable males to obtain a "softer" look. According to Holliday and Elfving-Hwang (2012), plastic surgery is another way of achieving a "soft" image. As Miller (2006) has observed, these practices of consumption and construction of masculinity are related to the display of the body and female desires (p. 126–127). This study considers beautification of the body not as a "feminization of men" but rather, as Miller (2006) has proposed, as an element of masculinity. This facilitates the proliferation of masculine identities and options for males to decide to incorporate beauty work components into their masculinity. The beauty work technologies that *kkonminam* use to maintain their appearance can be costly. For example, the first 25-year-old male mentioned JW (male, 25 years old), who identified himself as a former *kkonminam*, revealed that he had spent a substantial amount of money in his attempt to be one: "I spent maybe million Won [almost nine hundred U.S. dollars], per month to buy clothes or shoes and to dye my hair. Hair shops are very expensive in this area. Yeah, I tried and it worked."[6] Other interviewees noted the importance of clothing brands.[7] This is one reason why the respondents all remarked that *kkonminam* could likely be found in Hongdae and Sinchon, which are considered hip and trendy areas for fashion and young people, and in Gangnam around Garosu-gil, where there are international brands, such as Louis Vuitton, Prada, and independent designers. The informants' description suggests that there is not a specific physical location where *kkonminam* assemble, such as a particular clothing or makeup store. Usually, people buy clothing online and discuss fashion and related topics on blogs. An interesting idea for further research could be to examine online platforms in order to trace and participate in discussion about masculinities, including the implications and products that people attach to *kkonminam* and other masculinities.

Soft Masculinities: Embodiment and Limitations

Although soft masculinities are popular in the media, young Koreans encounter limitations when they attempt to adopt soft masculinities, especially *kkonminam* aspects, in "real life." The projections of these fictional protagonists in "real life" are the so-called *kkonminam*, or "flower boys," who comprise a distinctive group that forms part of an elite. Therefore, they are difficult to find and gain access to without economic power. Nevertheless, the commodities (e.g. accessories, fashion, makeup) related to these projections have a significant effect on people's perception of the male body. For instance, despite the low rank of the Korean gender gap index in 2017 (118th out of 144, according to World Economic Forum, 2017), changes have surfaced in the adaptation of *kkonminam* and other soft masculinities to "real life."

Homosexuality and Kkonminam

An example related to the commodification of *kkonminam* is that the protagonists' image can be associated with homosexuality. According to Kwon (2016), the commodification of gay culture in Korean popular culture is not due to the popularity and open acceptance of homosexuality but rather derives from the fandom of female subculture (p. 1576–7). When regarding *kkonminam* in popular culture, Kwon (2016) has explained that some Koreans associate their appearance with the gay body, which makes women (and men, according to this study's data) able to accept gay identities (p. 1571). In other words, it is because people tend to appreciate *kkonminam* in media and because of the product consumption associated with *kkonminam* that they thus accept gay identities in popular culture. This suggests that homosexuality in Korea is being somewhat accepted by young Koreans,[8] and that *kkonminam* could be used as a way of "blending into" society for male homosexuals, as some interviewees confirmed that all of their *kkonminam* friends are gay.

Kkonminam masculinity and the adaptation of other types of soft masculinities embrace Anderson's (2005, 2009, 2010, 2012) suggestion that masculinities are becoming more "inclusive," which reflects the notion of increased tolerance towards "feminine-related" activities, such as applying makeup and presenting a "weak" appearance, in the case of Korea. A key term in his research is "homohysteria," which he explains has been progressively changing. Homohysteria refers to a fear of being denominated as homosexual by other people, causing individuals to avoid certain behaviors. Anderson (2009) has defined "inclusive masculinities" as a position within masculinities whereby heterosexual men can "demonstrate emotional and physically homosocial proximity" (p. 8).

However, this behavior can also be considered part of what Hall (2015) has categorized as "feminized" masculinities, such as metrosexual or (*kkonminam*) soft masculinity. Metrosexual men take care of their appearance by means that are considered "feminine." Focusing mainly on the appearance, this "feminized" masculinity behaves according to the normative ideas of "manly" attitude (Hall, 2015). On the other hand, *kkonminam* masculinity extends to behavior (predominantly in media) and appearance. Hall (2015) has stated that these soft masculinities could be considered traditional masculinity reconfigured for today's society, wherein consumerism is the driving force (p. 4). When considering *kkonminam* in the context of Korea's consumer-oriented society, a determined group of young adults adapt traditionally masculine elements to modern models of masculinities, which embrace the consumption of products that are related to soft masculinities, such as makeup. This simultaneously generates another (multi)dimension of masculinity itself, which is the ability to be regarded as a commodity, too, in addition to the capacity of creating new types of soft masculinities.

Furthermore, soft masculinities carry traditional masculine elements, as they are a hybrid of *seonbi* and other types of masculinities. *Seonbi* masculinity is a traditional Neo-Confucian Korean masculinity that encourages the cultivation of the body. Men emphasized intellectual and spiritual development, rather than focusing on the body (Kim, 2003, p. 100–101). It highlights education, thus pertaining to elite groups, and ignores physical strength and household work (Moon, 2002; Jung, 2011; Kim, 2003). *Seonbi* masculinity drastically differs from strong, martial type of masculinity that a South Korean military dictatorship promoted in previous eras (Moon, 2005; Kim, 2004). The author of this essay proposes that *kkonminam* is a reaction to such a previous, martial/military type of "strong" masculinity. In other words, with *kkonminam*, *seonbi*-type of soft masculinity has made a comeback, or perhaps a continuation. Yet, consumerism in South Korea's contemporary society tends to commodify it and emphasize its looks only.

Kkonminam masculinity differs from traditional masculinity that is reframed for modern consumer individuals, as soft masculinities co-exist with hegemonic masculinities. This implies, then, the concept of "inclusive" masculinities. The hegemonic one is not imposed, leaving space for the creation and adaptation of other available (soft) masculinities. However, in a closed and regulated environment, such as in the military, hegemonic masculinities are imposed (see next section). In this case, *kkonminam* masculinity embraces several dimensions that situate this model of masculinity in a broad spectrum within the very concept of masculinities. Informants have opposed *kkonminam* masculinity and compared it to homosexuality, hard masculinity (including hegemonic masculinity), and the "fantasy-like" soft masculinities that are visible in the media. This opposition and comparison renders *kkonminam* masculinity in society an interesting case, as its "in-betweenness" allows for its presence not only in other types of masculinities but also outside the image of masculinity as a commodity to be sold and acquired.

Negative Connotations and Maturity

As mentioned earlier, *kkonminam* are not always viewed as a favorable interpretation of masculinities in society. Unlike the image the media advances (sweet, cool, pretty and handsome male who takes care of his lady and knows what to say at the right time), some people signaled negative aspects of the *kkonminam*. For instance, a 27-year-old female Vanessa (27 years old) used to like *kkonminam*, but a few experiences with them made her realize they can be arrogant. What was interesting was that she called them both "genies" and "weapons": the former conveys that *kkonminam* are knowledgeable of a girl's desires and fulfils them like a genie by being sweet and caring, while the latter refers to the negative side of the "genie-illusion," as she commented that *kkonminam* sometimes use girls for money or sexual relationships.

Youtuber Korea Junkies has portrayed this situation in the video, "10 Types of Korean Guys You Will Meet," which presents the *kkonminam* as a "gold-digger." The video uses another translation—*aegyo jaengi*—which refers to a person who engages in *aegyo*, i.e., cute expressions, such as a high tone of voice and gestures. In the video, the boy asks his girlfriend to buy some figures for him. She initially refuses, but after the boy performs some *aegyo*, she gives him her credit card. However, this cannot be interpreted as a whole reference to the *kkonminam*; the relevance here is that more people in the popular media acknowledge the stereotype of flower boys profiting from certain features that they possess.

Other respondents characterized *kkonminam* as "players," *nappeun namja*/ "bad boys," or *kisaeng orabi*. *Kisaeng* were Korean court ladies who entertained royal guests and also offered sexual services. The phrase *kisaeng orabi* is a slang term which associates the activities of *kisaeng* with their beauty, and it is generally used to describe a man who frequently goes to bars and clubs to pick up girls (Choe and Torchia, 2002, p. 53). Moreover, there is an impression that (heterosexual) *kkonminam* are sometimes arrogant, unfriendly, rude, unrealistic, and fake.

Respondents additionally suggested that *kkonminam* masculinity is positioned at the top of the beauty pyramid: an almost-ideal beauty that is difficult to achieve (see Figure 2). In fact, it is an almost unattainable ideal of a "natural" beauty, and a few young Koreans have pursued it through meticulously work on their appearance and spending large sums of money in order to maintain the look. Appearance is taken into account when adopting the *kkonminam* look, but behavior is not considered in its totality. Kindness towards women was mentioned as a "tool" to fulfill other desires, such as those of a material or sexual nature.

For young Koreans, the adoption of such masculinity could offer several benefits, as people associate beauty with upward social mobility (Edmonds, 2010). In order to achieve the "beautiful-soft look," males can opt for beauty work on their bodies. However, because certain people do not view the "real life" *kkonminam* as a positive model, numerous young Koreans have chosen not to follow it. In this case, the interviewee's personal experiences[9] contribute to the negative connotations associated with the *kkonminam* model, but it may be more complex than personal experiences, as culture plays an important role. With the sale of items such as clothing and makeup related to *kkonminam* masculinity, consumers do not have to adapt the model in its entirety–only elements of it. Therefore, they acquire certain upward social mobility or favorable outcomes in society, as evident from JW's, the first 25-year-old male's, experience.

As individuals adapt aspects of soft masculinity models, they construct other interpretations. The *kkonminam* model changes over time (age), which involves the transition into adulthood (maturity, responsibility). Furthermore, some individuals consider the "flower- boy look" to be a negative issue and an almost inaccessible beauty ideal. Hence, through these "limitations" of *kkonminam* masculinity, individuals can construct other interpretations, such as *hunnam* (considered a kind, warm and handsome person; see Figure 2). This and other models of soft masculinities (which change with the age of the individual) are often compared to *kkonminam* masculinity, as the latter remains at the top of the "beauty pyramid." The *kkonminam* masculinity's dimension reaches to discourses of beauty ideals and other types of masculinities.

As observed in this section, the *kkonminam*'s image in society is often associated with unfavorable behavior and good looks, while the media-portrayed image is sympathetic and attractive. However, it is important to consider why and how the *kkonminam* images differ. A possible explanation lies in the life trajectories of young Korean people, as they have to face responsibilities when they grow up. Specifically, there are two notions of *kkonminam* masculinity: one is related to the media image (positive), while the other concerns associations with the *kkonminam* interpretation (positive and negative connotations). Individuals adapt commodities pertaining to this soft masculinity model by purchasing items and services, e.g., makeup, haircuts, and clothing that are related to images promoted by celebrities. They even resort to plastic surgery. However, some individuals take behavior into account, as it seems that the projection of *kkonminam* is adapted, not its full content. Therefore, *kkonminam* masculinity could be regarded as "inclusive" and, as this paper proposes, multidimensional, as *kkonminam* embraces various dimensions such as media, fashion, marketing, beauty ideals, behavior, masculinities, and includes sensitive topics such as makeup into its model of masculinity.

The sensitivity of the matter of makeup is evident in the adapted presentation of products for men. Some cosmetic brands, such as Innisfree (see Figures 1 and 2), have opted for *Transformers*-themed makeup (as it is usually considered a boys' film) and military-themed cosmetics in order to evoke the idea of masculinity, as military service is associated with "being a man" and hegemonic masculinity[10] (Moon, 2002). However, the struggle with hegemonic subversion is clear in the use of military-related items, which is a component of hegemonic masculinities in Korea often found in the military realm (Moon, 2002, p. 84). Although, the stereotyped image of a Korean soldier might not be linked with household chores or self-sufficiency, here it is argued that young Korean males can take pride in engaging in household labor rather than "overshadowing" these chores, as Moon (2002) has suggested. In this sense, the idea of being "soft" shifts to being responsible. It is the connotations attached to age, military service, and masculinity that play

Figure 1: *Cosmetics for men.* Military-themed makeup for men at the Innisfree cosmetic shop in Sinchon.

Figure 2: *Cosmetics for men. Transformers*-themed facemask for men at the Sinchon Innisfree shop.

a relevant role in the transition from *kkonminam* to other interpretations of (soft) masculinities.

Another key factor in this transition is the notion of which duties men should have in society, which is determined by the state's and society's ideas about maturity. Moon (2002) has emphasized that even the state has a different regard for men who have completed their compulsory service, viewing as "true citizens" those who are willing to defend and die for their nation (Moon, 2002, p. 102).

This could be why some people view *kkonminam* as merely an adolescent phase that will disappear upon reaching adulthood.[11] The interviewees' notions of maturity reflect the idea that one who cannot assume responsibilities is not yet a man, and even women presume that *kkonminam* are not mature yet as *kkonminam* seem young, financially unreliable, and "weak." If compared to the Korean dramas, this notion does not match the media image, as the protagonists often take the lead in their relationships, and the Korean dramas present them as making the decisions and saving the female protagonists. Therefore, the protagonists portray characteristics of responsibility and maturity. Although these notions are divergent, younger people are still adopting the *kkonminam* interpretation of soft masculinity. When young Koreans opt to incorporate soft masculinities into their lives (be it superficially—only looks; or fully—looks and characterization), they still encounter certain limitations, such as those described in this section. Another limitation exists in the realm of military service, where men feel pressure to conform to the idea of manhood in the military. These limitations intertwine with various dimensions that engage in discourses of beauty, social pressure, and delimit and shape *kkonminam* masculinity in "real life."

The Military Service and the "Standardization" of Men

When young boys enter the military, they not only become more "mature" and responsible, but also confront several challenges, such as peer pressure and bullying. As four interviewees noted, experience in the military is relevant for relationships among men.

A third 25-year-old male SH indicated an example of experience and the feeling of uniformity in military service. In a similar vein, a 27-year-old male JY mentioned this "standardization" of men in noting that, for him, it was sometimes challenging to work with people who had not engaged in military service as men who participate in the army think alike in a certain way. As Moon (2002) has suggested, hegemonic masculinity is often associated with military service (p. 84). Hence, the "standardization" of men can be regarded as a component of hegemonic masculinity in contemporary Korean society.

Hegemonic masculinity can be identified in three notions and practices (Moon, 2002), which originally were understood as models that allowed the domination of men over women (Connell and Messerschmidt, 2005, p. 832). The first form is related to patriarchal gender roles (as in men being able to provide for the family), followed by military service, and *seonbi* masculinity (the distancing of men from the household work) (Moon, 2002). These practices are often associated with certain behaviors men should follow, for example, being competitive, tough, aggressive, successful, adventurous, courageous, and stoic in order to not show emotions (Connell and Messerschmidt, 2005), as opposed to the soft images of *kkonminam* in popular Korean dramas. In contrasting soft masculinities with hegemonic masculinities that are found in the disciplinary military realm, it is apparent that soft masculinities are particularly oppressed, as they are considered "weak" and sensitive. However, Moon (2002) has explained that military service does not establish military hegemonic masculinities per se (p. 91), which this essay proposes, might allow for the construction of other models of (soft) masculinities from which young Koreans can choose, establishing another dimension of the *kkonminam* masculinity.

Conclusion

The author of this essay analyzed portrayals and understandings of soft masculine men in Korean dramas and in society ("real life") by assessing ethnographic research data and applying textual analysis to three popular and key male protagonists in Korean dramas concerning *kkonminam* masculinity in Korea. While conducting the ethnographic research, the researcher noted that one of the limitations that this study encompassed is the language barrier. This study adds nuance and re-considers the definitions of soft masculinities within media studies (Shin, 2013; Jung, 2011; Maliangkay, 2010), as this essay has proven that the behavior of *kkonminam* does not have to be considered "effeminate," as the ethnographic research and discussion of the main male characters in Korean dramas reject the latter assumption.

The author of this essay argues that *kkonminam* masculinity is multidimensional. As young Koreans adopt only the surface, i.e., the looks of *kkonminam* masculinity, it results in the commodification of this type of masculinity, encouraged and limited by cultural and moral factors. In other words, *kkonminam* masculinity embodies social pressures that delimit and shape its image and content, becoming multidimensional (from image, to embodiment of social and moral expectations, to a commodity and vice versa). As Kim (2003) and Jung (2011) suggest, the hybridization of male and female features in the *kkonminam* figure satisfy the longing of both genders, which this research argues target the consumption of products derived from *kkonminam*, as both genders are affected by the hybrid features of *kkonminam*.

Furthermore, *kkonminam* have connotations in "real life" that diverge from those in media-related images. In "real life," *kkonminam* are recognized as "bad boys" or "players," which contradicts the attitude in Korean dramas: polite, tender, mature, responsible, and caring. Furthermore, when this masculinity is adopted, *kkonminam* do not behave differently, except toward women, as they use their looks as a tool for approaching women. At the same time, Korean masculinities embrace "inclusiveness" (Anderson, 2009); thus, activities that are considered feminine, homosexual or both are becoming gradually more accepted for men in contemporary Korea. However, there is a certain "standardization" of men, which regulates the development of soft masculinities.

Moreover, existent limitations when adapting this type of masculinity, such as the "standardization" of men in the military, the subsequent transition into adulthood, and negative connotations, enable the construction of other models of soft masculinities derived from the *kkonminam* figure, as the latter is seen as an unreachable beauty ideal that projects a consumer-related and media-centered masculinity. Therefore, conceptualizing *kkonminam* as multidimensional allows addressing the desires of consumers and the relevance it has for Korean youth today, as it embodies desires and anxieties of this group related to beauty and life trajectories.

Appendix

This section is an example of basic guiding questions; they were alternated and differed per individual and situation. These flexible questions were adapted according to each individual's English level and gender. However, the last seven interviews during the research period concerned specific topics such as military service, the importance of beauty in Korea, *kkonminam*'s beauty, make-up, and plastic surgery.

Interview questions for everyone (basic information)

1. What is your name?
2. How old are you?
3. [Only males] Have you already done your military service?
4. What is your occupation? [If student] Where do you study? [If employee] Where do you work?
5. Why did you choose to work/study there? Would there be another place where you would like to work/study, and why?

6. Where are you from?
7. Have you ever been abroad? Where?

Interviewing men and women about general topics

1. How would you define masculinity?
2. How would you define femininity?
3. What do you think are the characteristics of 'being a man'?
4. Do you consider a masculinity to be just looks, or does it involve other elements, such as social class, manners, culture, education, etc? Why?
5. How would you describe the relationship between appearance and employment in Korea?

Interviewing men

1. Do you watch Korean television dramas?
2. What do you think about the *kkonminam*? / How do you see them?
3. How would you describe *kkonminam*?
4. How do *kkonminam* behave?
5. Do you think *kkonminam* are androgynous? In which way?
6. Do you think *kkonminam* are homosexual? How and why do you think that?
7. What do you consider *kkonminam*'s "masculine" characteristics? How do you see that?
8. Are you friends with a *kkonminam*? Would you be friends with one?
9. Why are you friends with a *kkonminam* or why wouldn't you be friends with one?
10. Do you see *kkonminam* on the streets? If yes, where can I find a *kkonminam*?
11. How popular are they?
12. Why do you think girls like or dislike *kkonminam*?
13. Why do you think boys like or dislike *kkonminam*?
14. Would you like to have their style and why?
15. Which qualities of the *kkonminam* do you like, and which ones you dislike?
16. How would you describe the image/style of the *kkonminam*? Do you see different types of *kkonminam*? In which ways?
17. Why do you think *kkonminam* adapt their particular look? How come?
18. Who can be a *kkonminam;* students, adults, etc.?

19. Can you be a *kkonminam* if you wear wholesale clothing for example? Or does it have to be a specific brand or just a well-known brand?
20. Do *kkonminam* wear make-up? If a boy wears make-up, how would he be considered?
21. Why do you think *kkonminam* adopt this type of masculinity?
22. What are the reasons to behave like they do?

Interviewing women

Almost the same questions as the ones for boys, adding the following:

1. Have you ever dated a *kkonminam* boy? If yes, how was the experience? What was different about dating *kkonminam* and other boys?
2. If not, would you ever date a *kkonminam* boy, why?

Interviewing *kkonminam*

(In this research just one case occurred of a self-proclaimed "former" *kkonminan*)

Similar questions as "interviewing boys," including the following:

1. Why do you choose the style of *kkonminam*?
2. What are you aiming to achieve through this fashion/look?
3. Have you ever felt "looked at" because of your fashion/look?
4. How did that feel? What were the reasons for people to stare at you, or comment something to you?
5. How do girls react among you, regarding your fashion/look?
6. How do boys react among you, regarding your fashion/look?
7. How did you feel?
8. Where do you go out? Which club is your favourite, and why?
9. How would you describe your behavior?
10. What is your ideal type of person for a relationship? (What is your sexual preference?)

Causal questions in a cosmetic shop

1. Which are the products boys buy?
2. Which is the most popular? Who advertises this product?

Casual questions in a manicure and beauty salon

1. What type of clients do you have in a day?
2. What do your male clients ask for? (Style, procedure)
3. What kind of work do they do?

Interviewing men and women about the media image of *kkonminam*

1. Who is a role model for you? Who inspired you to adapt your look/fashion?
2. Do you watch television dramas? Which one is your favourite and why?
3. Who is your role model among Korean idols, and why?
4. How big do you think is the influence of visual media on *kkonminam*?
5. Have you ever bought a beauty product related to a certain idol just because of the person promoting it? Why, and who was the person in the advertisement?
6. How do you think men are portrayed in visual media?

Notes

1. The "original" referred here concerns the beginning of the 2000s, when young men wore skinny jeans, semi-long hair and were very thin. A prime example of this image is the K-pop group Shinee when they debuted.

2. "Other" refers to people who are looking for a job or who are studying to enter a university, or who are taking a break because they are going into military service soon. Casual interviews are not included in the interviewees' profile breakdown.

3. The interviews were conducted in English; however, sometimes the respondents seemed to have difficulty finding the right word. The issue was easily solved with the use of online dictionaries and sometimes through interpreters. One interviewee even called a friend to ask how he could express a certain word. Another respondent, W. (male, 28 years old), after the interview sent an email with his opinion on the questions that had just been asked to him. He wanted to make sure that what he mentioned was understood (these were his words).

4. The names of the interviewees are abbreviated for privacy reasons. Other participants gave an English name that could be used in this paper.

5. When the phenomenon of *kkonminam* gained sudden popularity, back in 2009 because of *Boys Over Flowers*, it was referred to by media as a "syndrome," given that young teenage girls seemed obsessed with *kkonminam* by purchasing products and talking on SNS (Social Networking Services) about them (Jung, 2010).

6. He says "it worked," because he started getting noticed by women. For instance, he had more blind dates (which are common in Korean culture, called *sogaeting*).

7. According to Nixon (1996), the primary cultural sites that allow the dissemination of masculine representations are men's clothing shops, TV advertisements, press advertisements, and men's magazines. Television series such as Korean dramas were a huge success in the early 2000s (Shim, 2006), providing the opportunity for soft masculinities to be represented and rise to fame. For example, the most iconic portrayal of soft masculinities is the character played by Bae Yong-joon in *Winter Sonata* (*Gyeoul yeonga* 2002).

8. In fact, several polls have revealed that young Koreans are more accepting of homosexuality (Denney, 21 October 2014, *The Diplomat*; Kwaak, 21 June 2013). An example is entertainer Hong Seok-cheon, who in 2000 became the first openly homosexual celebrity. After this announcement he lost his job, but he recovered his popularity in 2012 by getting invited as a guest to and hosting TV programs.

9. People appreciate the media image while disliking the *kkonminam* they encounter in reality. Nevertheless, not all stereotypes are true; for instance, JW (male, 25), a self-proclaimed former *kkonminam*, did not use girls for money but used the look to approach them.

10. Hegemonic masculinities are perceived as normative notions in Korea, meaning that the practices associated with masculinities become part of a certain society, which go unnoticed and seem natural. Hegemonic masculinity can be identified in three notions and practices (Moon, 2002), which originally were understood as models that allowed the domination of men over women (Connell and Messerschmidt, 2005, p. 832). The first form is related to patriarchal gender roles (as in men being able to provide for the family), followed by military service, and *seonbi* masculinity (the distancing of men from the household work) (Moon, 2002). These practices are often associated with certain behaviors men should follow, for example, to be competitive, tough, aggressive, successful, adventurous, and courageous, and to not show emotions (Connell and Messerschmidt, 2005).

11. If the person, now adult, is still considered to be a "pretty" mature man, then the term changes and becomes *kkotjungnyeon*, literally meaning "flower middle-aged man."

References

Abelmann, N. (2003). The melodrama of mobility: Women, talk, and class in contemporary South Korea. Honolulu: University of Hawai'i Press.

Ainslie, M.J. (2017). Korean soft masculinity vs. Malay hegemony: Malaysian masculinity and Hallyu fandom. *Korea Observer, 48*(3), 609–638.

Anderson, E. (2005). Orthodox and inclusive masculinity: Competing masculinities among heterosexual men in a feminized terrain. *Sociological Perspectives, 48*(3), 337–355.

Anderson, E. (2009). Inclusive masculinity: The changing nature of masculinities. New York: Routledge.

Anderson, E. (2010). In the game: Gay athletes and the cult of masculinity. New York: SUNY Press.

Anderson, E. (2012). Shifting masculinities in AngloAmerican countries. *Masculinities & Social Change, 1*(1), 40–60.

Beauty. (2018). In *the Oxford Dictionary*. Retrieved from http://www.oxforddictionaries.com/definition/english/beauty.

Binkley, C. (2014, April 30). A Jimmy Choo shoe's path to being a global best seller: The Abel sells out in Asia after an appearance on a Korean show. *Wall Street Journal*. Retrieved from http://www.wsj.com/articles/SB10001424052702304178104579533840140883978.

Bryman, A. (2012). *Social research methods*. New York: Oxford University Press.

Choe, S., & Torchia, C. (2002). Looking for a Mr. Kim in Seoul: A guide to Korean expressions. Cincinnati: Infini Press.

Choma, B.L., Foster, M.D., & Radford, E. (2007). Use of objectification theory to examine the effects of a media literacy intervention on women. *Sex Roles, 56*, 581–591.

Connell, R.W., & Messerschmidt, J.W. (2005). Hegemonic masculinity rethinking the concept. *Gender and Society, 19*(6), 829–859.

Crazy9drama. (2014, March 14). My Love from the Star: Do Min Joon's fashion. *Crazy9Drama*. Retrieved from https://crazy9drama.wordpress.com/2014/03/14/my-love-from-the-stars-do-min-joons-fashion/.

Denney, S. (2014, October 21). South Koreans more accepting of LGBT community. *The Diplomat*. Retrieved from http://thediplomat.com/2014/10/south-koreans-more-accepting-of-lgbt-community/.

The Economist. (2011, December 17). The one-shot society: The system that has helped South Korea prosper is beginning to break down. *The Economist*. Retrieved from http://www.economist.com/node/21541713#sthash.MtZdwvcJ.dpbs.

Edmonds, A. (2010). Pretty modern: Beauty, sex, and plastic surgery in Brazil. Durham, NC: Duke University Press.

FlorCruz, M. (2015, May 19). South Korea's plastic surgery boom lures Chinese as Korean pop culture gains popularity. *International Business Times*. Retrieved from http://www.ibtimes.com/south-koreas-plastic-surgery-boom-lures-chinese-korean-pop-culture-gains-popularity-1930132.

Gimlin, D. (2002). *Body work: Beauty and self-image in American culture.* Los Angeles: University of California Press.

Hall, M. (2015). *Metrosexual masculinities.* New York: Palgrave Macmillan.

Holliday, R., & Elfving-Hwang, J. (2012). Gender, globalization and aesthetic surgery in South Korea. *Body & Society, 18*(2), 58–81.

Jun, R. (2014, February 15). Everyone wants to wear what Jun Ji Hyun and Kim Soo Hyun wear, product placement in dramas. *Soompi.* Retrieved from http://www.soompi.com/2014/02/15/everyone-wants-to-wear-what-jun-ji-hyun-and-kim-soo-hyun-wear-product-placement-in-dramas/.

Jung, S. (2009). The shared imagination of Bishōnen, pan-East Asian soft masculinity: Reading DBSK, *YouTube.com* and transcultural new media consumption. *Intersections: Gender and Sexuality in Asia and the Pacific, 20.* Retrieved from http://intersections.anu.edu.au/issue20/jung.htm.

Jung, S. (2010). Chogukjeok pan-East Asian soft masculinity: Reading Boys Over Flowers, Coffee Prince and Shinhwa fan fiction. In D. Black, S. Epstein, and A. Tokita (Eds.), *Complicated currents: Media flows, soft power and East Asia.* Melbourne: Monash University ePress, 8.1–8.16.

Jung, S. (2011). Korean masculinities and transcultural consumption: Yonsama, Rain, Oldboy, K-Pop idols (Vol. 1). Hong Kong: Hong Kong University Press.

Jung, S.Y. (2015, May 26). Rising wave popularity of Hallyu goods ongoing. *Business Korea.* Retrieved from http://www.businesskorea.co.kr/article/10741/rising-wave-popularity-hallyu-goods-ongoing.

Kim, C. & Lee, S.H. (2018, March 15). South Korea proposes extra budget, bigger subsidies to address youth unemployment. *Reuters.* Retrieved from https://in.reuters.com/article/us-southkorea-economy-budget/south-korea-proposes-extra-budget-bigger-subsidies-to-address-youth-unemployment-idINKCN1GR0HH.

Kim, E.H., & Choi, C. (Eds.). (1998). *Dangerous women: Gender and Korean nationalism.* New York: Routledge.

Kim, J.Y., & Lee, J.O. (2014). Korean pop culture: A decade of ups and downs. *International Journal of Multimedia and Ubiquitous Engineering, 9*(3), 129–134.

Kim, K. (2013, February 17). How Korean girls like to be pretty (Korean beauty standards). *Seoulistic.* Retrieved from http://seoulistic.com/video/how-korean-girls-like-to-be-pretty-korean-beauty-standards/.

Kim, K.H. (2004). *The remasculinization of Korean cinema.* Durham, NC: Duke University Press.

Kim, S., Long, P., & Robinson, M. (2009). Small screen, big tourism: The role of popular Korean television dramas in South Korean tourism. *Tourism Geographies, 11*(3), 308–333.

Kim, S.H. (2012). *Lookism in the Korean business world and the role of business management* (Unpublished doctoral dissertation). The University of Arizona, Tucson, AZ.

Kim, T. (2003). Neo-Confucian body techniques: Women's bodies in Korea's consumer society. *Body & Society, 9*(2), 97–113.

Korea Junkies. (2015, May 16). *10 types of Korean guys you will meet.* [Video file]. Retrieved from https://youtu.be/KLmex3SDnjM.

KOSIS. (2018, July 23). *Korean Statistical Information Service.* Retrieved from http://kosis.kr/statHtml/statHtml.do?orgId=144&tblId=TX_14401_A041.

Kwaak, J.S. (2013, June 12). Poll shows Koreans warming to homosexuality. *Wall Street Journal.* Retrieved from http://blogs.wsj.com/korearealtime/2013/06/12/poll-shows-koreans-warming-to-homosexuality/.

Kwon, J. (2016). Co-modifying the gay body: Globalization, the film industry, and female prosumers in the contemporary Korean mediascape. *International Journal of Communication 10,* 1563–1580.

Lee, C. (2011, December 30). Remembering 'Winter Sonata,' the start of Hallyu. *Korea Herald.* Retrieved from http://www.koreaherald.com/view.php?ud=20111230000497.

Lee, S. (2012). The structure of the appeal of Korean Wave texts. *Korea Observer, 43*(3), 447–469.

Lin, A.M., & Tong, A. (2007). Crossing boundaries: Male consumption of Korean TV dramas and negotiation of gender relations in modern day Hong Kong. *Journal of Gender Studies, 16*(3), 217–232.

Louie, K. (2012). Popular culture and masculinity ideals in East Asia, with special reference to China. *The Journal of Asian Studies, 71*(04), 929–943.

MacDonald, J. (2014, January 22). Why Kim Soo Hyun is number one in China. *KDrama Stars.* Retrieved from http://www.kdramastars.com/articles/14600/20140122/why-kim-soo-hyun-is-number-one-in-china.htm.

Maliangkay, R. (2010). The effeminacy of male beauty in Korea. *IIAS Newsletter, 55,* 6–7.

Maliangkay, R. (2013). Catering to the female gaze: The semiotics of masculinity in Korean advertising. *Situations, 7*(1), 44–61.

Miller, L. (2006). *Beauty up: Exploring contemporary Japanese body aesthetics.* Los Angeles: University of California Press.

Min, E., Jinsook, J., & Kwak, H.J. (2003). *Korean film: History, resistance, and democratic imagination.* Westport, CT: Praeger Publishers.

Metrosexual. (2018). In the *Cambridge Dictionary.* Retrieved from https://dictionary.cambridge.org/dictionary/english/metrosexual.

Moon, S. (2002). The production and subversion of hegemonic masculinity: Reconfiguring gender hierarchy in contemporary South Korea. In L. Kendall (Ed.), *Under construction: The gendering of modernity, class, and consumption in the Republic of Korea.* Honolulu: University of Hawai'i Press, 79–133.

Moon, S. (2005). Militarized modernity and gendered citizenship in South Korea. Durham, NC: Duke University Press.

Nixon, S. (1996). Hard looks: Masculinities, spectatorship and contemporary consumption. New York: UCL Press.

Oh, C. (2015). Queering spectatorship in K-pop: The androgynous male dancing body and Western female fandom. *Journal of Fandom Studies, 3*(1), 59–79.

Oh, C. (2017). "Cinderella" in reverse: Eroticizing bodily labor of sympathetic men in K-pop dance practice video. In X. Lin, C. Haywood, M. Mac & M. Ghaill (Eds.), *East Asian Men* (pp. 123–141). London, UK: Palgrave Macmillan.

Paechter, C. (2006). Masculine femininities/feminine masculinities: Power, identities, and gender. *Gender and Education, 18*(3), 253–263.

Shiau, H.C., & Chen, C.C. (2009). When sissy boys become mainstream: Narrating Asian feminized masculinities in the Global Age. *International Journal of Social Inquiry, 2*(2), 55–74.

Shim, D. (2006). Hybridity and the rise of Korean popular culture in Asia. *Media Culture and Society, 28*(1), 25–44.

Shim, S. (2016, May 26). What it's like growing up with Korean beauty ideals. *i-D. VICE.* Retrieved from https://i-d.vice.com/en_us/article/what-its-like-growing-up-with-korean-beauty-ideals.

Shin, J. (2013). Male homosexuality in the "King and the Clown": Hybrid construction and contested meanings. *Journal of Korean Studies, 18*(1), 89–114.

Son, A. (2014, January 26). GD and Kim Soo Hyun wear the same clothes. *KDrama Stars.* Retrieved from http://www.kdramastars.com/articles/14811/20140126/gd-and-kim-soo-hyun-wears-the-same-clothes.htm.

Stanley, A. (2015, March 8). Kim Soo Hyun is selected as the global model for Caffe Bene. *KDrama Stars.* Retrieved from http://www.kdramastars.com/articles/77333/20150308/kim-soo-hyun-is-selected-as-the-global-model-for-caffe-bene.htm.

Sung, S.Y. (2015, March 17). Kim Soo-hyun to model for Jeju Air. *Korea JoongAng Daily.* Retrieved from http://koreajoongangdaily.joins.com/news/article/Article.aspx?aid=3001954.

Tai, C. (2017, July 24). South Korean men having plastic surgery to get "pretty boy" looks and macho physiques of their K-pop and K-drama idols. *South China Morning Post.* Retrieved from http://www.scmp.com/lifestyle/fashion-luxury/article/2103854/cutting-edge-beauty-male-plastic-surgery-south-korea.

World Economic Forum. (2017). Global gender gap index 2017. *World Economic Forum.* Retrieved from http://reports.weforum.org/global-gender-gap-report-2017/data explorer/.

Yang, H.C. (2013). Flower boys on campus: Performing and practicing masculinity. *Journal of Gender Studies, 23*(4), 391–408.

Yang, J. (2007). Globalization, nationalism, and regionalization: The case of Korean popular culture. *Development and Society, 36*(2), 177–199.

Yang, J. (2012). The Korean Wave (Hallyu) in East Asia: A comparison of Chinese, Japanese and Taiwanese audiences who watch Korean TV dramas. *Development and Society, 41*(1), 103–147.

Yonhap News. (2014, February 21). China media sees lessons in S. Korean TV dramas. *Yonhap News*. Retrieved from http://english.yonhapnews.co.kr/culturesports/2014/02/21/12/0701000000AEN20140221002400315F.html.

Part 3

Co-Production and Adaptation

Chinese-Korean TV Drama Co-Production

Representations of International Romance and the Potential of Multiculturalism

ELAINE W. CHUNG

As *hallyu* nowadays is arguably evolving into its 4.0 version (B. Kim, 2015), after a decade of extensive studies on the circulation of K-dramas in East Asia (J. Kim, 2014), scholarly focus on the phenomenon has gradually shifted to the global reach of other Korean cultural products. However, in mainland China, the earliest and largest terminus of *Hallyu*, there has been a transmuted form of K-drama craze since the early 2000s—the boom of Chinese-Korean TV drama co-production—which remains virtually overlooked. To shed light on this piece of history, this essay interrogates how far TV drama co-production between China and Korea can bridge cultural understanding between the two countries. Framed by the approach of critical multiculturalism, the author of this essay closely analyzes the representations of international romance and kinship in two Chinese-Korean dramas *Modern Family* (*Modeng Jiating*) from 2002 and *Master Lin in Seoul* (*Lin Shifu Zai Shouer*) from 2012, situating them in the specific political-economic contexts of production. Special attention is placed on the tropes of Korean women they commonly employed to generate a China-centric discourse of multiculturalism. On a whole, the author of this essay argues that being a de facto strategy for Chinese TV industry to imitate yet localize K-drama, and ultimately to build the brand of "C-drama," hardly can Chinese-Korean drama co-production live up to its potential of multiculturalism.

The question of whether drama co-production can help "bridge" cultural understanding obviously implicates a presumption that there is a "gap" to be filled. Since the normalization of the Sino-Korean relationship in 1992, mainland China (China hereafter) and South Korea (Korea hereafter) have rapidly developed close political, economic, and socio-cultural connections, creating a favorable environment for cross-border encounters of their peoples. As of 2016, their citizens have been each other's largest group of foreign-born residents, tourists, and international students. This enormous reciprocal flow, unfortunately, has been disproportionately underrepresented in both Chinese and Korean screen media.

With a long-established myth of a "single-blood nation," not until the year 2005, due to the significant growth of migrant laborers and (mail-order) brides, the Korean government began to develop its policies of multiculturalism. However, rather than to encourage diversity, they have aimed primarily to maintain a patriarchal hegemony, by calling for the assimilation of foreign brides into Korean housewives while excluding male migrant workers from the national multicultural blueprint (Ahn, 2012; 2013). This gender-biased multiculturalism is also in operation with the country's entertainment media outlets including films (S. Kim, 2009; Rhee, 2016; Ryu, 2010; Oh & Oh, 2016) and TV shows (M. Lee, 2010) in which, underprivileged Southeast Asian women are often vulnerable yet obedient wives under the protection of Korean men. K-dramas, certainly, are no exceptions with the cycle of "foreign-bride-dramas" like *Bride from Hanoi* (2005) and *Golden Bride* (2007), which are romantic stories between pure Vietnamese women (played by Korean actresses) and Korean men, obscuring the social problems of mail-order brides and the complexities of international marriage in reality (Kim & Han, 2009; Y. Kim, Yoo, & Kim, 2009). Whereas Korean cinema repetitively equates Chinese immigrants (especially those of Korean descent) to brutal criminals (Jung, 2017; "Chinese-Korean," 2017), K-dramas rarely touch on the stories of Chinese dwellers in Korea, even though migrant brides and workers from China outnumber those from any other country. In the racial hierarchy K-dramas have created, between the admired white men and the victimized Southeast Asian women at the opposite poles, Chinese people receive only limited and brief representations through minor characters, playing walk-on parts (Ju & Noh, 2013).

Unlike the single-ethnic discourses in Korea, China, on the other hand, proclaims itself to be a multi-ethnic state with fifty-five officially recognized ethnic minorities, which account for approximately 8% of the total population other than the Han majority. Described by scholars as "pluralistic unity" (Tsung & Bai, 2015), "state-multiculturalism" (Z. Zhao & Postiglione, 2010), and "culture of pluralistic integration" (J. S. Park, 2013), multiculturalism in China is highly subjugated by the one-party state. Fundamentally, choosing which ethnic minorities would be formally acknowledged as one of the official fifty-five was itself a decision made by the newly established Communist government in the 1950s. Officially re-translating the Chinese term *shaoshuminzu* from "national minority" to "ethnic minority" in English in the 1990s (Wang, 2015), the Chinese government has been making constant efforts to contain multiculturalism under the umbrella of a Han-dominated Chinese identity. Popular culture in China, in line with state-led multiculturalism, often highlights the exotic and uncivilized images of non–Han people, legitimizing Han superiority and assimilation over them (Gladney, 1994; Kaldis, 2013). Multiculturalism in China, however, after the country reopened its door to the outside world in the 1980s, is no longer an exclusively "internal matter" between Han and non–Han, as people across the world began to rush into China for travel, work and study. Still, the notion of "pluralistic unity" remains valid. Various programs on Chinese TV, for instance, routinely idealize foreign residents in China as docile newcomers in the "Chinese family" who are eager to learn Chinese language and culture (Gorfinkel & Chubb, 2015). For TV dramas particularly, the 1990s witnessed the rise of a cluster of "transnational TV dramas" in China (Zeng, 2008), defined by their cross-cultural stories about Chinese people in Western countries, as well as Western people's lives in China. *Beijinger in New* York (*Beijingren Zai Niuyue*) from 1993, *Russian Girls in Harbin* (*Eluosi Guniang Zai Ha'erbin*) from 1993, and *American Babes in Beijing* (*Yangniu Zai Beijing*) from 1995 are a few high-profile forerunners. In Lu's interpretation (2000), these stories about Chinese men's romantic and career triumphs over Western men are nationalistic forms of imagination to reverse the economic and political power disparity between China and the Western world. In the new century, Chinese TV continues to produce these kinds of transnational stories. Rather than Chinese people's mobility overseas, however, more recent cases tend to focus on incoming foreigners, especially women who go to China for better job or marriage opportunities and willingly assimilate into the Chinese society. *Foreign Children Chinese Dad* (*Waiguo Xiaohai Zhongguo Ba*) from 2003 and *Marry In and Get Married* (*Qujinlai Jiachuqu*) from 2010 are some of the examples. Given that the "foreigners" who take the lead in these "transnational dramas" tend to come from America and Europe, Asians who share more proximate culture and have much closer connections with Chinese people in everyday life are unduly underrepresented.

If TV dramas target mainly national audiences and help develop an imagined identity of a nation (Chan, 2011), Chinese and Korean TV dramas do have their roles to play in reproducing selective images of certain types of foreigners, negotiating them into the collective Chinese/Korean identities. Nonetheless, provided that national media can "exoticize and otherize" culture, transnational media can possibly "deterritorialize" the imagined communities and promote multicultural coalitions (Shohat & Stam, 1996, p. 145). Internationally co-produced TV dramas, which involve talents from more than one country and cater to audiences across national borders, is a form of transnational media that can potentially help overcome stereotypes and promote cultural understanding between the partnering nations. The three earliest co-produced dramas between Korea and Japan from 2002 to 2004 to celebrate the World Cup (2002) which they also co-hosted are representative cases in the inter-Asian context. These contemporary love stories between Korean and Japanese youngsters, according to Gossmann and Kirsch (2014, p. 164), did bring the two countries together, submerging their past traumas and conflicts from colonial legacies. This essay, hence, is prompted by the question whether TV drama co-production can similarly act as a cultural broker between China and Korea, filling their gap of mutual representation in media.

To seek the answers, this essay closely studies two Chinese-Korean romantic TV dramas—*Modern Family* (*Modeng Jiating*) from 2002 and *Master Lin in Seoul* (*Lin Shifu Zai Shouer*) from 2012. Closely reading their narratives on international romance and kinship, the author of this essay intends to excavate the multicultural discourses they have encoded. Textual analyses of the dramas lie under the framework of critical multiculturalism (Kellner, 1995, pp. 96–97) which emphasizes the need for a "multiperspectival" analysis in two-fold. First incriminating an aim to identify oppressions in all aspects of social life, it is important to consider a range of cultural constituents including class, gender, sexuality, ethnicity, and their interconnections. Amongst them, the entwinement between ethnicity and gender is especially apparent. As Nagel (2000) stated, "ethnic boundaries are also sexual boundaries" (p. 113), women in popular culture are always "national allegory" (Lu, 1997, p. 20) who are assigned the role of symbolic and discursive bearers of their nations. The victimized Southeast-Asian brides in K-dramas and eroticized white women in Chinese dramas aforementioned, evidently, reconfirm the universal archetype which equates gender dominance over "their women" in fictional romance to the envisioned superiority over another nation (Kirsch, 2015). Seeking to reveal the intersection of gender and nationality in the politics of media representation, the analyses to follow mainly focus on the leading female characters in the two Chinese-Korean love stories. Another "multiperspective" underscored in critical multiculturalism is the contextualization of individual texts into the historical, socio-political, and economic situations (Kellner, 1995, pp. 102–103). As Meyer and Stern (2007) rightly mentioned in their article analyzing the American TV series, *Lost* (2004–2010), that an American production made for American viewers will not fully realize its potential to include characters of more diverse ethnicities (p. 326), it is always necessary to consider the influence of political economy on media contents. In this sense, the studies of TV texts below are to be accompanied by a historical overview of the production contexts behind Chinese-Korean drama co-production. However, rather than ambitiously mapping the spider-network of "texts, audiences, media industries, politics and the socio-historical context in specific conjunctures" (Kellner, 1995, p. 37) which may lose sight of specific meanings of the texts in radical contextualization, the two selected dramas are the mainstays of this essay, unravelling the multicultural discourses framed in their specific representations of international romance.

Modern Family (Modeng Jiating): *Korean Woman as an Ideal Daughter-in-Law*

Upon its entrance to the World Trade Organization (WTO), China in the early 2000s was in full speed to commercialize its cultural and media industries. However, even acknowledging their commercial nature, the Chinese government continues to hold a firm grip with its system of censorship and regulation, leading to a unique market logic of "bureaucratic monopoly capitalism" (Y. Zhao, 2003, p. 62). Internally, although private actors are encouraged to join the game, state-owned broadcasters such as CCTV, CETV, and CNTV still enjoy privileges from government policy and in return take a hard line to propagate the party's ideologies. Externally, although foreign enterprises are welcome to invest in the Chinese TV industry, they can rarely gain official consent to produce their own cultural content, an ideologically sensitive activity for the Chinese government. To maximize the synergy with foreign capital and talents while ensuring the "appropriateness" of the content they produce, it is common for high-level national broadcasters, who are close to the central government, to form strategic partnerships with foreign players, as the latter can be granted larger rooms of creativity under the guidance and guarantee of the former (Fung, 2008). This combination also characterizes the early development of Chinese-Korean drama co-production, with *Modern Family (Modeng Jiating)* from 2002, *Just Like a Beautiful Flying Butterfly* (*Jiuxiang Meili Hudie Fei*) from 2003 and *Beijing My Love* (*Beijing, Wode Ai*) from 2004, which respectively engage China's state-owned companies, CCTV, Legal Daily, and CETV, as examples. As all these early Chinese-Korean dramas depict love stories between young Chinese and Koreans against the real cityscapes of Beijing and Seoul as backdrops—at first sight, they seemingly could embrace and reconcile the perspectives of multiculturalism of both countries. Scrutinizing their production practices in greater details, however, demonstrates that none of these dramas can conveniently be regarded as "genuine co-production" if it means "all important positions were held by representatives of each country" (Gossmann & Kirsch, 2014, p. 156). For example, though CCTV co-produced *Beijing My Love* with Korean public broadcaster KBS, it shared only twenty percent of the costs and was responsible only for location shootings in China (S. Lee, 2003). The remaining two, on the contrary, were led by the Chinese side. The political economy behind these initial attempts of Chinese-Korean co-production in the early 2000s, intriguingly, is interwoven with the pattern of textual representation. The uneven sharing of investment and production responsibility are found affecting the gender representation of international romance, as the partner with greater control always masculinize its own nation while feminizing another one. That is, the Korea-led *Beijing My Love* is between a Korean man and a Chinese woman, whereas the other two dramas run by China reverse the protagonists to be Chinese men and Korean women.

Modern Family, the first co-produced drama between Chinese (China Central Television) and Korean (Munhwa Broadcasting Corporation) broadcasters, is a China-led project in which the Korean crew including the co-producer and co-director were in charge of only the scenes filmed in Korea, one of the four shooting locations. When the drama was aired in China, their names were even absent in both the opening and closing credits.

Being a China-led co-production, the international couple in *Modern Family*, then, is between a Korean woman and a Chinese man. The 33-episode drama centers on an old couple Mr. and Mrs. Xiao in Beijing, whose son and two daughters are all abroad and in love with foreigners. Parallel to the two daughters in Malaysia and Australia, their son Yuntian (played by Liu Yijun), who works as a software engineer in a Korean corporation located in Seoul, falls in love with his supervisor, a Korean woman, Park Yeon-hee (Lee Taeran). In her first appearance (episode 1), Yeon-hee is captured in a spacious hall, confidently presenting a new mobile-phone model and then receiving large praise from the top management, as well as her juniors including Yuntian. Her image as a career woman, however, is short-lived, quickly fading after she dates and decides to marry Yuntian (episode 3), which triggers Mrs. Xiao's hasty trip to Seoul to stop her son from marrying a foreign woman (episode 8). At first, with a master plan to scare Yeon-hee off, she behaves nastily and declares a list of "ten criteria of a good daughter-in-law" according to "Chinese values," including "being good at cooking," "taking care of in-laws," and "giving birth." Yeon-hee, nonetheless, does not retreat despite Mrs. Xiao's harsh nitpicking. Her best endeavor to fulfill the demanding "requirements" eventually allows Mrs. Xiao to satisfyingly accept her as a part of the Xiao family before returning to Beijing. Before Mrs. Xiao appears in Seoul, Yuntian in fact faces the exactly same trouble as Yeon-hee's Korean parents at first strongly object to letting their "well-educated and pretty" daughter marry a Chinese man who is not well-off enough (episode 4). Feeling "humiliated," as he describes it, Yuntian is reluctant to tolerate or to beseech Yeon-hee's parents. After storming out of the flat and venting his anger to Yeon-hee, he even evades her and considers ending the relationship. In the end, it is still Yeon-hee who rebels and convinces her family not to stereotype Chinese people and says to them, "You don't really know China" (episode 4). In contrast to Yeon-hee's relentless effort to appease Mrs. Xiao, having failed to overcome his pride and self-esteem, Yuntian continues to keep a distance from them and flatly refuse to "flatter" his in-laws (episode 23).

Continuing to adhere to Mrs. Xiao "standards" immediately after their wedding (episode 10), even though her position in the company is more secure and generates a higher income than Yuntian, Yeon-hee resigns and becomes a full-time housewife. After that, the camera finds her mostly at home doing household chores. Preparing a full table of dishes, taking out Yuntian's shoes while seeing him off to work at the doorway, and waiting for him to come home from work until midnight, are some of the repetitive tasks the script assigns to her. Yuntian's annoyance at Yeon-hee's trivial talks during dinner makes a perfect foil to her changing routine and worldview, which are increasingly confined to domestic issues.

More than just her willing dedication to housework, the factor which further consolidates the characterization of Yeon-hee as an "ideal" wife/daughter-in-law is her selfless and stoic disposition, which is particularly magnified during times of family crisis. A scene from episode 17, in which she holds a passbook in hand and generously suggests Yuntian financially assisting his single-mother elder-sister, is only a prelude to episode 19, when this time it is her husband who falls into bankruptcy after an investment failure. Knowing the news last minute and seeing Yuntian lose his job and in debt, Yeon-hee does not complain or get outraged for a single second. Even when the loan sharks break into her parents' home and nearly hurt her younger sister, Yeon-hee continues to back up Yuntian by voluntarily contributing everything she has, including her pension, her parents' savings (episode 22), and her wedding jewelry (episode 23).

Instead of gratitude, however, this unconditional support overwhelms Yuntian with sorrow and shame, causing him to run away and ask for a divorce. Yeon-hee nonetheless continues to chase after him and moves into his dilapidated flat without his consent. In their new home, she happily continues to perform her responsibilities and routines as a housewife—doing the laundry and preparing a full breakfast for Yuntian. In this manner, her "virtues" of tolerance, self-sacrifice, and faithfulness remain static throughout the ups and downs in her marriage life. Such personalities are distinctly dramatized by the fact that her desperate search for Yuntian takes place after her miscarriage, which leads to her secret attempt to resume working to ease the family financial burden.

In the last scene in Seoul, sitting in a luxurious restaurant, the couple appears to regain their previous living standards as Yuntian is successfully starting his own software business. Although Yeon-hee's ideas and knowledge made a definitive contribution, this time, rather than presenting the ideas herself as she did in her first appearance in the drama, she merely chitchats with another woman about their husbands on the side, allowing Yuntian and his Chinese partner to discuss their "serious things" (episode 33). That means, for Yeon-hee, who is now a family-oriented woman, a "happy ending" is less dependent upon her personal achievement than on the well-being of her husband and family.

While it may seem unrealistic that a foreigner can conform so seamlessly to the "Chinese standard" of a traditional woman, the drama consciously attempts to rationalize such character development by Yeon-hee's "Koreanness." In the story, Korean cultural artifacts are continually juxtaposed with Chinese ones, with statements such as "their food [is] much like Southern cuisine" (episode 8), "Korea is more like us, [they] use chopsticks and eat rice," "[their] houses [are] like those in Beijing" (episode 9). More importantly, in intangible aspects, the two countries' family and gender values are indistinguishable. For example, Yeon-hee's mother, who stated that "We Korean women do not work after marriage as we must take care of the family" in her first appearance (episode 2), shows no problem in endorsing Mrs. Xiao's demand for "ten criteria." These mutually-agreed-upon norms about married woman then allow Yeon-hee to be "just like a Beijing daughter-in-law" (episode 16), if not "more lovable than Beijing girls" (episode 33). The other Chinese leading female characters in the drama are more deviant from traditional womanhood than Yeon-hee—Yuntian's eldest sister is a single mother wandering overseas, and his younger sister is a carefree college student who flew to Australia for her unfaithful lover. As Yeon-hee herself also defines the role of wife in a conservative way, "a man who works hard is longing for a warm home where a woman waiting for him," the idealization of a Korean woman as a traditional daughter-in-law in a Chinese family is justified by the drama via an assumed cultural proximity between the two countries, particularly in terms of gender and familial values.

Since "giving birth and extending the Xiao family tree" is the last and ultimate criterion in Mrs. Xiao's list of good daughter-in-law attributes, only by fulfilling this final task can her role as an ideal daughter-in-law in the drama be completed. Certainly, she does so by becoming pregnant in the "happy ending" of the drama. Yet, more inherent than her fertility, what made her a perfect candidate to give birth for the Xiao's family is her Asian ethnicity, since her "black hair/eyes and yellow skin" (episodes 2 and 9) will not disturb the "Chinese bloodline." This mentality is recapped again at the closing scene when Mr. and Mrs. Xiao excitingly respond to the news of Yeon-hee's pregnancy by saying: "It is great as long as this grandchild will have yellow skin and black eyes" (episode 33). A division of foreigners according to skin color become conspicuous here. This line, on one hand, shows that until the end of the story, the old couple still cannot dispel their discomfort with their eldest daughter's Chinese-Italian son with white skin and blonde hair, who is called by Mrs. Xiao as *xiaozamao* (little hybrid) throughout the drama. As defining the "Others" is always a process of self-definition, on the other hand, affirming that Yeon-hee's baby, though a Chinese-Korean, would be less alien to a Chinese family, this drama about a multicultural family wraps up ambivalently with an essential, biologically-determined definition of Chinese.[1]

Hailed as the "most cosmopolitan TV drama ever produced in China" (Song, 2015, p. 108), *Modern Family* without a doubt is made with a message that in the age of globalization, Chinese people should be open-minded to foreign cultures and willing to seek opportunities overseas. This is effectively delivered by sketching how the originally xenophobic Mrs. Xiao becomes happy with her family akin to "The United Nations" (episode 33). But beneath this overarching theme, the degree of tolerance and welcomeness vary among different racial/ethnic and gender combinations. The inter-Asian couple between a Chinese man and a Korean woman is depicted as the most "acceptable" in comparison to the inter-racial ones, since Korean culture is like "ours," their women inherit the same set of traditional family values treasured in "our society," and will not give birth to a "mixed" baby since their physical appearance is the same. The multicultural romances and families represented in the drama, all in all, are crafted from a China-centric position to divide different "Others" hierarchically, allowing Chinese audiences to imagine how some categories can be more conveniently molded in "our" culture and identity.

Master Lin in Seoul (Lin Shifu Zai Shouer): Korean Woman as a Chaste Lover

China entered the World Trade Organization (WTO) in 2001. Shortly after in 2005, the Chinese one-party state began to re-tighten its once relaxed policies for foreign players. One of the reasons for doing so was the growing anxiety concerning China's cultural trade deficit, for which to some extent they can blame on the rocketing popularity of K-dramas. The K-drama, *Jewel in the Palace* (*Dae Jang-geum*; from 2003, but first aired in China on Hunan TV in 2005) is the most remarkable watershed. As a result, the Chinese government began to be suspicious that *Hallyu*, which was once welcomed as an "Eastern culture like us" (Jang, 2012), would be a "cultural-economic imperialism" (Huang, 2009). *Jewel in the Palace* (2003) tells the story of Jang-geum (fl. early 16th century), the first female physician in Korean history, which stood at the helm of *hallyu* by breaking all the rating records set by preceding K-dramas in Taiwan, Hong Kong, China, and Japan. The drama "embarrassed" China, in Keane's (2015) words, since its "former vassal territory, Korea, has been able to successfully generate cultural exports by mixing traditional aesthetics with postmodern popcultural sensibilities" (p. 64). More importantly, as a historical epic, it has been the best-selling genre of Chinese TV drama.

However, the regional craze of *Jewel in the Palace* alarmed China that *hallyu* products would lead to lower prices and sales figures of Chinese dramas in the global market (Keane, 2015, pp. 64–65). As an aftermath, internally, in 2006, the censorship body abruptly reduced the number of imported TV dramas that could be broadcasted during prime time, aiming to protect homegrown products against foreign competitors implicitly, namely K-dramas. Externally, the intention to compete with foreign media products both at home and abroad also shaped China's cultural policies from the mid-2000s, which prioritized the push for moving local media culture to foreign markets, not only for market expansion and profit-making, but also for the dissemination of "China's voice and cultures across the world" (Yang, 2016, p. 83). Nonetheless, if Chinese drama showrunners want to attract both domestic and international audiences, they paradoxically must learn from and imitate their foreign counterparts, which also is paradoxically incompatible with *tbahe* mission to foster and promote "Chinese culture."

This dilemma and struggle for a solution also left traces on the development of Chinese-Korea TV co-production. Having been hungry for profit since the mid–2000s, the fast-growing private production houses and provincial/municipal channels in China have become active in aligning with Korean companies in making trendy "Korean-style" Chinese dramas. For example, the showrunners for *Love at the Moment (Ai, Zai Libieshi)* from 2010 touted itself as the Chinese version of the renowned 2000 K-drama, *Autumn in My Heart (Gaeul donghwa)*, involving the latter's Korean producers and cinematographers to create a similar story in a similar style (Hong, 2006). Since the mid–2000s, for Korean actors who have been cast in these projects, if any, have commonly been assigned to homogenous roles that resemble the typical male leads in K-dramas—wealthy and good-looking young men who are plagued by childhood trauma and waiting for true love to heal them.[2] Despite the catchwords of "Korean-style," the content of these dramas do not really have anything to do with Korea. The male roles resonating with K-drama protagonists above, for example, are all Chinese roles in Chinese stories. Considering these features, many so-called Chinese-Korean "co-productions" since the mid–2000s have veritably been "Chinese dramas" whose producers simply hired individual Korean crew members and actors to recycle and localize their K-drama knowledge/image to build the brand of "C-drama" or "Hanliu drama" (Han-Chinese Wave drama). Imitating "K-dramas" and "*Hallyu*" respectively, these "phenomena" have been hyped by Chinese media, especially those affiliated with the party state, to celebrate, if not exaggerate, the international popularity of Chinese drama. Undoubtedly, the terms have yet to be acknowledged internationally, but their creation indicates that the K-drama is always going to be a reference point in the overseas projects of Chinese dramas, which is simultaneously a role model it has to learn from (Wang, 2015) and a rival it has to and allegedly is going to outcompete (Wan, 2016). Hence, to put it more vividly, co-production should be understood as a strategy for the Chinese TV industry to "learn from the barbarians to subdue the barbarians"[3] (Er, 2015), for example, to acquire the Korean drama-making technology while retaining the centrality of China's national interests.

As Chinese-Korean "co-productions" since the mid–2000s have been predominantly telling Chinese stories which localize K-drama aesthetics, storytelling style, and actors, that leaves no room for representation, let alone facilitation of cultural exchange. Nonetheless, works that have directly engaged with China's top national broadcaster, CCTV, are still persistent in telling cross-cultural stories, including *Heaven Show* (*Tiantang Xiu*) from 2012 and *Master Lin in Seoul* also from 2012. With backdrops of Seoul, Jeju Island, and Chengdu, *Master Lin in Seoul* again is a love story between a Chinese man, Lin Fei (Lin Yongjian), and a Korean woman, Park Seon-hee (Jang Seo-hee). The latter, who graduated from a "prestigious university," is initially a manager of a chain-brand hotel in Seoul. But the death of her father forces her, the eldest daughter of the family, to resign and take care of his Sichuan restaurant. Seon-hee shows her strong will in handling the family business but becomes desperate as she is totally ignorant about cooking. To make things worse, a competitor is also maliciously plotting to take over the restaurant. Lin, a celebrated chef in Sichuan, who is taking a short trip to visit his Chinese fiancée, Jianing, who is working in Seoul, coincidently meets Seon-hee and helps her save the restaurant. As the story develops, after breaking off his engagement with Jianing, who has fallen in love with a Korean man, Lin and Seon-hee gradually feel the attraction for each other and become the lead couple of this drama.

In terms of Seon-hee's character development, although the death of her father forces her to change her career, it is the romantic attachment to Lin that imposes a greater impact on her life as well as disposition. In the opening episodes, Seon-hee demonstrates her mental and physical toughness as a professional leader—either in the scene in which she is guiding her subordinates at the hotel, the scene in which she beats up a nasty customer, or the scene in which she cheers up the restaurant's employees after her father's death. However, instead of her own struggles, what genuinely sets her free from the family crisis is the arrival of Lin, whom she describes as the "savior of the Park family" (episode 4). Acting as if he is the owner of the restaurant, Lin not only boosts the reputation of the restaurant with his extraordinary dishes, but he also negotiates with their cunning competitors, trains the unqualified Korean staff, plans new menus, and represents the restaurant by participating in cooking competitions to save the restaurant from falling into the wrong hands. As Seon-hee says in episode 18, knowing that Lin is planning to return home, "It is like the sky has collapsed when I know I have to carry the burden again." This shows Seon-hee fully entrusts her family business to him.

Or from another perspective, with Lin's presence, Seon-hee is now liberated from the duty that was forced on her. Retreating from the restaurant's kitchen yet not returning to her original position as hotel manager, Seon-hee is gradually displaced from her workplace and more frequently spotted at home, a traditional Korean house akin to the traditional Chinese complex (*siheyuan*) of the Xiao family in *Modern Family*. In this place where cooking is more like domestic work than a business after her culinary skills and knowledge are proven unsuitable to run a restaurant, she is found happily preparing meals at home. The Chinese dumplings she especially made for Lin (episode 23) and the full table of food served to Lin's foster mother (episode 14), for instance, are well appreciated. Besides the settings in which the audience finds her, Seon-hee's personality also undergoes a vital change after Lin takes over. Unlike her initial image of a working woman, Seon-hee transforms into a weak woman who requires sympathy and care, as highlighted by the sights of her screaming at a raw fish and later crying and passing out after a long time of cooking (episode 12).

The growing femininity of Seon-hee is denoted also in her attitude towards romantic relationships. Although this 30-episode drama proclaims itself as a "transnational love story," it is not until episode 22 that the couple finally confirms their relationship. Before that, romantic moments between the duo are forcefully fabricated by people around them, mainly Lin's former fiancée, Lin's foster mother, and Seon-hee's younger sister, who puts a drunk Lin and Seon-hee into the same bed (episode 12), gives them presents in each other's name (episode 16), sends them on a holiday, and forces Lin to buy a diamond ring with which to propose to Seon-hee (episode 21). Their encouragement, however, is mostly ineffective as throughout the drama, Lin is hesitant and indecisive regarding his fondness for Seon-hee. Multiple times, even once after their engagement, Lin abruptly announces that he is leaving for China, yet returns later without prior notice. Notwithstanding repeated disappointment and prolonged waiting, Seon-hee never harbors a grudge against him nor does she ever beg him to stay.

On the other hand, her reluctance to actively fight for Lin's heart does not mean her feelings for him are not deep enough, as Seon-hee repeatedly rejects other wealthy Korean suitors while waiting for Lin's unknown return. The happy ending of the drama, following this manner of interaction between the pair, is expectedly a result of Lin's unilateral decision to return to Seon-hee and marry her (episode 26). Yet, in the last four episodes, Lin's one-sided decision once again puts their relationship at risk. Right before their marriage, Jianing, Lin's former fiancée, suddenly takes a trip to Lhasa alone without telling anyone, after having been cheated on by her Korean boyfriend. Treating Jianing as a family member now, Lin cannot concentrate on his wedding preparation and abruptly heads to Lhasa after leaving a note for Seon-hee. This time, in the final scene, Seon-hee atypically claims her active agency. However, rather than expressing her sadness and jealousy, she chooses to surprise Lin by appearing on the same flight he is taking. This can be viewed as a declaration that she is willing to not only wait for him, but also follow him anywhere, regardless of whether she is his legal wife or not.

Different from the strong emphasis on the proximity between Chinese and Korean cultures in *Modern Family*, *Master Lin in Seoul* pays greater attention to the cultural differences, which are underscored by Lin's constant utterance and explanation of Chinese idioms to his Korean fellows, his firm request to use made-in-China ingredients to make Chinese dishes, and his insistence on holding a wedding ceremony in China since "Chinese people must return to their roots" (episode 29). The delayed romance between Lin and Seon-hee is indeed caused by Lin's worries about the cultural gap they must overcome, including the language barrier between him and Seon-hee (though the dialogues fully dubbed in Chinese cannot effectively visualize this point). They also need to think about what language their future child should speak and where they would live after marriage, etc. Whilst his frustrations do address some realistic difficulties concerning international marriage and multicultural families, it is important to remember that all of them are addressed solely from the standpoint of Lin as a Chinese man, who meditates and reaches the best solution alone without discussing it with the woman he thinks he is going to marry. As her voices on the issues are not heard, these anxieties about cross-cultural romance seemingly are inapplicable to Seon-hee, as if marrying Lin is in her natural and designated trajectory, as long as it is when Lin agrees to do so.

As their nearly identical names may tell, despite the ten-year gap, Park Seon-hee in *Master Lin* strikingly resembles her predecessor Park Yeon-hee in *Modern Family* in two particular ways. Firstly, while both of them first appear on screen as highly-educated career women, once falling in love with a Chinese man, their domestic roles loom largely and outshine their former social roles. In the romantic relationship that increasingly preoccupies their lives, Yeon-hee and Seon-hee are presented as flawless characters who are unconditionally loyal and supportive of their lovers. By analyzing the two cases, it is evident that transformation into conservative femininity upon romantic encounters with Chinese men is a recurring trope representing Korean women in Chinese-Korean romances/marriages. In fact, in an interview, *Master Lin*'s director Yu Chun considers his drama an updated version of *Beijinger in New York* (B. Zhao, 2010), a Chinese drama from 1993 that traces the painful struggle of a Chinese man for his American dream in New York City. If *Master*

Lin in Seoul aligns itself with *Beijinger in New York*, then the minimal agency granted to Seon-hee can be easily explained, since the spotlight is cast on a Chinese man who strives for career success in a foreign country. As mentioned earlier, in the cycle of "transnational Chinese TV dramas" in the 1990s (Zeng, 2008; Lu 2000), Western and white women are often reduced to a group of sexually open and attractive characters for the spectacle and pleasure of Chinese men. In the same sense, the Korean women in these two cases can be placed into another category of "foreign women"—feminine, virtuous, and thus ideal candidates for wives, who can reinforce the masculinity Chinese men have lost when crossing over to Korea (signified by Yuntian's insecurity and low position in the Korean company and Lin's loss of his fiancée to a young Korean man). It is thereby safe to conclude that, despite their transnational nature as co-produced dramas, in representing international romance and multicultural family, both *A Modern Family* and *Master Lin* maintain the same China-centric standpoint upheld by their domestic predecessors in the nineties.

Produced by China International Television (CIT), a studio owned by CCTV, and Communist Party Foreign Publicity Office at Chengdu, *Master Lin in Seoul* declared itself as a celebration of the twentieth anniversary of normalized Sino-Korean relationship. Notwithstanding direct sponsorship from the state government and its grand diplomatic mission, CIT chose only to collaborate with other local partners instead of any Korean investor or studio. According to the director, Yu Chun, *Master Lin in Seoul* is aimed at "promoting traditional Chinese cuisine, cultures, and values" to the world, and the theme of cooking is inspired by the success of the K-drama, *Jewel in the Palace* (B. Zhao, 2010). His words make it crystal clear that from the outset, the use of "Korean elements" is simply to decorate and marketize a Chinese story with the proven lucrative K-drama formula. This intention sufficiently explains why, other than leading female character Seon-hee, all of the other Korean characters are played by Chinese actors, since the pursuit of faithful and realistic representation is a low priority in the producer's agenda. In a nutshell, through providing increasingly rare narratives of Chinese-Korean romance to audiences, *Master Lin in Seoul* is only a part of the broader phenomenon in China to localize K-drama. Against such production backgrounds, naturally, the drama has little motivation to alter or complicate the cookie-cut tropes of the "beautiful and virtuous" Korean wife.

Chinese-Korean Co-Production and Its Multicultural Potential: An Uncertain Future

Although some of the abovementioned co-productions achieved considerable popularity within China, so far they are seemingly ineffective in making Chinese dramas more "exportable." Besides the only Korea-led project, *Beijing, My Love*, none of them have ever been presented to Korean audiences on major TV channels. To seek other paths, since the mid–2010s, the trend to localize K-drama via co-production has evolved into some new forms. The practice of co-production has emerged as more Korean producers have relocated to China and have converted their successful K-dramas into Chinese versions. Korean media conglomerate CJ E&M, for example, sent a team to assist Hunan TV (China) to remake its high-rating K-drama *Queen In-hyun's Man* (*Inhyeon wanghuui namja*) from 2012 into *Love Weaves through a Millennium* (*Xiangai Chuansuo Qiannian*) in 2015, by adapting the story into a Chinese setting with an all-Chinese cast. Realizing that these Chinese narratives permeated with K-drama features make it difficult to lure audiences outside China, Chinese media moguls at the same time begin to directly finance star-studded and big-budget K-dramas such as *Descendents of the Sun* (*Taeyang ui huye*) and *Saimdang, Memoir of Colors* (*Saimdang, bichui ilgi*) from 2016.[4] Although these dramas did generate much larger profits across national boundaries, given the absence of Chinese cultural specificity in the narratives, they are still ineffective in promoting Chinese dramas globally. As an alternative option, some Chinese practitioners have taken more radical attempts by erasing the nationality of the dramas with whom they co-produced, namely Korea. *Best Couple* (*Zuijia Qinglu*) from 2017, is a characteristic example. Starring both Chinese and Korean actors as leading roles, from the visual signs including the street-views and props like newspaper and name cards, its Korean setting is more than conspicuous. However, when released exclusively online in China, the drama ambiguously assigned all the characters with Chinese names and dubbed their voices into Mandarin Chinese, not providing a concrete national background of the story throughout the 16 episodes.

These diverse forms of drama co-production demonstrate the Chinese TV industry's eagerness to replicate the global success of K-drama by internalizing it. Therefore, more co-produced experiments are foreseeable in the near future. Coincidentally, China's ongoing ban on Korea cultural products from July 2016 to the end of 2017 due to the THAAD conflict has also accelerated the process to localize K-drama in China[5] as more Chinese production houses have chosen to remake, imitate, and even plagiarize K-dramas by themselves, without involving the now "sensitive" Korean workforce. How far would this localization of K-dramas proceed? How would the changing production context affect the making of cross-cultural stories between China and Korea? Can some more recent dramas on Chinese-Korean romance, such as *My Goddess, My Mother* (*Wodinushen Wodima*) (A family drama about a Chinese man, his mother, and his Korean wife, which was completed in 2016 but delayed from broadcasting due to the Korean-media ban) generate novel reprsentations different from their predecessors? Are the pre-existing tropes of Korean women applicable to Chinese chracters played by Korean actresses too? While the author of this essay focuses only on two cases that directly address international romance/marriage and involve China's state broadcasters, to continue writing the history of Chinese-Korean TV drama co-production, these questions demand further investigation along with cases of more diverse production backgrounds.

Conclusion

This piece of insight from Baltruschat (2002) would be more than enough to conclude this essay: "Co-productions have the potential to reflect upon globalization processes, such as the hybridization of cultures and their diversification; however, due to their commercial focus, they target international audiences as consumers rather than citizens" (p. 1). Although their crossing-borders nature always made them probable cultural brokers, in practice, most internationally co-produced films, as TV dramas, can hardly live up to their multicultural potential, owing to the divergent, sometimes conflicting interests between the partnering countries. TV dramas co-produced between China and Korea, including the two cases examined in this essay—*Modern Family* and *Master Lin in Seoul*—are not exceptions. Notwithstanding their stories of international romance that were written ten years apart, the cookie-cut tropes they employed to depict Korean women as ideally virtuous wives reveal a China-centric perspective of multiculturalism, along with an obliviousness to bridging cultures via media representations. After all, given that Chinese-Korean TV drama co-production is a commercial activity predominated by the Chinese TV industry, which primarily seeks to recycle K-drama creativities to polish and build the brand of "C-dramas," the more up-to-date, realistic, and thus critical representations of multiculturalism it offers are indispensably few. The latest and accelerated process to localize K-drama in China, very possibly, will only take the multiculturalist prospects of co-production farther away.

Notes

1. As Chinese president Xi Jinping bragged about the longevity of the Chinese civilization to U.S. president Donald Trump at the Forbidden City in November 2017: "We people are the original people, black hair, yellow skin, inherited onwards (Hernández & Zhao, 2017)." Essential biological features have been and will continue to be central to the state-sponsored myth of Chinese identity.

2. If one looks at the synopses of the Chinese-Korean dramas co-produced since the mid–2000s, one can see that the roles played by Korean actors are highly coherent to each other. To name but a few, Cha In-pyo is a successor of a large corporation in *Love at the Moment*

(*Ai, Zailibieshi*) from 2006, who has difficulty communicating with others after the death of his mother during his childhood; Kim Jeong-hoon in *Love Strategy* (*Lianai Bingfa*) from 2008 is the heir of a conglomerate, who ran away from home only to find his lost puppy love in China; and also Kim Jeong-hoon in *Love on Tiptoe* (*Dianqi Jiaojian Wendaoai*) from 2013 is a mysterious man who strives to be a top model to gain recognition from his mother.

3. Originating from late-nineteenth-century China in the face of Western imperialism, this notion was upheld by a group of intellectuals who urged the central government to acquire military and industrial technologies from Western countries. However, they emphasized that learning from the West would only be a strategy to stop their encroachment on China, never an endorsement of Western cultural values. In recent years, amid the growing popularity of K-dramas in China, some figures in the Chinese TV industry, including Wu Yi, the producer of *Love Strategy*, and star-actor, Zhang Han (Zhou, 2007; Er, 2015), openly adopted this saying to express their view on collaborations between K-drama and Chinese drama.

4. The growing influence of Chinese capital and the Chinese market have caused some scholars to worry that this might not only alter the production practices of K-drama but also drain local talents to the filming sites of China. See Shim (2016) for further details.

5. Since July 2016, to object to the deployment of the U.S. Terminal High Altitude Area Defense (THAAD) in South Korea, a missile defense system that allegedly targets North Korea, China has put an unofficial ban on all Korean cultural products. Not only were all K-dramas removed from TV channels and online streaming platforms, Chinese-Korean co-production projects also came to a halt overnight. Numerous domestic Chinese films and dramas that casted Korean actors were delayed from release and broadcasting too.

References

Ahn, J. (2012). Transforming Korea into a multicultural society: Reception of multiculturalism discourse and its discursive disposition in Korea. *Asian Ethnicity*, *13*(1), 97–109.

Ahn, J. (2013). Global migration and the racial project in transition: Institutionalizing racial difference through the discourse of multiculturalism in South Korea. *Journal of Multicultural Discourses*, *8*(1), 29–47.

Baltruschat, D. (2002). Globalization and international TV and film co-productions: In search of new narratives. Presented at the Media in Transition 2: Globalization and Convergence, MIT, Cambridge, Massachusetts, U.S.A. Retrieved from http://cmsw.mit.edu/mit2/Abstracts/DorisBaltruschat.pdf.

Chan, B. (2011). Home, identities and transnational appeal: The case of Singaporean television dramas. *Critical Studies in Television: The International Journal of Television Studies*, *6*(2), 114–126.

Chinese-Korean = criminals? "Midnight Runner," "The Outlaws" angered the Chinese Koreans. (2017, September 30). *BBC Korea*. Retrieved from https://www.bbc.com/korean/41357319.

Er, M. (2015, September 14). Zhang Han huiying "shiyichangjiyizhiyi" zhengyi: Wo shi shan yi di [Zhang Han responds to the controversy of "Learning from the Barbarian to Contain the Barbarian": It is from good intention]. *Phoenix TV News*. Retrieved from http://ent.ifeng.com/a/20150914/42491983_0.shtml.

Fung, A.Y.H. (2008). Global capital, local culture: Transnational media corporations in China. New York: Peter Lang.

Gladney, D.C. (1994). Representing nationality in China: Refiguring majority/minority identities. *The Journal of Asian Studies*, *53*(1), 92–123.

Gorfinkel, L., & Chubb, A. (2015). When foreigners perform the Chinese nation: Televised global Chinese language competitions. In R. Bai & G. Song (Eds.), *Chinese television in the twenty-first century: Entertaining the nation* (pp. 121–140). New York: Routledge.

Gossmann, H., & Kirsch, G. (2014). Crossing borders, building bridges: "Asian stars" in Japanese TV drama. In J. Kim (Ed.), *Reading Asian television drama: Crossing borders and breaking boundaries* (pp. 147–168). New York: I.B. Tauris.

Hernández, J.C., & Zhao, I. (2017, November 10). Trump's visit to China provides a propa-

ganda. *New York Times*. Retrieved from https://www.nytimes.com/2017/11/10/world/asia/china-trump-visit-propaganda.html.
Hong, M. (2006, September 4). Pinglun: Tianshiyi Di "Ai, Zai Libieshi" [Review: Angel Wang Yi's "Love at the moment"]. *Sina Entertainment*. Retrieved from http://ent.sina.com.cn/r/m/2006-09-04/14181230339.html.
Huang, X. (2009). "Korean Wave"--The popular culture, comes as both cultural and economic imperialism in East Asia. *Asian Social Science*, *5*(8), 123–130.
Jang, S.H. (2012). The Korean Wave and its implications for the Korea-China relationship. *Journal of International and Area Studies* (2), 97—113.
Ju, H.Y., & Noh, K.W. (2013). Multiculturalism and representation of racial others in Korean TV dramas. *Cartoon and Animation Studies*, 32, 335–61. https://doi.org/10.7230/KOSCAS.2013.32.335.
Jung, M. (2017, September 11). Chinese urge suspension of "Midnight Runners." *The Korea Times*. Retrieved from http://www.koreatimes.co.kr/www/nation/2017/09/177_236284.html.
Kaldis, N. (2013). Couching race in the global era: Intra-Asian racism in Crouching Tiger, Hidden Dragon. In J. Kuo (Ed.), *Contemporary Chinese art and film* (pp. 209–228). Washington, D.C.: New Academia Publishing.
Keane, M. (2015). *The Chinese television industry*. London, UK: British Film Institute.
Kellner, D. (1995). Media culture, cultural studies, identity, and politics between the modern and the postmodern. New York: Routledge.
Kim, B. (2015). Past, present, and future of Hallyu (Korean Wave). *American International Journal of Contemporary Research*, *5*(5), 154–160.
Kim, J. (2014). Introduction: East Asian television drama: A story of booms, fevers and waves. In *Reading Asian television drama: Crossing borders and breaking boundaries* (pp. 1–26). New York: I.B.Tauris.
Kim, J., & Han, H. (2009). Study on female marriage immigrants' representation in TV drama: A semiological analysis of SBS 'The Golden Bride.' *Busan Kyeongnam Society for Journalism and Communication*, *70*, 45–81.
Kim, S. (2009). Politics of representation in the era of globalization: Discourse about marriage migrant women in two South Korean films. *Asian Journal of Communication*, *19*(2), 210–226.
Kim, Y., Yoo, D., & Kim, J. (2009). Disarticulated dynamics of ethnicity, gender, and class: Analysis of transnational love narrative and capitalism discourse in TV "multicultural dramas." *Media & Society*, *2*, 2–41.
Kirsch, G. (2015). Contemporary Sino-Japanese relations on screen: A history, 1989–2005. London, UK: Bloomsbury Publishing.
Lee, M. (2010). Marriage migrant women represented in rural soap opera, "In Nam-Chon over a mountain." *Journal of Multi-Cultural Contents Studies*, *8*, 153–177.
Lee, S. (2003, April 16). "Interview" China-Korea co-production drama "Beijing My Love" KBS Lee Gyu-Wook PD. *PD Journal*. Retrieved from http://www.pdjournal.com/news/articleView.html?idxno=5256.
Lu, H. (2000). Soap opera in China: The transnational politics of visuality, sexuality, and masculinity. *Cinema Journal* (1), 25–47.
Lu, S. (1997). Transnational Chinese cinemas: Identity, nationhood, gender. Honolulu: University of Hawai'i Press.
Meyer, M.D.E., & Stern, D.M. (2007). The modern(?) Korean woman in prime-time: Analyzing the representation of Sun on the television series "Lost." *Women's Studies*, *36*(5), 313–331.
Nagel, J. (2000). Ethnicity and sexuality. *Annual Review of Sociology*, *26*, 107–133.
Park, J.S. (2013). Nationalism and multiculturalism: A case analysis of Chinese multiculturalism culture of pluralistic integration. *Korean Political Science Review*, *47*(2), 5–23.
Park, S. (2017, October 7). China's brazen plagiarism of Korean TV shows hits new heights. *The Korea Times*. Retrieved from http://www.koreatimes.co.kr/www/art/2017/11/688_237317.html.
Rhee, J. (2016). Gendering multiculturalism: Representation of migrant workers and foreign brides in Korean popular films. *The Asia-Pacific Journal*, *14*(7(9)), 1–20.

Ryu, C. (2010). A study on the representational images of immigrant workers in the Korean films in the 2000s–Focusing on searching for Ronny and Bandhobi. *Journal of Multi-Cultural Contents Studies, 3*, 137–152.

Shim, D. (2016). China's cultural rise and Korean cultural industries: Can Hallyu overcome Chinese capital? *Inmun Sahwe, 7*(4), 833–858.

Shohat, E., & Stam, R. (1996). From the imperial family to the transnational imaginary: Media spectatorship in the age of globalization. In R. Wilson & W. Dissanayake (Eds.), *Global/Local: Cultural production and the transnational imaginary* (pp. 145–170). Durham, NC: Duke University Press.

Song, G. (2015). Imagining the other: Foreigners on the Chinese TV screen. In R. Bai & G. Song (Eds.), *Chinese television in the twenty-first century: Entertaining the nation* (pp. 107–120). New York, NY: Routledge.

Tsung, L., & Bai, Y. (2015). The discourse of unity in diversity in Contemporary China. In W. Wang & L. Tsung (Eds.), *Contemporary Chinese discourse and social practice in China* (pp. 201–220). Philadelphia: John Benjamins Publishing Company.

Wan, Y. (2016, May 17). Zhongguo dianshi daidong Hangguo Hanliu [Chinese dramas drive Hanliu in Korea]. *People's Daily.* Retrieved from http://world.people.com.cn/n1/2016/0517/c1002-28355167.html.

Wang, L. (2015). The identification of minorities in China. *Asian-Pacific Law & Policy Journal, 16*(2), 1–21.

Wang, Z. (2015, November 4). Li Keqiang cu Hanfeng jingchui Hanliu chongdong [Li Keqiang urged Hanfeng to blow the Korean Wave]. *Xinhua News.* Retrieved from http://www.xinhuanet.com/world/2015-11/04/c_1117037682.htm.

Yang, Y. (2016). Film policy, the Chinese government, and soft power. *New Cinemas: Journal of Contemporary Film, 14*(1), 71–91.

Zeng, L. (2008). Global imaginary, local desire: Chinese transnational serial drama in the 1990s. In Y. Zhu, M. Keane, & R. Bai (Eds.), *TV drama in China* (pp. 61–72). Hong Kong: Hong Kong University Press.

Zhao, B. (2010, December 16). "Lin Shifu Zai Shouer" jian Chengdu meishi Zhang Ruixi diaokan Lin Yongjian ["Master Lin in Seoul" recommends Chengdu cuisine Jang Seo-hee makes fun of Lin Yongjian]. *Sina News.* Retrieved from http://dailynews.sina.com/bg/ent/tv/sinacn/20101216/17242087058.html.

Zhao, Y. (2003). Transnational capital, the Chinese state, and China's communication industries in a fractured society. *Javnost-The Public, 10*(4), 53–74.

Zhao, Z., & Postiglione, G.A. (2010). Representations of ethnic minorities in China's university media. *Discourse: Studies in the cultural politics of education, 31*(3), 319–334.

Zhou, Y. (2007, March 12). Zhonghan hepai dianshiju maidabu "Lianai Bingfa" paozhuanyinyu [A great leap of China-Korea co-production "Love Strategy" is expected to breed more great works in the future]. *Sina News.* Retrieved from http://ent.sina.com.cn/v/m/2007-03-12/12181475320.html.

An Eastern Perspective on Western Dramas

A Korean Take on American Television Dramas

Daniela Mazur, Melina Meimaridis *and* Afonso de Albuquerque

For several decades, American television shows have been sold abroad in a unidirectional flow (Sinclair, Backa & Cunningham, 2000; Waisbord, 2004). In many countries—especially those from the so-called Third World—these shows have provided the backbone of national television schedules. In addition, American studios have bought the rights to several foreign television series, but instead of airing these shows, they are adapted in hopes of their becoming more palatable to American viewers, such as *Hatufim* (2010–2012), an Israeli drama adapted by Showtime known as *Homeland* (2011–), *The Good Doctor* (2013), a South Korean production that has been adapted by ABC in 2017 with the same title, and *Como Aproveitar o Fim do Mundo* (2012), a Brazilian dramedy adapted by the CW network called *No Tomorrow* (2016–2017). Recently, however, this trend has been reverted in South Korea where TV networks have started to make their own versions of American television series, such as *The Good Wife* (CBS, 2009–2016) and *Criminal Minds* (CBS, 2005–).

The authors of this essay take these two productions as a focus to discuss how western narratives are adapted and translated for a distinct, South Korean (and, in a broader sense, East Asian) cultural environment. In practical terms, this involves a double effort to understand both how this happens, in terms of narrative strategies, and what it potentially means from a changing global order perspective. By doing so, this analysis articulates text and context. From a contextual viewpoint, the authors of this essay consider the problem with reference to the phenomenon that several authors have referred to as a global shift in the international media landscape (Aouragh & Chakravartty, 2016; Iwabuchi, 2010; Zhao, 2014), with the rise of alternative centers of media production beyond the western world, notably in East Asia (Keane, 2006; Shim, 2008), from which South Korea is among the most influential ones (Joo, 2011; Ryoo, 2009).

Otherwise, the textual analysis refers to the strategies employed by South Korean television to adapt the original American product for a very different cultural environment. The first aspect to consider here refers to a general circumstance that provides the basis of the very possibility of adapting television shows: the popularity that television formats have progressively acquired since the 1990s. Formats provide a more sophisticated solution to the globalization of television business. The issue started to become the focus of scholarly research in the 1990s with Moran's (1998/2005) influential work, *Copycat TV: Globalisation, program formats, and cultural identity*. More recently Keinonen (2014) has argued that "television formats, just like genres, are bound and shaped by both cultural parameters and material conditions defined by political economy, network structures, work routines and other factors" (p. 2). Thus, she suggests that "television formats should be understood and studied as a process of cultural negotiation in which global influences and local elements amalgamate on various levels of television culture" (p. 1).

Scripted television dramas have a strong national presence, especially within East and Southeast Asia, where each country incorporates local particularities in order to not only connect to their target audience, but also to differentiate themselves in the regional market of television products (Chua & Iwabuchi, 2008; Dissanayake, 2012). Hence, South Korean television dramas (hereafter referred to as K-dramas) are currently the highlight of this market, endorsing domestic features that fuel national issues and reaffirm the country's current position as a fundamental pop culture influence in the region (Shim, 2008; Ryoo, 2009).

The adaptation process of American television series in the East is particularly intriguing, mainly because of the legitimizing authority shifts from the United States to Korea, since the power to adapt a narrative to one's reality means to define oneself as the center of an established order. This centrality is relevant because South Korea positions itself as hub of pop culture in East Asia, in which the audiences in these countries still resist great changes and look for products that are culturally suitable and familiar (Joo, 2011). Therefore, Korean versions of American shows are more likely to be received favorably than their western counterparts.

Here, the authors of this essay analyze the cultural adaptation of two South Korean dramas: *The Good Wife* (*Gut waipeu*) from 2016 and *Criminal*

Minds (*Keurimineol maindeu*) from 2017. Despite being of different genres, a legal procedural and a police procedural, respectively, both of these South Korean versions have something in common—they are both produced by the cable channel Total Variety Network (tvN, hereafter). The manner in which these productions have been adapted is quite revealing of Korean television's political economy, since tvN has adapted these long-running American series into single-season stories with 16 to 20 episodes, condensing the original narratives to fit the country's conventional television formats. At the same time, the American series' episodes have around 42 minutes while the Korean versions run a little over an hour. In this sense, the network has taken some liberties extensively modifying *Criminal Minds*' original narrative structure. More than just adapting these western dramas structures, the new versions must be adapted to domestic cultures (Keinonen, 2014; Moran, 1998; Waisbord, 2004) and, in this way, the western reality, governed in this case by U.S. standards, has been adapted to South Korea's local and cultural backgrounds.

It should be noted that these products are not restricted to South Korean borders, but have been circulated overseas, first throughout East Asia, and later in other regions of the world, as a part of the Korean Wave (*hallyu*, hereafter). In particular, a number of scholars have suggested that a core factor behind the initial expansion of *hallyu* in East Asia was cultural proximity (Iwabuchi, 2002; Lee, 2004; Straubhaar, 1991, 2003), due to the influence of beliefs associated with Confucianism in the region, which presents a value system that emphasizes family, hierarchy and collectivism (Chua, 2004; Kim, 2003; Park & Kim, 2003). According to Shim (2008), Korean dramas "touch the right chord of Asian sentiments, such as family values and respect for elders" (p. 27).

With this in mind, the authors of this essay discuss recent adaptations of American television series into Korean dramas, by focusing on the means employed in translating these products into terms culturally familiar to South Korean (and secondarily other East Asian) viewers. In order to do this, the authors have divided this essay into three sections. First, the authors will introduce the issue of television formats and global flows. Next, the authors will cover specific aspects of Korean television, its political economy, as well as the history of *hallyu*. Last, two adapted Korean television dramas will be analyzed, considering their similarities and differences to their original American productions.

A Shifting Paradigm in the Global Television Market

Television global flows have experienced a notable change in the past few decades. During the 1970s and 1980s, television flows mainly extended "from the West to the rest" of the world, specifically from the United States and the United Kingdom (Hall, 1992; Sinclair, Jacka & Cunningham, 2000; Waisbord, 2004). At this time, television and communication scholars worried about the supposed cultural effects of these global flows of television programs. For example, *Dynasty* (ABC [USA], 1981–1989) and *Dallas* (CBS [USA], 1978–1991) have been studied in the theoretical framework of "cultural imperialism" or "media imperialism" (Boyd-Barret, 2018; Sinclair, Jacka & Cunningham, 2000). What this means is that they were concerned about the cultural domination (specially by a nation's values, life styles, and moral code) of the so-called center over the periphery, worrying about the homogenizing outcome on culture through globalization and unidirectional flows of cultural products, in particular the media ones.

This situation has progressively changed since the 1990s, as other centers producing media content emerged—for instance, Brazil becoming a global exporter of telenovelas (Crane, 2016; Davis, Straubhaar, & Ferin Cunha, 2016). More recently, other countries have joined the trend, such as Turkey, who recently became the second biggest exporter of TV shows in the world, attracting especially the Arab League (Berg, 2017; Yanardagoglu & Karam, 2013) and South Korea. On the other hand, South Korea distinguishes itself from other peripheries because it encompasses a universe of cultural strands that disseminates not only its pop culture, but also a South Korean lifestyle, mediated especially by its television shows. For the last decade, the country has consolidated itself as one of the largest producers and exporters of TV programs within Asia, reinforcing its status as a stable source of cultural influence in the region (Jin, 2007; Joo, 2011; Ryoo, 2009).

The adaptation of television products provides an interesting angle in the international format television market, as it implies converting cultural conventions from one society to another. Historically, the United States has exerted a leading role in adapting foreign television content, reflecting the imperial status of the country as a global superpower, providing it with "a global influence through its soft power based on the appeal of its values and culture, and perhaps more importantly as a consequence of its pivotal position in the global economy" (Curran, 2011, p. 11). In fact, in the 1980s and 1990s, the global influence of the United States was so remarkable that globalization and Americanization were usually supposed to be the same thing (Antonio & Bonanno, 2000; Mueller, 2004). This allowed Americans to present specific traits of their culture as endowed with a universal character.

Yet, in the beginning of the 2000s, the American dominance in global culture became growingly challenged by the emergence of other players that associated their native cultural/media products to strategies of nation-branding, in a process of renationalization of culture and communication (Iwabuchi, 2018). As a matter of fact, South Korea exerted a prominent role here.

Instead of claiming a "universal" voice, South Korean strategy relies mostly on the dynamics of cultural proximity to other countries in East Asia (Kim, 2004; Ryoo, 2009; Shim, 2006; Suh, Cho, & Kwon, 2013). Historical patterns of interactions, established over several centuries, shared collective memories, and geographic adjacency contributed to the fostering of a sense of cultural identity (or "Asian values") among East-Asian countries (Iwabuchi, 2002), providing a fertile ground for *hallyu*. Contrary to what happened to the United States, South Korea's influence was facilitated due to the fact that the country had never performed a leading role in the region—and therefore is not associated with historical traumas in a relatively recent past, as Japan (2002)—nor with a present emerging superpower status as China (Zhao, 2014). By avoiding association of themselves to a very strong nationalistic discourse and initially putting in practice a low-prices policy, *hallyu* products became considerably palatable abroad, even in Communist China (Huang & Kwang, 2009; Jiang & Leung, 2012). However, it is worth noting the fact that the growing popularity of South Korean's pop culture has fostered anti-*hallyu* movements in some countries (Chen, 2017).

The South Korean Television Industry

In the late 1990s, South Korea built itself as a hub of pop culture production and became a center of cultural influences, not only as a source of media products, but also of a lifestyle (Joo, 2011; Ryoo, 2009). South Korean pop music (K-pop, hereafter) is now probably the most recognizable product of the country's media industries, whose influence has expanded beyond East Asia and has conquered fans in other continents (Jin & Yoon, 2017). Its influence abroad happened hand in hand with the success of K-dramas, especially in East Asia (Hanaki, Singhal, Han, Kim, & Chitnis, 2007; Shim, 2006). Initially, the development of a domestic cultural industry aimed merely to reduce the dominance of foreign productions in South Korean television (Joo, 2011; Shim, 2008). However, the disastrous impact of the Asian financial crisis, in 1997, motivated those in South Korea to review its development model, while it called attention to the importance of investing more in the nation's cultural industry (Joo, 2011; Kwon & Kim, 2013; Yang, 2007). In order to do this, those in South Korea invested time in figuring out how to make their cultural products cheaper than the average content available in the regional market at that time. In fact, K-dramas were a quarter of the price of Japanese dramas and one tenth of Hong Kong dramas (Shim, 2006, 2008). As this strategy proved a success, those in South Korea raised its ambitions beyond merely economic objectives and took the exportation of cultural products as a basis for a systematic nation branding effort (Huang, 2011; Iwabuchi, 2018).

"Trendy Dramas," a Japanese genre that conquered the export market, was a major influence on Korean narrative strategies. Such strategies centered on more contemporary and urban issues, focusing on younger audiences, specifically through their casts. Romantic stories centered on love triangles played by beautiful actors and actresses, paradise-like locations, and a soundtrack filled with the latest pop music (Huang, 2011; Ota, 2004). This narrative formula has made room for stories that dialogue with less specific and more relatable issues, embracing young consumers who are interested in current issues. Moreover, the consumption and dissemination of these productions have also been facilitated by the use of dubbing and subtitling tools (Chan &Wang, 2011; Kim, 2005).

The international spread of K-dramas allowed a new, re-franchised South Korean identity to circulate overseas, which did not emphasize the specificities of the Korean culture, but instead, promoted a more cosmopolitan identity associated with a more general idea of East Asian modernity (Kim, 2008). In this sense, South Korean television products have presented the East and Southeast Asian markets with an alternative that balances a traditional regional culture with Western influences. The traditional elements have been shared among these countries and their societies while the Western influences have reached them through the process of globalization.

Korea's Take on Western Narratives

The debate on cultural imperialism provides a fertile starting point to discuss the rise of South Korea as an international pole of production and distribution of television content. The debate on cultural imperialism originated in the 1970s, in association with the debate of the construction of a New World Information and Communication Order (NWICO), and has remained a highly controversial issue ever since. Writing in the early 2000s, Elasmar contended that cultural imperialism is chiefly a "conspiration theory," grounded on hypodermic model premises, and therefore is an outdated paradigm. In fact, after losing its influence along the 1990s and early 2000s, the concept gained new breath, associated with the criticism raised by others, such as the BRICS group—which Thussu (2015) describes as a "NWICO 2.0." Moreover, according to Bourdieu and Wacquant (1999), "cultural imperialism rests on the power to universalize particularisms linked to a singular historical tradition by causing them to be misrecognized as such" (p. 41). Since the end of World War II, the United States has strived to establish itself as the world's leading storyteller, dictating narrative genres, patterns, and formats, all the while promoting their peculiar points of view as universally appealing.

By producing its own adaptations of American shows, South Korea subverts this order as it challenges the premise of American culture's universality, and at the same time, it claims for itself a more important position in the global television market. Adaptations of foreign products are not extraneous to the South Korean cultural industry although traditionally this has happened to regional narratives (especially Chinese and Japanese ones) enjoying cultural proximity with the country (Lee, 2003; Lim, 2008). Regarding this motive, the adaptation of Western products represents a step further in relation to the standard practices of South Korean television. The comedy sketch show, *Saturday Night Live Korea* (tvN, 2011–) and the reality TV program, *Korea's Next Top Model* (OnStyle, 2010–) provide two pioneer examples. Both are not K-dramas per se, but they still reveal the initial shift in television adaptation flows.

In 2016, the Korean cable channel tvN began to adapt American series. Launched in 2006, tvN recurred to differentiating strategies—just like HBO's motto, "It's not TV. It's HBO" strategy in the 1990s and early 2000s (Leverette, Ott, & Buckley, 2008)—in order to differentiate itself from the older, more established broadcast channels. The challenges behind this adaptation effort were considerable due to the fact that American series are often long-form narratives produced to last for as long as the show still has decent ratings—*Law and Order* (NBC, 1990–2010) remained on the air for two decades and has over 450 episodes—and, in contrast, Korea's television dramas rely on single-season programming. Initially tvN produced adaptations of *Criminal Minds* (2005–) and *The Good Wife* (2009–2016), both multi-season shows from CBS, an American broadcast network, that have approximately 22 episodes of 42 minutes each season.

In order to better understand how the Korean versions adapted Western narratives, *Keurimineol maindeu's* 20-episode season and *Gut waipeu's* 16-episode season were analyzed. Both shows were evaluated through a comparison with the original American productions, which were also analyzed for this study. The analysis below is made up from the researchers' observations of the original shows and their adaptations, while considering the specificities of the K-drama format and the current global scenario, in which cultural counterflows are changing the global TV game. Looking at the dynamics involved in translating a "core" narrative into a "peripheral" one, the authors of this essay can observe some insights about regional cultural markets and adaptations in the current global order. Specifically through the lenses of a non-core country as South Korea that has established itself as a powerful pop culture source in East Asia and now, it claims the power to adapt an American narrative into its own cultural codes, and in this sense, challenge the globalization forces.

With *Criminal Minds*, tvN tackled the challenging feat of adapting a show that is still on the air in the United States and that already has, as of right now, 299 episodes in 14 seasons. Another difficulty that arose for them is the fact that unlike *The Good Wife*, the American version of *Criminal Minds* (and its spin-offs) were already airing (and widely consumed) in South Korea. The original version chronicles the day-to-day running of an FBI investigation team that solves crimes through behavioral profiling. The narrative has a procedural structure, in which each episode focuses on the resolution of a specific criminal case. Throughout the show's run, a couple of more serialized narrative arcs propel the narrative forward, as well as, contribute to the development of the drama's main characters.

The American series *The Good Wife* is centered on Alicia Florrick (Juliana Margulies), a housewife married to a politician, Peter Florrick (Chris Noth), who is accused of corruption and a sex scandal. After her husband's imprisonment, Alicia is forced to go back to work and she gets a job as a junior litigator at a law firm. The show spans throughout seven seasons, consisting of 156 episodes. The legal drama has a mostly procedural structure that allowed the firm in the story to focus on intriguing legal cases each week, which ranged from criminal law to major class actions against Big Pharma. A typical episode in the show's first seasons would focus on a specific "case of the week" in which Alicia and the other lawyers at the company would have to defend or fight for a client. However, in the show's later seasons the narrative structure becomes more and more serialized. For example, in the show's sixth season, one of the main lawyers in their firm, company lawyer Cary Agos (Matt Czuchry), is arrested, and a great deal of the season is dedicated to the aftermath of his imprisonment. Cary's troubles with the law are present from the first episode of the season, "The Line" to the eleventh episode, "*Hail Mary*," which makes up half of the show's episodes that season. Even though the narrative is focused on Agos's personal troubles, there are still episodes that deal with a "case of the week." However, the procedural logic has given way to a more serialized narrative structure.

Adapting these American dramas for a Korean audience presents a considerable challenge given that Korean dramas have a more melodramatic style and serialized form in which each episode advances the narrative, most ending with cliffhangers. At the same time, K-dramas largely have only one season comprised of, on average, 16 to 20 one-hour episodes. However, the fact that tvN is a Korean cable channel and is therefore subject to fewer restrictions than the major networks, allows its adaptations to become more similar in tone to the original American versions. Yet, a question arises: How does a team adapt *The Good Wife*'s 156 episodes into a season of just 16 episodes, or how can the team convert *Criminal Minds*' 299 episodes into just 20 episodes? And how do showrunners make these dramas more appealing to a Korean and East Asian public?

Because the two American shows differ in nature—again with one being a police procedural drama and the other being a complex legal melodrama—two opposed strategies have been employed in order to adapt these narratives to K-drama's production system: one is to make the narrative more complex, while the other is to simplify it. The American version of *Criminal Minds* has an episodic structure with a narrative closure at the end of each episode. Because the story is centered on how these characters solve crimes, there is little character development during most of the episodes, usually with the exception of the last episodes in each season, which need to keep the viewer hooked and engaged during the show's hiatus. Yet, since the vast majority of K-dramas run for only one season, the showrunners of the Korean version of *Criminal Minds* have to make it more complex than its American counterpart, adding serialized elements in order to tell a complete story in only a couple of episodes. In this sense, the writers of *Keurimineol maindeu* have mixed serial and episodic structures, intertwining short- and long-term narrative arcs throughout the drama's 20-episode season.

On the other hand, the original version of *The Good Wife* employs a complex narrative that blends episodic and serialized structures across the seasons. Due to this complexity in the original show, the showrunners of the Korean adaptation chose to oversimplify the complex American drama by focusing only on the personal lives of its three main characters, Kim Hye-kyung (Jeon Do-yeon), her husband Lee Tae-joon (Yoo Ji-tae), and her boss Seo Joong-won (Yoon Kye-sang). Being true to K-drama form, these characters make up a dramatic and messy love triangle in which Hye-kyung has to decide if she's the "good wife," who stands by her sometimes-unethical husband Tae-joon, or if she chooses to be with her former-lover-now-boss Joong-won. Although this love triangle, is common in both shows, it gains more attention from the Korean version's narrative by eliminating the storylines surrounding the other supporting characters. While changing the format leads to shifts, the showrunners modifying the cultural background of the show also affects how these narratives are adapted. The romantic foundation that underlies these narratives is a direct reflection of this ideological inheritance that values the representation of a pure love between a man and a woman, the valorization and centrality of the family, respect for hierarchy, and emotional stability (Kim, 2003; Yang, 2012).

In order to best present an evaluation of how both western shows were adapted in Korean television, the authors of this essay have divided the analysis into two distinct parts: "The minds of Korean criminals" and "A good Korean wife." They intend to shed some light on aspects concerning the four television products (two American originals, and two Korean versions) in order to understand how "peripherical" content, consisting of adaptations of shows originally from "core" countries, can mediate power.

The Minds of Korean Criminals

At first glance, the Korean version of *Criminal Minds* seems to share a lot of the original show's backbone. A team of investigators strive to solve crimes and stop those responsible for them, using suspect profiling techniques. However, the narrative strategies differ significantly. Firstly, the Korean depiction of crimes is more graphically violent than in the original show, probably because it airs on a cable channel rather than on a commercial national broadcast network in the United States.

The original version is fundamentally a procedural, yet *Keurimineol maindeu* has two long-running arcs that tie the narrative from start to finish: the case of the serial killer "Reaper"[1] and the case of "Nadeul River." Although this is a more serialized aspect, the show still develops shorter arcs throughout the season by investigating different criminals using a variety of cases from different seasons of the original show. Unlike the American version that has a procedural logic, some cases are resolved before the end of the episode, and those final minutes are used to introduce a criminal and/or his crimes from the next episode. However, in other cases, it takes the investigation team more than one episode to apprehend the criminal, extending the case to over two episodes and therefore allowing two very important narrative devices in K-dramas to be maintained: cliffhangers and flashbacks.

Flashbacks have become more and more common on contemporary American television (Ames, 2012). The use of flashbacks and other temporal narrative devices are usually associated with the narrative complexity framework (Mittell, 2006; Booth, 2010) and are characterized by Booth (2010) as one of the devices that promotes a "temporal displacement of contemporary narrative action" (p. 2). One popular example is *How I Met Your Mother* (CBS, 2005–2014), a show conceived as an *extensive flashback* into protagonist Ted Mosby (Josh Radnor) and his search for his wife. Another example would be *Lost* (ABC, 2004–2010), a show that presented a group of survivors of an airplane crash on a mystical island. Flashbacks were used in the show's first three seasons to provide backstories to the survivors. In Korean television, flashbacks are also a staple of the K-drama format because they reveal a character's past and the secrets they carry. In this way, they help to create more curiosity and, at the same time, constantly reaffirm the love between the main couple and the happy moments they have shared together (Han, 2008; Yang, 2012). K-dramas frequently use flashbacks because it is an important characteristic of these narratives, used mainly to keep the plotlines progressing. One prominent example is the *Reply* (*Eungdaphara*) series and its extensive use of flashbacks. Each of the show's three seasons represent the years of 1997, 1994, and 1988, respectively, flashing back and forth from the main characters' past into their present. Despite the fact that some of the reasons behind the extensive use of flashbacks in K-dramas overlap with reasons why this narrative device is used in American productions, it should be noted that K-dramas rely more often on this strategy, to the point in which it has become a common feature of the K-drama format.

Because K-dramas have fewer episodes than the American ones, *Keurim-ineol maindeu* focuses more on developing its main cast than investigating the intriguing cases in each episode. Therefore, the personal and family lives of Kim Hyun-joon (Lee Joon-gi), Kang Ki-hyung (Son Hyun-joo) and Ha Sun-woo (Moon Chae-won) are at the center of the narrative, while the details of their professional world are less explored. In order for the show to remain a police drama, the narrative will constantly involve the investigators themselves or their families in criminal cases by having the culprit target them. Although the American version sometimes puts the investigators' loved ones in jeopardy, the Korean version takes this one step further by creating a dramatic atmosphere throughout the season that becomes more potent through the familial bonds existing between the investigators and the victims.

Although the Korean drama's first episode revolves around a very similar criminal case, when compared to the original American pilot, the main story is developed differently in the Korean version. The case of the week has the team of investigators looking for a serial killer who kidnaps women, keeps them in a cage, and kills them after four days of torturing them. The team of investigators tries to understand the criminal's mind and the patterns behind the abductions in order to capture the serial killer. In the American version, the team of investigators is able to apprehend the culprit, while also saving the innocent woman by the episode's end. In the Korean version, however, this victim is not saved; she is killed midway through the episode. The rest of the episode shows the serial killer going after his next victim, who happens to be Kim Hyun-joon's *dongsaeng* (a Korean term for a family or friendship, that refers to a younger brother or sister, who may or may not be related by blood). Kim Hyun-joon is now more invested in stopping the serial killer from killing his *dongsaeng* and is only able to apprehend the criminal in the show's second episode. The narrative, therefore, starts involving the investigators' personal lives and relationships, thus deepening the drama of the crime under investigation on a personal level. The interrogations are longer and more detailed, as the team is looking for clues that may lead to the actual culprit and thus save Hyun-joon's *dongsaeng's* life. Also, the criminal's past actions are more scrutinized than in the original. The interrogation reveals why he entered the world of crime using specific flashbacks as well as how the team of investigators reached their current positions. After the case is resolved, viewers can see its impact upon the investigators' lives.

K-dramas highlight the dichotomy between good and evil, moral value, and sentimentality in abundance. These features are consistent with a set of conventions that different authors (Brooks, 1976; Ang, 1985) associate with the melodrama matrix. Melodrama has been commonly criticized for its lack of realism (Smith, 1973; Ang, 1985), and used pejoratively to indicate a "lesser" genre (Brooks, 1976; Dissanayake, 1993), usually associated with a female audience (Brunsdon, 2000). However, we caution the thoughtless use of concepts coined from Western experience as universal (Yau, 1987; Yeh, 2011) since melodramas have gained global reach in the wake of the globalization process, but they also enter into dialogue with other narrative conventions. K-dramas have been seen as an excessive and over sentimentalized genre, shaped by heterosexual romantic love, monogamy, and intimacy in the private sector, but they have had a steady popularity largely because of their enormous affective power (Lee, 2004). However, the cop-drama aesthetics lend a tone of seriousness to this melodramatic structure, controlling its excessive nature by focusing the story on timely criminal cases. Dialoguing more directly with the original version, social issues specific to the South Korean context appear rarely; the cases investigated are mostly universal.

In *Keurimineol maindeu*, the romantic sentimentality characteristic of K-dramas is not present. There is no development of a romantic arc, since the narrative is directly related to the crimes that are part of the professional environment in question as well as the familial bonds created between these characters. Here, the melodramatic root is organized by the police workplace drama's narrative structure. Despite the showrunners using content from multiple seasons of the original show, the last episode focuses on the Reaper case by finally capturing and killing him off. The K-drama's final scene then is formed by the investigating team's efforts in taking care of Ki-hyung's child, therefore uniting as a work family. Ultimately, a crucial cultural characteristic of the adaptation is its strong sense of collectivism that exceeds the individual, associated with the Confucian ideology that has exerted a remarkable influence in Korean culture, especially with respect to intra-group relationships, as in family and neighborhood community (Kim, 2003). This strong sense of collectivism reflects on TV's fictional narratives, especially in K-dramas. *Keurimineol maindeu* is not an exception to the rule, although the team investigates crimes, while also bringing a professional/institutional quality to the story—they are more than interchangeable colleagues; they are a (work) family.

A Good Korean Wife

As with the Korean version of *Criminal Minds*, the adaptation of *The Good Wife* undergoes some changes because of the country's television formats (especially K-drama) as well as modifications in order to adapt the narrative to Korea's cultural background. While the original show from the United States has several supporting characters, *Gut Waipeu* mainly focuses on the love triangle formed by Kim Hye-kyung, Lee Tae-joon, and Seo Joong-won, due to the drama's limited number of episodes.

The very first scene of episode one is extremely similar to the original, with Lee Tae-joon resigning as a prosecutor during a press conference following corruption charges and a sex scandal. Kim Hye-kyung, his wife, stands by his side, seemingly dazed by the journalists and cameras. The scene is almost identical, except for the fact that in the original when Alicia and her husband are leaving, she slaps him in the face. In the Korean version, Tae-joon starts to apologize to Hye-kyung, and the scene flashes back to the day the scandal first broke on the news. Because of the original show's procedural structure and its focus on the day-to-day workings of a law firm, flashbacks are an uncommon narrative device in the American version. There are only a few flashbacks throughout the show's seven seasons. A noticeable example is in the episode "A Few Words" from Season 5, when Alicia has to give the keynote speech on op-out moms returning to the workplace. While she writes her speech, we see her looking back on some of her early pre–Lockhart-Gardner interviews (episode 14). These moments were not in the show's first season. In this sense, even though they are flashbacks, they are made up of new scenes and more information for the viewer. However, flashbacks are widely used throughout the K-drama as a way to prolong the narrative and explain backstory, since each episode is approximately twenty minutes longer than the original. Although flashbacks are used commonly in the show, they can sometimes become excessive and repetitive, for example flashing back to a previous moment from the same episode, thus not providing new information, but reinforcing previous plotlines.

When analyzing *Gut waipeu*, the authors of this essay observed that the Korean adaptation tends to be more realistic than other K-dramas. In order to best explain this observation, the authors of this essay will focus on two main distinctions: (1) Focus on workplace dramas; (2) a more realistic notion of love. First, traditional K-dramas' proximity to the melodramatic matrix translate into narratives that tend to focus on a character's personal life being influenced by several dramatic conflicts (Ang, 1985; Baldacchino, 2014). However, because the American show is a workplace legal drama, its narrative structure provides dramatic tension mainly in the form of legal cases that Alicia, or Kim Hye-kyung in the adaptation, must handle each week, thus professional drama. It can, nonetheless, also present dramatic tension between her personal and family life with the demands from her job. The difference is that while the narrative in traditional K-dramas are subordinate to excess and sentimentality, workplace dramas revolve around fictional institutions that tend to rein in the excess by presenting institutionalized perspectives of human experience.

At the same time, understanding that one of K-dramas' most prominent themes is the modern ideology of romantic love (Baldacchino, 2014), in which love, romantic love, is the character's main achievement, *Gut waipeu* can also be considered more realistic than traditional K-dramas because it reveals a more pragmatic and less romantic notion of love. Although the writers of *Gut waipeu* do focus on a romantic triangle, Kim Hye-kyung's main struggle is between reason and emotion, in which she tries to keep her emotions and feelings under control for her cheating husband and for her former-lover-now-boss. By the show's end, Kim chooses to stay by her husband because of her own career and political interests, a charade of a marriage, while she has also declared her real feelings for her boss. None of this, however, adheres to the modern ideology of romantic and pure love.

In spite of this, *Gut waipeu* is still more exaggerated than the original show. For example, in the eighth episode, Hye-kyung's life is threatened by a hitman sent by Jo Gook-hyun (Go Joon). Despite the fact that the show does not have a clear antagonist or villain because it is a legal procedural, Jo Gook-hyun is presented as an unethical and immoral businessman who does tend to exhibit some features of a typical villain archetype. Despite the harrowing death of a character in the fifth season of *The Good Wife* (season 5, episode 15), there are very few moments in the original show when the viewer fears for someone's life. In fact, Alicia's life is never intensely threatened like this in all of the drama's 156 episodes. While in the original show there are characters with questionable morals and unethical attitudes, none of them are made out to be as villainous as Jo Gook-hyun is in the Korean version. The use of a villainous antagonist is very common in K-dramas, due to its melodramatic influence, specifically the dichotomy between good versus evil, which is uncommon in American legal workplace dramas, in which the narrative mainly presents a more complex understanding of right and wrong, focusing on each character's personal struggle with his or her own ideas of morality and humanity.

As often happens to characters within K-dramas, the notion of family and unity is central in the stories, as a reflection of the national cultural background and value system that has been dominated for thousands of years by Confucian principles (Kim, 2003). *The Good Wife*'s adaptation strives to find balance between Kim Hye-kyung's work life and her home life with her kids. Likewise, Hye-kyung's romantic triangle between her husband and boss is the driving force of the adaptation's narrative. Personality-wise, Kim Hye-kyung is more forthcoming[2] than her American counterpart, challenging the stereotypical notion that Korean women are more submissive and restrained than women in the west. A possible explanation can be that the character only has sixteen episodes to develop, which is different from Alicia, whose empowerment and development is seen throughout the show's 156 episodes (Orgad, 2016). During a pivotal moment in the fourteenth episode, Hye-kyung declares her love for Joong-won, in which she presents herself as a woman who wants to break free from the shackles of her troubled marriage in spite of the possible negative ramifications and decides to put her feelings and needs first in a way Alicia never seems to fully accomplish. In the original show, Alicia has somewhat of a dark ending in the series finale. She throws her former boss and friend Diane under the bus in order to help Peter, her husband, evade a new prosecutorial misconduct conviction. When her efforts fail, however, Alicia is given the choice between love and staying with Peter. For her own selfish reasons, Alicia again chooses to stand, unhappily, by her husband and reap the benefits from his connections.

The importance of the concept of family, on the other hand, translates into another element in the show's narrative, with Hye-kyung's law firm being a *chaebol*, i.e., a family-controlled conglomerate. Chaebols dominate the South Korean economy—they are a unique national business practice characterized by family administrations, a direct reflection of the Confucian heritage that lives in the South Korean culture (Campbell II & Keys, 2002). The sense of collectivism and the importance of family above the individual are a big part of the national sphere, and this is also reflected in their economy. Hence, legacy is a very important national facet, and the chaebols prove that (Kim & Park, 2003).

In this sense, the Korean version of the show presents Seo Joong-won's Will Gardner (played by Josh Charles) and Seo Myung-hee's Diane Lockhart (played by Christine Baranski) as siblings, and Seo Jae-moon's Jonas Stern (played by Kevin Conway) as their father. In this sense, Jae-moon's children are co-managing partners that run the family business. This characteristic complicates some of the original show's dynamics. Every argument these characters have is more relevant since their familial bonds bring additional tension to the narrative. In the original, Will constantly fights and mocks Jonas; however, in the Korean version, Joong-won has to temper his voice because Jae-moon is his father. Another example can be seen in the final two episodes when Joong-won is investigated for bribing judges, a situation that leaves his sister in the awkward position of deciding whether she should stand by her brother or forsake her partner's mistakes in order to protect the company. This storyline is present in the first half of the American show's third season. In the original, although Diane is put in the same delicate position, she is not Will's sister. In this sense, she does not have a familial obligation to condone his behavior. Nevertheless, she does choose to stand by her long-time friend and partner.

Lastly, how *Gut waipeu* ends is also significant. During the K-drama's 16 episodes, producers used narrative arcs from the first three seasons of the original show. Just like in the American version, the legal drama started out with a more procedural structure in its first episodes, focusing on specific legal cases and then shifted to a more serialized one by the end of the drama, with Joong-won's bribery accusation and trial. In the end of the show, Hye-kyung is still married to and living with her husband, just like her American counterpart in the seventh season, having agreed to an arrangement in her marriage that supposedly advances both of their careers. In spite of the fact Hye-kyung never truly divorces her husband, she still ends up being involved with her boss, which is different from Alicia's situation because Will dies in the fifth season of the American drama.

Conclusion

The authors of this article took the adaptation of two American television shows—*Criminal Minds* and *The Good Wife*—in light of a more general problem: the rise of emergent poles of production and distribution of television content and its impact upon the television international market. For many decades, the United States has reigned as the undisputed leader in such a manner that Globalization was commonly associated with Americanization (Antonio & Bonanno, 2000; Mueller, 2004). This allowed the United States to present some peculiar characteristics of its culture as endowed with a universal value (Bourdieu & Wacquant, 1999), and therefore to exert tremendous influence through soft power (Curran, 2011). The asymmetry resulting from this has been criticized as a form of media imperialism (Sinclair, Jacka, & Cunningham, 2000; Boyd-Barret, 2018). One of the most important manners by which the United States has exerted its dominance over the world is through the adaptation of foreign shows and, subsequently, their commercialization to the rest of the world. By doing this, the United States has claimed for itself the status of a universal interpreter with respect to television and cultural products.

Yet, recently the emergence of new regional centers of production and international distribution of television shows has challenged the American dominance. One of the most powerful among them is South Korea. The authors in this essay have argued that the adaptation of American shows by South Korean television signifies a very relevant development in the game's rulebook, as it signalizes that South Korea is challenging the United States' dominance, since the power to adapt a narrative to one's reality means to define oneself as the center of an established order. By adapting American shows to its reality, South Korea then turns the American "universal" into "particular," while at the same time, claims for itself a more relevant status as a cultural mediator in the global arena. Although it still lacks the capacity to challenge the United States on a more global scale, South Korea has managed to become a dominating force in Eastern and Southeastern countries by translating "foreign" American products into something more familiar from the perspective of East Asian culture.

Adapting cultural practices is not a simple process, however. American and South Korean cultures are not only distinct in many significant aspects, but their audiovisual industries have their own production practices, which are different from each other. Both of the shows discussed in this essay face similar challenges and provide different solutions in order to be adapted from the American format to the Korean one. These difficulties presented in this essay can be summed up through three main issues: (1) Political economy of TV series; (2) Narrative strategies; (3) Cultural background. The first issue revolves around the issue of converting long-form narratives, made to last for several seasons in a particular television logic, into narratives that usually end in just one season. The American version of *Criminal Minds* is currently on its fourteenth season and has at least 299 episodes. The Korean version, *Keurimineol maindeu,* not only had to compact these 299 episodes into a season of only 20 hour-long episodes, but also had the difficult task of providing an ending for a show that is still on the air in the United States. On the other hand, the American version of *The Good Wife* has 156 episodes divided into 7 seasons, while the Korean version, *Gut waipeu*, only has 16 hour-long episodes to the story.

The second issue the showrunners of Korean adaptations of American shows face is simply put, from a narrative strategy point of view, translating an open narrative structure, made to last indefinitely, into a closed narrative. *Criminal Minds* has a procedural narrative structure that focuses on a different criminal each week, yet *Keurimineol maindeu* is more serialized in expanding narrative plots throughout two or three episodes, thus making the show's narrative structure more complex. On the other hand, *Gut waipeu* focuses on a specific love triangle and ignores most of the supporting characters' narrative arcs from the original, therefore simplifying the original show's complex narrative structure.

Third, and more importantly, the cultural background of the countries involved present particular challenges within the adaptation process. In this specific Korean case, the narratives shift the notion of the individual in favor of family and the collective. Bringing these American shows into the South Korean reality, in modern Seoul, with Korean actors and highlighting important national cultural traces, like hierarchy, sense of collectivism and discipline, makes it easier to attract viewers, not only in Korea, but also in the neighboring countries that also consume K-dramas on a daily basis. And, in conclusion, this reveals the importance of the emerging cultural mediators in the global scenario, especially in favor of adapting different national contexts into palatable ones for peripheral regions, creating new meanings and media dialogues in the globalized world.

Notes

1. In the original show, the Reaper's case actively develops over eleven episodes of the fourth and fifth season, until he is ultimately killed. His actions, however, still haunt the investigators during the show's most recent seasons.

2. Because of this decisiveness, the issue of divorce becomes a central theme in the show, an uncommon feat by K-drama standards, since the issue is still taboo in Korea. Divorce is unrepresented in television or shown unrealistically, with couples who are divorced at the start of a K-drama and get back together by the end of the show, such as in *Cunning Single Lady* (MBC, 2014) and *Emergency Couple* (tvN, 2014).

References

Abelmann, N. (2003). The melodrama of mobility women, talk, and class in contemporary South Korea. Honolulu: University of Hawai'i Press.

Ames, M. (2012). Time in television narrative: Exploring temporality in twenty-first-century programming. Jackson: University Press of Mississippi.

Ang, I. (1985). Watching Dallas: Soap opera and the melodramatic imagination. London, UK: Methuen.

Antonio, R.J. & Bonanno, A. (2000). A new global capitalism? From "Americanism and Fordism" to "Americanization-Globalization." *American Studies, 41*(2/3), 33–77.

Aouragh, M., & Chakravartty, P. (2016). Infrastructures of empire: Towards a critical geopolitics of media and information studies. *Media, Culture & Society, 38*(4), 559–575.

Baldacchino, J.P. (2014). In sickness and in love? *Korea Journal, 54*(4), 5–28.

Berg, M. (2017). The importance of cultural proximity in the success of Turkish dramas in Qatar. *International Journal of Communication, 11*, 3415–3430.

Booth, P. (2011). Memories, temporalities, fictions: Temporal displacement in contemporary television. *Television & New Media, 12*(4), 370–388.

Bourdieu, P., & Wacquant, L. (1999). On the cunning of imperialist reason. *Theory, Culture & Society, 16*(1), 41–58.

Boyd-Barrett. O. (2018). Cultural imperialism and communication. *Oxford Research Encyclopedia of Communication.* doi:10.1093/acrefore/9780190228613.013.678. Retrieved from http://communication.oxfordre.com/view/10.1093/acrefore/9780190228613.001.0001/acrefore-9780190228613-e-678.

Brooks, P. (1976). The melodramatic imagination: Balzac, Henry James, melodrama, and the mode of excess. New Haven, CT: Yale University Press.

Brunsdon, C. (2000). "Women's genres and female agency." In Brunsdon, C. (Ed.), *The feminist, the housewife, and the soap pera.* (pp.19–42). Oxford, UK: Clarendon Press.

Campbell II, T.L., & Keys, P.Y. (2002). Corporate governance in South Korea: The chaebol experience. *Journal of Corporate Finance, 8*(4), 373–391.

Chan, B., & Wang, X. (2011). Of Prince Charming and male chauvinist pigs: Singaporean female viewers and the dream-world of Korean television dramas. *International Journal of Cultural Studies, 14*(3), 291–305.

Chen, L. (2017). The emergence of the anti-hallyu movement in China. *Media, Culture & Society, 39*(3), 374–390.

Chua, B.H. (2004). Conceptualizing an East Asian popular culture. *Inter-Asia Cultural Studies, 5*(2), 200–221.

Chua, B.H., & Iwabuchi, K. (2008). *East Asian pop culture: Analysing the Korean Wave* (Vol. 1). Hong Kong: Hong Kong University Press.

Crane, D. (2016). Culture and globalization: Theoretical models and emerging trends. In D. Crane, N. Kawashima, & K.I. Kawasaki (Eds.), *Global culture: Media, arts, policy, and globalization.* (pp.1–28). New York: Routledge.

Curran, J. (2011). *Media and democracy.* London, UK: Taylor & Francis.

Davis, S., Straubhaar, J., & Ferin Cunha, I. (2016). The construction of a transnational Lusophone media space: A historiographic analysis. *Popular Communication, 14*(4), 212–223.

Dissanayake, W. (1993). Introduction. In W. Dissanayake (Ed.), *Melodrama and Asian cinema.* (pp.1–8). Cambridge, UK: Cambridge University Press.

Dissanayake, W. (2012). Asian television dramas and Asian theories of communication. *Journal of Multicultural Discourses, 7*(2), 191–196.
Elasmar, M.G. & Bennett, K. (2003). The cultural imperialism paradigm revisited: Origin and evolution. In M.G. Elasmar (Ed.), *The impact of international television: A paradigm shift.* (pp.1–17). Mahwah, NJ: Lawrence Erlbaum Associates.
Hall, S. (1992). The West and the rest: Discourse and power. In S. Hall & B. Gieben (Eds.), *Formations of Modernity.* (pp. 185–227). Cambridge, UK: Open University Press.
Han, B.M. (2008). Reliving Winter Sonata: Memory, nostalgia, and identity. *Post Script, 27*(3), 25.
Hanaki, T., Singhal, A., Han, M.W., Kim, D.K., & Chitnis, K. (2007). Hanryu sweeps East Asia: How Winter Sonata is gripping Japan. *International Communication Gazette, 69*(3), 281–294.
Huang, S. (2011). Nation-branding and transnational consumption: Japan-mania and the Korean Wave in Taiwan. *Media, Culture & Society, 33*(1), 3–18.
Huang, Y., & Kwang, K.N. (2009). Cultural proximity and distance: The reception of Korean films in China through the lens of My Sassy Girl. *Asian Cinema, 20*(2), 193–205.
Iwabuchi, K. (2002). Recentering globalization: Popular culture and Japanese transnationalism. Durham, NC: Duke University Press.
Iwabuchi, K. (2010). De-Westernization and the governance of global cultural connectivity: A dialogic approach to East Asian media cultures. *Postcolonial Studies, 13*(4), 403–419.
Iwabuchi, K. (2018). Globalization, culture, and communication: Renationalization in a globalized world. *Oxford Research Encyclopedia of Communication.* doi: 10.1093/acrefore/9780190228613.013.631. Retrieved from http://communication.oxfordre.com/view/10.1093/acrefore/9780190228613.001.0001/acrefore-9780190228613-e-631.
Jiang, Q., & Leung, L. (2012). Lifestyles, gratifications sought, and narrative appeal: American and Korean TV drama viewing among Internet users in urban China. *International Communication Gazette, 74*(2), 159–180.
Jin, D.Y. (2007). Reinterpretation of cultural imperialism: Emerging domestic market vs. continuing US dominance. *Media, Culture & Society, 29*(5), 753–771.
Jin, D.Y., & Yoon, T.J. (2017). The Korean Wave: Retrospect and prospect. *International Journal of Communication, 11*, 2241–2249.
Joo, J. (2011). Transnationalization of Korean popular culture and the rise of "pop nationalism" in Korea. *The Journal of Popular Culture, 44*(3), 489–504.
Keane, M. (2006). Once were peripheral: Creating media capacity in East Asia. *Media, Culture & Society, 28*(6), 835–855.
Keinonen, H. (2016). Television format as cultural negotiation: Studying format appropriation through a synthesizing approach. *VIEW Journal of European Television History and Culture, 5*(9), 1–12.
Kim, A.E., & Park, G.S. (2003). Nationalism, Confucianism, work ethic and industrialization in South Korea. *Journal of Contemporary Asia, 33*(1), 37–49.
Kim, H.M. (2005). Korean TV dramas in Taiwan: With an emphasis on the localization process. *Korea Journal, 45*(4), 183–205.
Kim, M. (2004). Cultural proximity and the type of Korean television programs in Asian market. *6th World Media Economics Conference* Centre, Montreal, Canada, 1–13. Retrieved from http://www.cem.ulaval.ca/pdf/kim.pdf.
Kim, S. (2003). Korean cultural codes and communication. *International Area Studies Review, 6* (93), 93–114.
Kim, Y. (2008). Media consumption and everyday life in Asia. New York: Routledge.
Kwon, S.H., & Kim, J. (2013). From censorship to active support: The Korean state and Korea's cultural industries. *The Economic and Labour Relations Review, 24*(4), 517–532.
Lee, D.H. (2003). A local mode of programme adaptation: South Korea in the global television format business. In M. Keane & A. Moran (Eds.), *Television across Asia* (pp. 48–65). New York: Routledge.
Lee, D.H. (2004). Cultural contact with Japanese TV dramas: Modes of reception and narrative transparency. In K. Iwabuchi (Ed.), *Feeling Asian modernities: Transnational consumption of Japanese TV dramas.* (pp. 251–274). Hong Kong: Hong Kong University Press.
Lee, K. (2004). Speak memory! Morae Sigye and the politics of social melodrama in contemporary South Korea. *Cultural Studies? Critical Methodologies, 4*(4), 526–539.

Leverette, M., Ott, B.L., & Buckley, C.L. (2008). *It's not TV: Watching HBO in the post-network era*. New York: Routledge.
Lim, T. (2008). Renting East Asian popular culture for local television: Regional networks of cultural production. Hong Kong: Hong Kong University Press.
Martín-Barbero, J. (1998). *De los medios a las mediaciones: Comunicación, cultura y hegemonía*. Bogotá, Colombia: Convenio Andrés Bello.
Mittell, J. (2006). Narrative complexity in contemporary American television. *The Velvet Light Trap*, *58*(1), 29–40.
Moran, A. (1998/2005). Copycat TV: Globalisation, program formats, and cultural identity. Bloomington: Indiana University Press.
Mueller, A.C. (2004). *German pop culture: How American is it?* Ann Arbor: University of Michigan Press.
Orgad, S. (2017). The cruel optimism of The Good Wife: The fantastic working mother on the fantastical treadmill. *Television & New Media*, *18*(2), 165–183.
Ryoo, W. (2009). Globalization, or the logic of cultural hybridization: The case of the Korean Wave. *Asian Journal of Communication*, *19*(2), 137–151.
Shim, D. (2006). Hybridity and the rise of Korean popular culture in Asia. *Media, Culture & Society*, *28*(1), 25–44.
Shim, D. (2008). The growth of Korean cultural industries and the Korean Wave. In C.B. Huat & K. Iwabuchi (Eds.), *East Asian pop culture: Analysing the Korean Wave* (pp. 15–32). Hong Kong: Hong Kong University Press.
Sinclair, J., Jacka, E., & Cunningham, S. (2000). Peripheral vision. In F.J.Lechner & J. Boli (Eds.), *The Globalization Reader* (pp. 301–306). Oxford, UK: Blackwell.
Smith, J.L. (1973). *Melodrama*. London, UK: Methuen.
Straubhaar, J.D. (1991). Beyond media imperialism: Assymetrical interdependence and cultural proximity. *Critical Studies in Media Communication*, *8*(1), 39–59.
Straubhaar, J.D. (2003). Choosing national TV: Cultural capital, language, and cultural proximity in Brazil. In M.G. Elasmar (Ed.), *The impact of international television: A paradigm shift* (pp. 77–110). New York: Routledge.
Suh, C., Cho, Y., & Kwon, S. (2013). The Korean Wave in Southeast Asia: An analysis of cultural proximity and the globalisation of the Korean cultural products. Paper presented at Korean Studies, a New Perspective toward Global Humanities Congress, Hawai'i. Retrieved from http://congress.aks.ac.kr/korean/files/2_1358476377.pdf.
Thussu, D.K. (2015). Digital BRICS: Building a NWICO 2.0? In K. Nordenstreng & D.K. Thussu (Eds.), *Mapping BRICS media* (pp. 242–263). London, UK: Routledge.
Toru, Ota. (2004). Producing (post-) trendy Japanese TV dramas. In K. Iwabuchi (Ed.), *Feeling asian modernities* (pp. 69–86). Hong Kong: Hong Kong University Press.
Waisbord, S. (2004). McTV: Understanding the global popularity of television formats. *Television & New Media*, *5*(4), 359–383.
Yanardağoğlu, E., & Karam, I.N. (2013). The fever that hit Arab satellite television: audience perceptions of Turkish TV series. *Identities*, *20*(5), 561–579.
Yang, F.C. I. (2012). From Korean Wave to Korean living: Meteor Garden and the politics of love fantasies in Taiwan. *Korea Observer*, *43*(3), 419–445.
Yang, J. (2007). Globalization, nationalism, and regionalization: The case of Korean popular culture. *Development and Society*, *36*(2), 177–199.
Yang, J. (2012). The Korean Wave (Hallyu) in East Asia: A comparison of Chinese, Japanese, and Taiwanese audiences who watch Korean TV dramas. *Development and Society*, *41*(1), 103–147.
Yeh, E.Y. (2010). Pitfalls of cross-cultural analysis: Chinese wenyi film and melodrama. In G. Wang (Ed.), *De-Westernizing communication research: Altering questions and changing frameworks* (pp. 111–127). New York: Routledge.
Yau, E.C. (1987). "Yellow Earth": Western analysis and a non-western text. *Film Quarterly*, *41*(2), 22–33.
Zhao, Y. (2014). Communication, crisis, and global shift: An introduction. *International Journal of Communication*, *8*, 275–300.

The East Meets the Middle East

Cultural Proximity, Audience Reception and Korean TV Adaptations on Turkish Televisions

YEŞIM KAPTAN *and* MURAT TUTUCU

Starting in the 2000s, Korean dramas (K-dramas) have become very popular among Turkish audiences. *Hallyu* or the Korean Wave arrived in Turkey when the state-owned national public television stations, Turkish Radio and Television Corporation (TRT), started broadcasting K-dramas. *Emperor of the Sea* (*Haesin*), broadcast in 2006, was the very first K-drama offered to Turkish viewers. However, *Jewel in the Palace* (*Dae Jang-geum*) became the first popular Korean drama bought by TRT in 2008. Turkish audiences first enjoyed watching historical K-dramas and viewing characters in traditional clothes. Within five years, more than six K-dramas were broadcast in daytime only on TRT1 (the first Turkish national television station among 15 government channels). Later, the Korean Wave influenced other multinational channels including Fox TV and Kanal D, which followed TRT in broadcasting K-dramas or their adaptations. Since then, many K-dramas have aired and are still airing on local, regional, and national Turkish TV channels broadcasting on satellite networks. In Turkey, terrestrial and satellite are the most important reception platforms with two widespread satellite networks: Digiturk and D–Smart; and one cable TV and internet service, Türksat. These platforms offer over 500 channels for people willing to pay for it (Akser, 2014). Today, national channels such as Fox TV, TRT 1, Show TV, Star TV, and local and regional TV channels such as Meltem TV, Olay TV, Mesaj TV, Ege TV, Kadırga TV are broadcasting K-dramas on these satellite networks. Some national channels including Fox TV and TRT 1 broadcast

K-dramas or their adaptations twice a day. Although undoubtedly K-dramas are the most popular cultural products of *Hallyu* in Turkey, after increasing popularity of K-dramas, a new type of television series emerged on Turkish TV channels: Turkish adaptations of K-dramas. Show TV was the first broadcasting company that aired an adaptation of K-dramas in 2011. Until today, more than fifteen Turkish adaptations of K-dramas have been broadcasted on Turkish TV channels. (See Table 1 in Appendix for selected TV drama adaptations.)

The authors of this essay explore the cultural reception of K-dramas and Turkish adaptations of K-dramas focusing on *Güneşi Beklerken* (2013–2014), a loosely-based adaptation of *Boys Over Flowers* (*Kkotboda namja*, 2009). Relying on the reception of Turkish viewers, the authors aimed to understand why Turkish audiences are passionately watching Korean adaptations such as *Güneşi Beklerken* and original K-dramas. Considering media texts as cultural transporters of social, political, and economic features of a specific society, the authors interrogated which hybrid cultural dynamics in adaptations of K-drama attract Turkish audiences and touch their sensibilities. In this context, the authors investigated the concept of cultural proximity (LaPastina and Straubhaar, 2005; Straubhaar, 1991; 2003). The authors argued that the participants in the study take a complicated and ambiguous position by discursively constructing similarities and commonalities in the Turkish remake of K-dramas by perceiving the series positively based on idealized values of middle-class, while minimizing differences between two distinct and different cultures.

In this essay, the authors primarily focused on *Güneşi Beklerken* (hereafter *Waiting for the Sun*), a loosely-based Turkish remake of a K-drama, *Boys Over Flowers*. While the show's writers have not directly said so, in addition to the interview participants in this study, many fans and fan sites find it very obvious that *Waiting for the Sun* was adapted from *Boys Over Flowers* due to its popularity in Turkey.[1] *Waiting for the Sun* is a high school love story drama about a poor rural girl, Zeynep, who receives a fellowship from a private high school in Istanbul. Zeynep, as a stubborn, strong-minded and kind-hearted newbie at school, stands up to Kerem Sayer, the rich and arrogant son of the owner of the private high school, who is a bully. Kerem's best friend, Barış, protects Zeynep from bullying. Zeynep develops feelings for Barış. Yet, in the meantime, former rivals Zeynep and Kerem fall in love with each other. Similarly, the hit Korean teen drama, *Boys Over Flowers* (*Kkotboda namja*), centers around the love and friendship story between a poor girl (Geum Jan-di) and spoiled rich boys (Goo Joon-pyo and Yoon Ji-hoo). *Boys Over Flowers* is a popular Asian melodrama which is an adaptation of Japanese and later Taiwanese dramas.

The authors chose *Waiting for the Sun* because as the most commercially successful adaptation of a K-drama in Turkey, *Waiting for the Sun* paved the way for more, subsequent K-drama adaptations. *Waiting for the Sun* was produced as a summer TV show in 2013, yet, after its great success, the series went on to broadcast 50 *more* episodes until July 2014. Since the TV series portrays a story of four teenagers and their friendships in a high school, the producers thought only young people would be interested in the series. However, high ratings of the show made it clear that adults were also watching it. In the next section, to gain insight about Turkish audiences' responses to K-dramas and their adaptations, the authors briefly discussed the broader socio-cultural context in Turkey. Then, the authors focus on the method of the study.

Interviews with Turkish Audiences

Straddling Europe, western Asia, and the Middle East, Turkey is a unique hybrid in terms of its geographical location, heritage, and history. With cultural connections to European, Middle-Eastern, and Asian cultures, Turkey is a modern country with a large Muslim population. By adopting Western values such as liberal democracy, secularism, and consumer culture in combination with Islamic conservatism, Turkey's modernization process is complex. Therefore, regarding Turkey's relationship with Islam, the East and Western modernity is a crucial, yet a deep and complicated one (Navaro-Yashin, 2002; Göle, 1997), including media consumption and television viewing practices. Since the 1980s, Turkish viewers have consumed both local and foreign television dramas including global American TV series such as *Dallas, Falcon Crest, The Flamingo Road*, and Latin American soap operas such as *Isaura the Slave Girl, Los Ricos Tambien Lloran* (*Zenginler de Aglar*), as well as local Turkish TV series (Eichner et al. forthcoming). Turkish audiences, particularly women, are fond of watching dramas on television. Based on the Turkish Radio and Television Supreme Council's (RTUK) research on Television Watching Trends, women are mostly watching television serials (87.5%), whereas men mainly prefer news (80.5%), and then television serials (66.6%) (RTUK, 2013). Kanal D, the broadcaster channel of *Waiting for the Sun* is the most preferred television channel (54.6%) among women because of its television dramas (RTUK, 2016).

As a data-collection technique, semi-structured one-on-one in-depth interviews teased out detailed information about the sensibilities of Turkish audience to the major themes of the K-dramas and their Turkish remakes. The authors used snowball sampling as a recruitment method employing research into participants' social networks to access specific populations to identify potential subjects (Marcus et al. 2017; Noy 2008; Browne 2005). The interviews were conducted between January and April 2015 in participants' homes, offices, or in university classrooms. All interviews were conducted in Turkish and translated to English by the authors. For this study, nineteen people, between 21 and 65 years old, were interviewed. The names of all participants were concealed to protect their privacy. All participants came from middle-class backgrounds and reside in Izmir, the third biggest city in Turkey. The occupations of the respondents varied from civil servants to graphic designers. However, seven out of nineteen informants were graduate and undergraduate students in various universities in Izmir. All participants were either high school or college graduates. The interviews lasted for an average of one hour. Since television viewing, particularly watching dramas, is a distinctly gendered experience in Turkey (RTUK, 2013), the majority of the participants were women. Only two male viewers participated in the study. The participants were not chosen randomly but were chosen based on their viewing preferences and their reflexive engagement with Korean TV adaptations or original K-dramas. All participants had watched Turkish adaptations of K-dramas such as *Waiting for the Sun* (*Güneşi Beklerken*), *Kiraz Mevsimi* (an adaption of *Shinsaui pumgyeok*), and *Kocamın Ailesi (Neongkuljjae gulleoon dangsin*). Respondents preferred to watch Turkish adaptations on TV in designated time slots and in private settings such as their homes or a friend's home. They watched original K-dramas either on TV or on the internet.

In this essay, the authors employed critical discourse analysis (CDA) to investigate the language used in the interviews. CDA, as an interdisciplinary approach, focuses on linguistic structures to explain overt relations of struggle and conflict (Wodak, 2001, p. 2) in socio-cultural contexts. As stated by Stubbs (1997), CDA helps people understand how the world is represented in texts and how people think about the world. Fowler (1996) states that "critical linguistics insists that all representation is mediated, molded by the value systems that are ingrained in the medium" (p. 4). Therefore, CDA focuses on the relationships between language, worldview, power and ideology. It is a useful method, in this study, to understand audiences' ways of thinking and talking about television representations, implicit and hidden meanings of the texts and interpretations of Turkish drama audiences. Given the significantly larger K-drama viewing population in Turkey, the authors do not claim the group under study represents Turkish audiences as a whole. This concept predominantly refers to participants of the study. Thus, rather than seeking a collective representative sample, the authors strived to achieve a grasp of Turkish audiences' consumption of transnational media texts, exploring ways that social construction of cultural proximity have affected viewing practices of audiences.

In our interviews, the authors found out that the following themes were appealing to the audiences regarding cultural proximity between Turkish and Korean cultures and media products: the portrayals of romanticism, representation of class differences via lifestyles, and social relations such as family ties. Straubhaar (2003) defined cultural proximity as "the tendency to prefer media products from one's own culture or the most similar possible culture" (p. 85). In this essay, the authors argue that Turkish audiences discursively construct cultural proximity when watching K-dramas and their adaptations by perceiving the series positively based on idealized values of middle-class. Turkish audiences who do not experience Korean culture firsthand create assumed commonalities between two communities based on media representations of Korean culture. Their statements showed that they tend to link their experiences reflexively to historical specificity of the Eastern societies such as a conservative form of romanticism or strong family ties by utilizing cultural texts (TV series) for similarities at the expense of ignoring and overlooking profound distinctions between Korean and Turkish cultures. In this context, a successful hybridization of Western, Turkish, and Asian values not only fosters Turkish audience anticipation for the cultural proximity between Turkey and Korea, but also plays an important role in the wide distribution of Korean cultural products in Turkey and their adaptations.

In the next section, the authors briefly discuss the concept of cultural proximity and transnational flows of TV program formats to provide the background and information necessary to an understanding of our approach to the subject. Later, the empirical findings of the study go under three major themes, composed of subsections of the essay: romanticism, differences and inequalities among social classes, and social relationships in terms of family relations. Based on audience responses, these categories emerged in personal interviews while discussing the K-dramas and their adaptations. These themes arose in the interviews as recurring aspects of cultural proximity. In the final section, the authors discuss major findings of the study and attempt to reconceptualize their findings in relation to Iwabuchi's (2002) ideas on cultural proximity. The study of Turkish audiences' consumption of K-dramas or their adaptations provides insights into understanding media consumption of non-western media products (K-dramas) in a non–Western society (Turkey) for analyzing a complex and contentious concept: cultural proximity.

Cultural Proximity, Format Adaptations and Multiple-Flows

Straubhaar (1991) defined cultural proximity as "nationally or locally produced material that is closer to and more reinforcing of traditional identities, based on regional, ethnic, dialect/language, religious and other elements" (p. 51). In other words, he stated that the audiences give priority to local TV programs, including the ones adapted from different TV formats. The audiences "tend to choose to watch television programs that are close, most proximate and must directly relevant to them in cultural and linguistic terms" (Straubhaar, 2005, p. 273). The first choice of the audiences is national programs produced in their own language and culture. If the cost of local programs is very high and these programs are not available to the local or national audiences, the alternative choices for the audiences are the programs which are closer or similar to their culture. Sinclair (1996) explained these common characteristics and similarities with the "cultural-linguistic concept" by referring to cultural, ethnical, religious, historical, linguistic and geographic, and other forms of proximity. Cultural proximity is a very complex concept because people have different, multilayered type and level identities as global, transnational, national, and local (Kaptan, 2018). Therefore, in this essay, the authors used Iwabuchi's (2002) approach to cultural proximity. From Iwabuchi's perspective, cultural proximity is not something "out there," but rather is something audiences should subjectively identify and experience. It is based on an impression and assumption of similarity rather than ontological cultural similarities (Berg, 2017; MacLachlan & Chua, 2004; Iwabuchi, 2002). Hence, audiences willingly create a sense of commonalities (or shared cultural values).

Cultural characteristics of a country, such as its traditions and sociocultural identities, are embedded into its cultural goods. For instance, one of the most powerful exporters of cultural products, without a doubt, is the Hollywood industry. Particularly during the 1980s, the United States was the most competitive exporter of TV programs and formats (Chalaby, 2012). Although the United States has been the most powerful exporter of TV dramas and TV formats, Latin American countries, such as Mexico and Brazil, started to sell soap operas to many countries around the world as early as the late 1980s. Until the 1990s, the United States dominated the format trade industry due to unidirectional cultural or media flow. However, in the last three decades, American media products have not been the only formats exported to different countries. In addition to Latin-American telenovelas and Indian Bollywood movies (Kavoori & Punathambekar, 2008; Punathambekar, 2005), Turkish TV series and program formats (Ghazzi & Kraidy, 2013; Kaptan, 2013; Yanardağoğlu & Karam, 2013), and Danish TV series (Jensen, 2007; Jensen & Waade, 2013) and their adaptations are distributed transnationally and watched by millions worldwide. In the last two decades, one more genre has been added to such multi-directional media flows: K-dramas.

Today, new countries, such as Turkey and South Korea, have been competing with the U.S. and Latin American countries such as Mexico and Brazil and the U.S. to export TV programs in a globalizing media industry. Within this current multi-directional flows of the global media market, public broadcasters of Turkey, such as TRT, introduced Turkish audiences to K-dramas, helping K-dramas rapidly become popular in Turkey.

In the next section, the authors discussed their investigation into this popularity through interviews with Turkish audiences. In the interviews, participants implied the logic of cultural proximity by stressing three major themes: romanticism, social class inequalities, and social relationships, particularly family ties related to protagonists' socio-economic classes.

A Conservative Form of Romanticism

While discussing *Waiting for the Sun* or its Korean original, *Boys Over Flowers*, one of the most popular and recurring themes among Turkish audiences is the concept of romance. The love story between Kerem and Zeynep is a "cliché" seen in classical Turkish movie plots of *Yeşilçam*. *Yeşilçam* was used as a general name for the Turkish cinema and the Turkish movie industry, but substantially it is a name which covers a period between the 1950s and 1980s (Yilmazok, 2012, p. 29, 30). In *Yeşilçam*'s romantic love stories, the most commonly used and repeated plot is the rich boy–poor girl love story (or the other way around). Many participants considered the plot a "cliché" without necessarily attributing negative connotations to the word. Three female participants elaborated on this concept while discussing *Waiting for the Sun*:

> **Female Subject #1:** I thought of it as a classical [story], but the classics always attract everybody's attention. Honestly, I love it!
>
> **Female Subject #2:** This is a cliché, but a very nice cliché for me.
>
> **Female Subject #3:** The love story between Kerem and Zeynep is the same [story] as in *Yeşilçam* movies. In those movies, the same cliché was also used. Even today, actually, similar topics are used. Just look at [the content of the TV series] and how [these] series could [have] rich [content] when other stories are connected to this topic [romance].

To put these participants' comments into a perspective, the authors briefly looked at common structures of *Yeşilçam* movies, and then the K-dramas and their Turkish adaptations. Turkish film companies produce movies around similar issues; similar scenes and similar speeches are repeated in the films. Turkish cinema researcher Ayça (1996) expressed that "in terms of *Yeşilçam* there is a common repertoire [of stories]" (p. 135). *Yeşilçam* movies are also based on "the star system." Hence, the protagonists are very important (Ayça, 1996). *Yeşilçam* melodramas have a narrative structure based on chronological and casual relationships. Generally, the plot is familiar, predictable, and simple in every movie. The story develops as follows: the male and female protagonists usually meet because of a coincidence, and they fall in love at first sight. However, they are separated due to acts of villains, misunderstandings between lovers, or social-class differences. Later, misunderstandings and obstacles are overcome, and there is a happy ending in almost every story. It is also typical that the relationship sparks hatred among protagonists, yet romance immediately replaces aversion. Love is idealized as "pure" or "supreme" love. An ideal love is defined as an honest, non-materialistic, naïve, non-sexual, sacrificial, selfless, and heteronormative form of love.

Yeşilçam movies emphasize "real and naïve" love, based on emotions and sacrifices rather than sexuality. Thus, they do not implicitly show the sex scenes, even kissing, making intimacy among protagonists confidential. The writers tend to romanticize and idealize love rather than sexualize it. Even in the love stories resulting in marriage, the writers do not invite the audiences to see any sexual acts between protagonists. With a conservative tone, the writers may even be warning audiences in an implicit manner to stay outside the bedroom. A conservative form of romanticism overlays upon the whole story. Generally, writers represent those who do engage in sex as "being selfish" and suitable for unemotional one-night stands. In classical *Yeşilçam* movies, however, writers imply and encourage the idea that sex should be only in compliance with conservative values when real love is at stake. They emphasize marriage as an appropriate form of love approved by the Turkish society. The scenes include only romanticized form of physical expression such as kissing, holding hands, or hugging.

In Turkish adaptations, the audiences recall the romantic melodramas of *Yeşilçam* in loosely-based K-drama adaptations such as *Waiting for the Sun*. According to these audiences, the *Yeşilçam* form of love, in participants' words, "pure love," signifies a more conservative, clean, non-sexual, virtuous type of love. Based on participants' interviews, this form of love has also been emphasized in original K-dramas. For instance, *Waiting for the Sun* and its original version, *Boys Over Flowers*, share a similar plot with Turkish movies. A 37-year-old officer and a fan of K-dramas, Female Subject #4, explains her familiarity based on familiarity with the generic, melodramatic structure (what Straubhaar [2007] calls genre proximity) with a Korean TV series as follows:

> [*Waiting for the Sun*] is a love story between a rich boy and a poor girl at the [high] school. A love born from hate. Previously, the boy seems troubled, but he loves her; he makes every effort to gain her love. It is the same story [in *Yeşilçam* movies].

Based on Obregon's discussion of genre proximity, Straubhaar (2007) defines the concept as the common structure of melodrama covering many cultures. Straubhaar (p. 199–201) says melodrama builds on underlying oral strutures, formulas, and archetypes that can be shared by cultures. Genre proximity refers to audiences' familiarity with a specific genre such as melodramas (Obregon, 1995 as cited in La Pastina & Straubhaar, 2005). It can influence preferences of the audiences (Ksiazek & Webster, 2008; La Pastina & Straubhaar, 2005). As a popular genre, melodramas, whether Korean dramas or Latin American telenovelas, share common characteristics that appeal to national audiences. The "basic premises of the genre (e.g. love stories, female heroines, social inequalities)," "flexible narrative structure," and "predictability" (Dorce, 2014) are distinctive styles of melodramas. Today, viewers frequently see aforementioned clichés in the classic narrative structure of K-dramas and their Turkish versions. The clichés in K-dramas create a sense of closeness to Turkish culture and spark a sense of familiarity among Turkish audiences. These noticeable similarities between Turkish movies or TV series and K-dramas point out "genre proximity." Similarly, Female Subject #4 also stated no surprise [for the audience] in the K-dramas or in their Turkish remakes. In her opinion, there are a lot of similarities not only between K-dramas and classical Turkish movies but also between the cultures of the two countries. She said, "Koreans put specific emphasis on love, romanticism and [romantic love] which are very important [concepts] in Turkish culture, too." She inferred that Turkish audiences feel familiar with K-dramas due to these similarities embedded in culture. To identify a sense of proximity, perceived or constructed by the audiences between Turkish and Korean TV series, the authors asked participants about the interplay between proximity and distance. Based on her multiple viewing experiences, Female Subject #4 defined a classical plot of K-dramas and familiarities with Turkish dramas:

> [In Korean dramas] [t]here is an exaggerated "pure" romanticism and it is weird. The girl and the boy are not shown together. There are not any scenes that they appear together. They torture each other due to misunderstandings and make peace with regret. They prioritize love. Kissing is shown rarely. They are represented as childish. They never show any affection or sexuality; [the TV series] just skips these scenes quickly. They show that love [means] suffering for someone and getting together at the end. There is a common understanding that patience is a virtue.

Female Subject #4's representation of K-drama is fundamentally essential to understanding genre proximity in media texts as well as cultural proximity in everyday experiences. Her objection, finding pure romanticism "weird," reveals not the divergence between Turkish and Korean media texts, but the unrealistic portrayal of love on TV contrary to audiences' mundane life experiences. However, when the authors asked her to make a comparison between Turkish and K-dramas regarding their similarities, she stated:

> For instance, in *Boys Over Flowers*, there was a scene in which the boy [Gu Jun-pyo] says he does not love her. We understand that he is telling a lie for the sake of the heroine. Actually, this is a cliche for Turkish movies, too. But [still] Korean series are much more convincing.

Ostensibly, Female Subject #4's responses seem contradictory considering that she finds K-dramas "weird" but "convincing." However, the authors can understand her statement on different planes of reality. On the one hand, she objects to the romanticism depicted in K-dramas as incongruous with everyday life. On the other hand, when she decodes cultural representations of interpersonal relations or romance to make a comparison among media texts, she assumes K- dramas are closer to reality to epitomize sentiments, desires, and emotions. She also adds other commonalities with Turkish culture including "loyalty, mercy, helping their lover (sometimes secretly), and giving up on a lover in tears for his or her own benefit." Other respondents point out these themes. Another female participant, 24-year-old Female Subject #2's statements supports Female Subject #4's's statement: "Their relationships are not very close, and the scenes do not evoke sexuality between women and men in the Korean series. I feel that they are experiencing a much more pure form of love." Female Subject #5 took a similarly romanticized approach to K-dramas when she gave her reason for watching them:

> There is loyalty. [Korean] male protagonists are protective, and they do not behave badly or are not making mistakes. They are always respectful to everyone. They are like this in all their relationships. The understanding of romanticism seems very close to our culture. Because they are not affectionate immediately, they are shy with each other. They don't confess their love to each other.

All the interviewees agreed that representation of romanticism in Korean and Turkish TV series is very similar in terms of delineation of obscenity. Even kissing does not appear often in Korean TV dramas. The relationships are based on non-sexual form of romanticism. This resonates with Turkish audiences' understanding of romance, especially complying with middle-age audiences who grew up watching *Yeşilçam* movies. Particularly during the golden age of *Yeşilçam* in the 1960s, the glorification of love and purity of love—excluding sexuality—has become one of the most frequent themes of Turkish cinema.

The other topic of cultural proximity brought up by respondents many times, and commonly called a cliché, is a transformation of Zeynep and Kerem's emotions from hate to love. The showrunners of *Waiting for the Sun* and *Boys Over Flowers* used similar clichés to guarantee the success of the drama. This point was observed by two participants of the study:

> **Female Subject #3:** There is a very famous anonymous quote: "Big loves begin with fights." The series is based on this idea.
>
> **Female Subject #5:** The first reason for my watching this series was the love

relationship between two people who previously did not like each other. It seemed impossible [that they (would) fall in love]. I wondered what would happen and if they could accomplish the impossible.

The "love-hate relationship" is one of the best ways to drive a plot not only in the series but also in the novels. Radway (1991) specified particular objectivities of love stories in the romance genre. Radway (1991) conducted interviews with women readers of romance novels. In the romance genre, in its inception, the hero and the heroine hate each other and argue a lot due to misunderstandings. Then, the hate turns into love. According to Radway, "hero and heroine are shown to despise each other overtly, even though they are 'in love' primarily because each is jealous or suspicious of the other's motives and consequently fails to trust the other" (1991, p.65). As in the traditional romance genre, in Korean and Turkish TV series love-hate relationships and romance exist only among heterosexual couples. Writers tend to exclude queer romance from mainstream Turkish and K-dramas such as *Waiting for the Sun* and *Boys Over Flowers* respectively. In both dramas, love relationships and sexual orientations of actors and actresses are between people of the opposite sex. However, none of the participants question or present a challenge to heteronormativity. The audience does not show any concerns that the Turkish and Korean media are essentially promoting and normalizing heteronormativity along the same line with the hegemonic discourse of gender and sexuality.

Similarly, a romantic, non-sexual, heteronormative relationship between a rich man and poor girl are prevalent themes of many Turkish TV shows and *Yeşilçam* movies. In the Turkish adaptations of K-dramas, the conflict and tension between the hero and the heroine predominantly arise from their social-class identities. Protagonists, coming from different social classes, who strive to achieve, as one participant puts it, an "impossible love," is another "cliché" used in the Turkish TV shows and K-dramas (Female Subject #5). Yet, it is also one of the main reasons why Turkish audiences watch K-dramas and their Turkish remakes. Therefore, in the next section, the authors discussed how media representations of different social classes resonate with the respondents of the study. Class difference is one of the conventional obstacles, in participants' words, "another cliché" commonly used in melodramas and romantic comedies.

Proximity Through Globalization: Class Differences and Luxurious Lifestyles

The participants of this study mentioned the class differences between the protagonists of the love story as another important theme in K-dramas and their Turkish adaptations. Audiences respond to the TV series demonstrating different lifestyles, particularly the conspicuous consumption lifestyles of the upper classes. A 36-year-old female participant, Female Subject #6 talked about *Waiting for the Sun* by referring to audiences' structure of feelings when watching the drama:

> If you watch this series, you can see that there are "two different worlds" in the TV series. There are rich people and people who are not rich. I know well the culture in private schools because that's where I came from. The richness and wealth attract young people's attention. This is the situation! There are people who are privileged, and at the same time these are the rich people. That's why jealousy occurs in society. This series [*Waiting for the Sun*] reflects this situation very successfully.

Female Subject #6's lexical choice revealed the contrast and tension between social classes both on TV and in society. She deliberately avoided saying "poor" and preferred to say "people who are not rich." This statement also brings the working class and the middle classes together as a unified category as opposed to the upper class. From her perspective, the jealousy and envy stem from portrayals of luxurious lifestyles in the media. A 23-year-old college student, Female Subject #7, showed a similar sensitivity through calibration of words while talking about family relations in the working class. "The poor, in other words, unjustly treated" have closer family ties, according to Female Subject #7 (Emphasis added). Similarly, the binary representation of classes on TV is strikingly disturbing for the audiences, yet it is considered very appealing for the very young TV viewers. Similarly, a 28-year-old female journalist, Female Subject #1 criticized the TV series in this vein:

> It's [very] negative. Young people wonder [about] or want to achieve this material wealth. Actually, nobody wants weak people in their lives. It is same in our lives, too. We want to see powerful people standing next to us. This is human nature! People want to watch rich lives or want to experience this type of life. But this affects society negatively. Everybody wants to obtain this lifestyle that they watch in the series. But many people do not have enough money [to sustain] this kind of affluent lifestyle.

The participants emphasized the feeling of dissonance these dramas create between their lived experiences and media representations. Female Subject #7 who regularly watch *Waiting for the Sun* stated:

> Honestly, it is really interesting and [also] distanced. [These are] extreme lives! When I am sitting in our living room, I am dreaming and am asking: "What's going on? Why don't we have a life like that?" I was a student at a private high school, but nobody had a Porsche! To me, this lifestyle seems too much of an exaggeration. My brother is in a high school. I was surprised when I saw the effect of the series on him. He is getting mad!

On the one hand, the representation of lives of the rich in *Waiting for the Sun*, especially Kerem's eye-catching lifestyle—sports car, unlimited spending, luxurious homes—were the point of attraction for the research participants. The audiences agreed on a spectacle value in watching wealthy lives different than their own. On the other hand, middle-class audiences also interpret it unfavorably. Aforementioned participants (#6, 7 and 1) emphasized that young people are attracted to the luxurious lives they see on the screen. The luxurious way of living represented in the series catches the fantasy of the young audiences and sparks an interest in the TV series. However, they described a gap between these visual images and personal experiences of the audiences. In addition, Female Subject #4 stressed that luxurious consumption and extraordinary lifestyles of rich protagonists are not just in Turkish dramas; Koreans also like to depict upper-class lifestyles in their dramas. In many K-dramas, luxury cars, affluent houses, brand-name clothes, and fancy places (cafes, restaurants, and entertainment places) appear as a symbol of prosperity and wealth. In this sense, perceived "modern" lifestyles are depicted with the use of luxury items and accessibility to expensive places, bringing about participation in modernity through consumption. The experience of modernity and consumption is very significant in the formation of identities (Savage and Warde, 1993; Hollands, 2017).

Hence, displaying fortune and abundance on TV is an element of familiarity shared between Turkish and Korean media products. Female Subject #4 stated that:

> I noticed when I was watching the Korean version: it is important that men are very handsome, very cool, and very strong … as if the men have to own everything. For example, knowledge of a second language is given more importance…. Like in the 1980s in Turkey, there was an affection towards foreigners and a need to show off. "I have money,[2] I can shop, I am versed in cultures, I can speak different languages." This attitude of awe and a feeling of lowliness of Turks also exists [in K-dramas]: it is important to have relations with people from abroad; they are treated as if they are superior. The same thing exists in Korean [culture]. It felt like I was in the 1980s in Turkey, the same kind of eagerness to experience new things.

In this sense, consumption, ability to speak foreign languages, and a privileged lifestyle relate to the issue of power. These commodities not only represent wealth but also the power which refers to the idea that money can buy anything. Therefore, the ability to afford expensive consumer goods, connecting with the world, and having a rich lifestyle are seen as being powerful and important in the society—a popular view commonly disseminated through television during the 1980s.

In the 1980s, globalization was closely related to consumption in Turkey (Ahiska & Yenal, 2006; Bali, 2002). After the acceleration of the multinational companies and foreign capital in the country, foreign brands started to appear in the supermarket shelves. From the clothing industry to fast-food restaurants, new brands have become prevalent and discernible everywhere in big cities. Consumption is a premise for obtaining a western lifestyle and identity. Accessibility of the products consumed in Western countries provide people a sense of belonging as if they are a part of Western culture and identity (Ahiska & Yenal, 2006; Bali, 2002). This sense of sharing of a common identity constitutes an important motivation for consumption. Therefore, the media promotes a need for the spectacle of the wealth and therefore conspicuous consumption. According to Ahıska and Yenal (2006), while the image of modernity, recognition of fashion and their coming into prominence were widely getting into circulation and increased the awareness, the desires, aspirations and dreams of the society are indexed to the consumption (p. 49).

Both in Korean drama and its Turkish adaptations, class differences deepened by conspicuous consumption have come into a reconciliation through the shared love of protagonists. Therefore, in the romantic dramas, writers emphasize happy endings as a form of peacemaking between classes. This is expected and demanded by the audiences. Female Subject #10, a 24-year-old student stated, "The situation of wealthy-ness and poorness of Kerem and Zeynep don't affect their love relationship in the series. It's okay that Zeynep's family is poor and Kerem's family is rich. Neither Kerem's family's richness nor Zeynep's family's poorness prevents their love."

Similarly, a 22-year-old college student, Female Subject #11 specified that Zeynep loves Kerem, not for his money but for his real character. She also stated, "Zeynep seems so close to us, she [her character] is more realistic, and she is one of us." In other words, the depiction of Zeynep's middle class lifestyle creates a sense of proximity and closeness for the viewers. Female Subject #5 echoed Female Subject #11's ideas: "Zeynep was a character like any [Turkish] girl. Her jealousy, her happiness is like as it should be, I feel she is very close to me." Therefore, the audiences want Zeynep to succeed in the TV series and feel satisfaction with the achievements of the protagonists. The lower or lower-middle class characters in the TV series are expected to become successful or to achieve their goals due to an identification or empathy of the audience to the characters. Therefore, the success of the characters creates satisfaction for the audience.

Family Matters: Reception of Social Relations

Turkish audiences, who prefer to watch K-dramas and their Turkish adaptations, demonstrate great receptivity to family ties and friendships in the popular dramas. Family ties, connectivity, belonging, loyalty, social and emotional support, and intimacy were recurrent themes in each interview. These themes also evoke cultural proximity between Korean and Turkish societies. According to participants, these subject matters and values mostly emerge from family TV programs. Therefore, as discussed above, audiences perceive such dramas as "family television series." The audience members self-reflectively watched these shows by comparing their families with Korean and Turkish families on TV and identify with the media characters they feel proximate.

As a point of comparison and contrast, informants immediately offered an analysis of the portrayal of the families of heroes and heroines. Differences among social classes come into play. The participants elaborated on protagonists' family relations by highlighting a lack of similarities between social classes represented on TV and real life. In addition, stereotypes based on class differences come into play during the narrative construction of family relations. Nearly all participants agreed that both *Waiting for the Sun* and *Boys Over Flowers* reinforced their belief that "rich people have weak family connections." Female Subject #8, a-22-year-old industrial designer, stated:

> Yes, there are many examples of that [in real life]. I know someone. He is not my close friend. I met him a couple of years ago. His mother and father are very rich, but they're divorced. They only send money to him, and he spends it on useless things. It's not weird to me because there are similar examples in real life. The reality is shown very well in those series. I liked it.

A-23-year-old college student, Female Subject #7, and a 45-year-old school teacher, Male Subject #1, interpreted the media text by pointing out the broken family ties of upper-class families because of wealth. She explained,

> I noticed in series that the more wealth and prosperity, the weaker family connections. Kerem's mother and father are not cheating on each other, but they are also not together. The poor, in other words unjustly treated, are more strongly connected with one another when we compare them with rich families. For example, Kerem's family seems to think that they can solve problems with money. But poor people are closer to each other.

In the interview, Male Subject #1 echoed this female participant's statement:

> We already hear about it, see on the media, and know that the family relations of rich people are weak. This was also the case in the TV drama. On the other hand, the relationship between Zeynep and her mother is very strong. There is always a problem in very rich families such as Kerem's family and his friends' families.

It is interesting to note both Female Subject #7 and Male Subject #1 relied on media representations and stereotypes rather than personal experiences and social encounters to compare social values and family relations of the hero and the heroine. They tend to embrace negative media images of upper classes and symbolic content of media to shape their beliefs about a social class. In this respect, they claim a similarity between Korean and Turkish societies. The viewers are familiar with negative representations of family relations of upper-class people. Thus, with only a few exceptions, these participants did not regard any distinctions between media representations and reality.

However, some informants criticized televised representation of social classes, particularly representation of the upper class. A 65-year-old retired teacher, Female Subject #9 exemplified the process of negotiated meaning while drawing on media representation by taking a cautious approach:

> To me, it seems very exaggerated. Or, I have not seen anything like this. But maybe there are very few [rich families] like that. In the series, the family is very rich, but their son is emotionally poor. He has a mother and a father, but they aren't there for him. Kerem is a lonely boy. Children [the young audience] are influenced by Kerem's rich [lifestyle]. However, they [also] see that Kerem's life is miserable. You feel sorry for Kerem as a character. When smart young people watch this TV series, they can learn a lot. If you think rationally, Kerem is a miserable example. The reason for Kerem's anger is being deprived of family love.

A 24-year-old interior architecture student, Female Subject #2 took a more critical approach by denying "unrealistic" representations of upper social class in K-dramas and their Turkish adaptations:

> This is an absolute prejudice. There are [rich] people who are not like this. I think this is an idea imposed by [the media]. The popular [representation] is that "if you are rich, you are free." You are rich, you have got a car, but the car is bought for you by your family. It is a show-off who says, "I'm rich, I'm free, nobody can tell me what to do." There are many examples [of people] who are rich and still have close connections with their families.

A media studies master's student, Female Subject #5 reflected on the significance of family values from a slightly different perspective. She stated that *Waiting for the Sun* highlights the love story rather than the socio-economic status of the characters. However, she declared that the depiction of wealth (luxurious properties, expensive cars, and limitless opportunities that money can buy) is one of the reasons for audiences to watch this series. She said, "The rich lifestyle of Kerem is concurrently foregrounded and backgrounded… In the TV series, [Kerem's] affluence is attributed negative connotations." She added that the series represents Turkish culture by referring to family values:

> I understand the importance of family. Kerem is a rebel; the reason behind it is his family. They are not bad people, but they are uncaring. We understand Kerem and empathize with him. However, Zeynep grew up in a good family although she does not have a father. She has a loving and caring family. She gives Kerem the love and warmth she received from her family. Kerem changes because of her love and care. We [the audience] perceived the significance of growing up in a happy family after watching Zeynep's [media] character.

Some respondents who watch Korean TV dramas regularly observed that Koreans also emphasized family relations in their TV shows. These informants claimed, without a doubt, family/family relations are one of the most prominent themes in K-dramas. Audiences noted that love and respect for family are constituent elements of the story and recur in the dramas. An ideal family stays together in integrity, protects family members, and supports one another when experiencing problems or calamity. Close family ties are one of the landmarks of Korean TV shows and also the element of cultural proximity for Turkish audiences. Female Subject #4 described K-dramas as follows:

> Family relations are important in the Korean TV series. For instance, family members who do not see each other [very often] come together because of an illness or at funerals. They act as it should be. It is not like we fight all the time or do not see [each other], do not feel anything [for our family]. Love is there all the time. Although wrongdoings happen, family members get together in difficult times. This is [the essence of being] family. It is the same for the rich and the poor.

In another interview, Female Subject #3 echoed Female Subject #4's argument and emphasized that she began to watch Korean TV series due to similarities between Korean and Turkish cultures. Female Subject #3 stressed,

> [Korean] family relations are very similar to the Turkish culture. I recognized powerful family connections in all Korean series that I watched. They give importance to family. There are well-structured hierarchical relations and respect among [family members]. These are the commonalities. In [Korean] culture, children are respectful towards their mothers and fathers [because of the way] they brought up. When I think about all these, I find similar hierarchies in Turkish families, too.

Also, other participants, regardless of their age, mentioned hierarchies within families by endorsing traditional roles in the family. Hence, despite generational differences, 26-year-old Female Subject #5 and 65-year-old Female Subject #9 were on the same page in terms of approving of the conservative messages of Korean adaptations as well as K-dramas. Female Subject #5 exemplified that as follows:

> The family is very important concept [in the Korean TV series]. Whatever happens, a mother is a mother, a father is a father, and a brother is a brother. I have the same feelings while watching Korean adaptations such as *Güneşi Beklerken*, *Kiraz Mevsimi*, and *Kocamın Ailesi*. Love and respect are substantial themes in all of these adaptations.

Her statement "a mother is a mother, a father is a father, and a brother is a brother" signified that every family member knows his/her responsibility, duty and his/her boundaries. Female Subject #9 invoked Female Subject #5's statement by emphasizing that everyone has a status and a role in the hierarchical structure of the family. She called attention to extended families and family ties between family members and the elders. She stated,

> There is an extended family in *Kocamın Ailesi*. It is a "normal" family lives in Turkey. Of course, today, a number of extended families are less than the past. Maybe they are not very common in the Western region [of Turkey], but there are extended families especially in the villages. Everybody in the family respects the grandmother. The father is a family member who is loved and respected. The mother is the one who keeps the balance in the family. She tries hard not to reflect any difficulties to the father. The role of the mother [in the TV series] is very similar to the mother in our daily lives.

According to Female Subject #2, close family relations, traditional roles, and hierarchies within families do not only mark similarities and create a point of cultural proximity between Korean and Turkish cultures, but also highlight differences between the Eastern and the Western cultures. She stated,

> Their family relations are very similar [to Turkish families]. They are close-knit families. There are close family ties, and there is a hardliner, strict family structure.... What I mean by hardliner, strict is ... they are not like American families who live largely and live more liberally.

She also added, "There is not any exaggerated [sexual] affection between men and women" in the K-dramas, yet there is "intimacy among friends and family members as opposed to the Western TV shows." In this sense, Female Subject #2 insisted on describing Korea and Turkey as similar societies and proximate cultures by lumping all differences.

As a patriarchal institution, the family and family relations depicted in the media reflect the complicated nature of the connections among media representations, audience reception and culture. It is striking that the traditional social construction of the family and relationships between family members are ascribed positive connotations by Turkish audiences while the audience seems to eagerly construct proximities between Korean and Turkish TV dramas. In other words, the traditional institutions of the Eastern societies including the family are idealized and authenticated within the context of patriarchal system to construct a proximity among Korean and Turkish cultures. Turkish audiences more eagerly approve the existing social order they see on TV when they compare it to the Korean culture. Turkish audiences relate to K-dramas through the reflective interpretation of the TV series, yet at the expense of internalizing socially conservative values and acknowledging the dominant cultural position of the patriarchy.

Conclusion

While K-dramas are becoming tremendously widespread and popular around the world including the Middle East, global media consumption of K-dramas and their re-makes varies in specific cultural contexts. In this study, the authors analyzed the media reception of K-dramas and their Turkish adaptations by employing the concept of cultural proximity. The analysis of Turkish media audiences' consumption of K-drama adaptations and original K-dramas help viewers in understanding a multidimensional and contentious concept—cultural proximity and media consumption of non-western media products with regards to multiple media flows of globalization.

In this study, the participants who watch original K-dramas made a better comparison and offered a more analytical framework considering commonalities, contradictions, and differences between Turkish and Korean cultural values including respect, loyalty, honesty, justice, and virtues. However, the Turkish respondents primarily identified three main themes in the Turkish adaptations of K-dramas: (1) romanticism, (2) social class differences in terms of inequalities, and (3) social relationships in terms of family ties. These topics were not only the cultural themes emerging from the interviews, but also are points of references for a feeling of close cultural proximity.

First, the Turkish audiences, amused by the cultural specific conceptualization of romanticism, based on common cultural values and clichés shared by classical Turkish movies (*Yeşilçam*) and K-dramas or their format adaptations. Korean and Turkish culture industries drive proximities by eliminating obscenity, promoting an ideal or "pure" love, erasing sexuality of heterosexual protagonists in the movies and soap operas. Global clichés such as a love story between the rich boy and the poor girl (or vice versa) or the melodrama structure of genre proximity cut across regional, national, and language barriers.

Second, the depiction of wealth and its spectacles were considered another aspect of proximity and crucial characteristic of format adaptations. The interviews showed that audiences appreciated the aesthetic spectacle value of the representation of wealthy lifestyles associated with the modernity and consumption. Thus, the spectacle of affluent lifestyles—gorgeous houses, latest model sports cars, designer clothes, etc.—caught audiences' attention both in the K-dramas and their adaptations. Luxurious consumption became a point of interest for the middle-class audience consumption and a privileged lifestyle as it relates to the issue of power.

Third, stereotypical displays of economic inequality and cultural differences between social classes—such as witnessing close family ties in lower-class and middle-class families and a lack of intimate family relations in upper classes and traditional values including respecting elders and considering family as a sacred institution—are other perceptible commonalities meeting the expectations of Turkish audiences both in the original K-dramas and their clones. Although no consensus lies among participants regarding the stereotypical understanding of social-class representations, Turkish audiences tend not to challenge these stereotypes.

While watching Turkish adaptations or the original K-dramas, informants of the study refrained from taking a critical approach to traditional family structures. On the contrary, these traditional, yet conservative, values remained cherished elements of proximities between Turkish and Korean cultures. Patriarchal values in K-dramas presented in line with the values of Turkish family structure. According to the participants, Korean male characters are powerful and potent. Both in Turkish adaptations and K-dramas, audiences accept conservative values compatible with traditions of the patriarchal Turkish society. In other words, cultural proximity is constructed and realized by Turkish audiences within Turkish and Korean cultures of the East/the Middle East.

The authors have argued that the popularity of K-dramas and Turkish adaptations of K-dramas among Turkish audiences cannot be explained by cultural factors associated with "language, shared histories and geographic proximities" (La Pastina & Straubhaar, 2005, p. 277–278). In the case of K-dramas and their Turkish adaptations, multiple proximities do not conjure up local-national spatial relationships, but transgress boundaries to contrive *imagined nation-to-nation proximities* by building on the proximity of values and imaginary cultural representations of the East. The Turkish audiences' viewing experiences of K-dramas and their adaptations link reflexive engagement with a cultural text to historical specificity of the Eastern societies. In other words, Turkish audiences discursively construct and simultaneously experience the concept of cultural proximity when they are watching K-dramas and their adaptations. Their experiences are reflexively linked to the historical conjunction of the flow of non–Western media texts. The participants utilized these media texts in order to assert salient cultural commonalities between Korean and Turkish cultures. One of the findings of the study was the inclination of participants to suppress distinctions among Korean and Turkish cultures in order to invent a consistent discourse of proximity. By "diminishing spatio-temporal distance" (Iwabuchi, 2002, p. 134) and suppressing and erasing profound distinctions between Korea and Turkey, they subjectively identified a successful hybridization of Turkish and Asian, as well as Western, values and articulate proximity between two societies. On the one hand, by recognizing the East and the Middle East as a broad and homogenous category against the West, yet, on the other hand by underpinning cultural differences between Turkey and Korea, the participants took a complicated and ambiguous position. Due to the juxtaposition of multiple and contentious perspectives, "culture proximity occurs *a posteriori*" (Iwabuchi, 2002, p. 134), and viewing experiences become a polysemic event in practice.

Appendix I

Korean Title	***English Title***	***Turkish Title***	***Turkish Broadcasting Channel***	***Year***
Bu Hwal	*Resurrection*	*Kış Güneşi*	Show	2016
Gajokggiri Wae Irae	*What Happens to My Family?*	*Baba Candır*	TRT1	2016
Yongmangeui Bulkkot	*Flames of Desire*	*Hayat Şarkısı*	Kanal D	2016
Pul-hauseu	*Full House*	*İlişki Durumu Karışık*	Show TV	2015
SarangdoDoni Dwoinayo	*Can Love Become Money?*	*Kiralık Aşk*	Star TV	2015
Wang-gwaneul Sseuryeoneun Ja, Geu Mugereul Gyeondyeora—Sangsokjadeul	*The Heirs*	*Çilek Kokusu*	Star TV	2015
Neongkuljjae Gulleoon Dangsin	*My Husband Got a Family*	*Kocamın Ailesi*	Fox	2014
Shinsaui Pumgyeok	*A Gentleman's Dignity*	*Kiraz Mevsimi*	Fox	2014
Oktapbang Wangseja	*Rooftop Prince*	*Osmanlı Tokadı*	TRT1	2013
Kkotboda Namja	*Boys Over Flowers*	*Güneşi Beklerken*	Kanal D	2013
Jeppangwang, Kim Takgu	*King of Baking, Kim Takgu*	*Aşk, Ekmek, Hayaller*	Show TV	2013
Gaeul Donghwa	*Autumn in My Heart*	*Paramparça*	Star TV	2013
Mianhada, Saranghanda	*I'm Sorry I Love You*	*Bir Aşk Hikayesi*	Fox	2013
Cheonsaui Yuhok	*Temptation of an Angel*	*Beni Affet*	Show TV	2011

Appendix II: Demographic Information About the Interviewees

Number	*Name and Surname*	*Job Title*	*Age*
1	Female Subject #1	Journalist	28
2	Female Subject #2	Student (MA)	24
3	Female Subject #3	Interior Architecture	28
4	Female Subject #4	Officer	37
5	Female Subject #5	Translator	26
6	Female Subject #6	Italian teacher	36
7	Female Subject #7	Student	23
8	Female Subject #8	Industrial Designer	22
9	Female Subject #9	Retired Teacher	65
10	Female Subject #10	Student (MA)	24
11	Female Subject #11	Student (BA)	22
12	Female Subject #12	Graphic Designer	33
13	Female Subject #13	Student (MA)	24
14	Female Subject #14	Student (BA)	21
15	Female Subject #15	Officer	52
16	Female Subject #16	Teacher	44
17	Female Subject #17	Archive Specialist	38
18	Male Subject #1	Teacher	45
19	Male Subject #2	Student (MA)	23

Notes

1. For example, a contributor for MyDramaList, Whatteverr (2014), gave several reasons for why she thinks it is based on *Boys Over Flowers*: poor heroine, heroine is bullied by rich boy, heroine falls for rich boy's best friend, heroine and rich boy end up together. Regarding K-dramas around the world, particularly in Turkey and the Middle East, Daehan Drama (2016), a UK-based fanpage, also considers *Waiting for the Sun* to be an adaptation of *Boys Over Flowers*. Azade-ruh (2016), who blogs on Tumblr, admitted, "Okay, okay, so I know the Korean version is not even the original version of this story but I put it on this list because the Korean version was one of the most popular remakes." In a story about how Korea's CJ E&M is going to start a production unit in Turkey, TodoTV News (2017) pointed out that "The adaptation of Korean series in Turkey is nothing new" and listed *Waiting for the Sun* as the adaptation for *Boys Over Flowers*.

2. As stated by Female Subject #4, a similar understanding regarding the wealthy was popular in Turkey in the 1980s. After the 1980 military coup, the late Prime Minister, Turgut Özal, won the first democratic election. Özal supported the ideology of the free market economy and implemented neoliberal economic policies. During the 1980s and 1990s, Turkey

underwent a great transformation by adapting to the increasing globalization of the world economy and culture. In this period, while the state was abolished from the economic realm through privatization policies, the Turkish national economy and culture went global with the integration of transnational capital and global culture (Kaptan, 2016). New regulations urged foreign capital to make investments which are considered a free ticket for entering transnational markets. These were also the years that Turks witnessed the successful increase of consumer culture and global mass consumerism in Turkey. (Ahiska & Yenal, 2006; Boratav, 1991; Bora, 1994; Kaptan, 2016).

References

Ahıska, M., & Yenal, Z. (2006). Aradığınız kişiye şu an ulaşılamıyor: Türkiye'de hayat tarzı temsilleri 1980–2005. İstanbul: Osmanlı Bankası Arşiv ve Araştırma Merk.

Akser, M. (2014). Technology and the Turkish mind: Flash animation as counter culture. *CINEJ Cinema Journal*, *3*(2), 193–217.

Ayça, E. (1996).*Yeşilçam'a Bakış*. Türk Sineması Üzerine Düşünceler. İstanbul: Doruk Yayımcılık. pp. 129–148.

Azade-ruh. (2016). Turkish-Korean TV dramas. *Tumblr*. Retrieved from http://azade-ruh.tumblr.com/post/150153578252/turkish-korean-tv-dramas.

Bali. R.N. (2002). Tarz-ı hayat'tan life style'a: Yeni Seçkinler, Yeni Mekanlar, Yeni Yaşamlar. İstanbul: İletişim Yayınları.

Bora, T. (1994). Türkiyede milliyetçilik söylemleri. *Birikim*, Kasım 1994, sayı 67. İstanbul.

Boratav, K. (1991). 1980'li yıllarda türkiye'de sosyal Sınıflar ve Bölüşüm. İstanbul: Gerçek Yayınevi.

Browne, K. (2005). Snowball sampling: using social networks to research non-heterosexual women. *International Journal of Social Research Methodology*, *8*(1), 47–60.

Chalaby, J.K. (2012). At the origin of a global industry: The TV format trade as an Anglo-American invention. *Media, Culture & Society*, *34*(1), 36–52.

Daehan Drama. (2016, July 17). Kdramas around the World: Turkey & Middle East. *Daehan Drama*. Retrieved from http://www.daehandrama.com/kdramas-around-world-turkey-and-middle-east/.

Dorce, A. (2014). Latin American telenovelas: Affect, citizenship and interculturality. In M. Alvaradi, M. Buonanna, H. Gray, & T. Miller. (Eds.), *The SAGE Handbook of Television Studies* (pp. 245–268). Los Angeles: SAGE.

Ghazzi, O.A., & Kraidy, M.M. (2013). Neo-Ottoman cool 2: Turkish nation branding and Arabic language transnational broadcasting. *International Journal of Communication*, *7*, 2341–2360.

Göle, N. (1997). The quest for the Islamic-self within the context of modernity. In S. Bozdogan & R. Kasaba (Eds.), *Rethinking modernity and national identity in Turkey* (pp. 91–94). Seattle: University of Washington Press.

Hall, S. (2006). Encoding/decoding. In M.G. Durham & D.M. Kellner (Eds.), *Media and cultural studies: Keyworks* (pp. 171–173). Malden, MA: Blackwell Publishing Ltd.

Hollands, R. (2017). The restructuring of young Geordies' employment, household and consumption identities. In J. Tomaney & N. Ward (Eds.), *A region in transition: North East England at the millenium*. New York: Taylor and Francis.

Iwabuchi, K. (2002). Recentering globalization: Popular culture and Japanese transnationalism. Durham, NC: Duke University Press.

Jensen, P.M. (2007). Danish and Australian television: The impact of format adaptation. *Media International Australia Incorporating Culture and Policy*, *124*, 119–133.

Jensen, P.M., & Waade, A.M. (2013). Nordic noir challenging 'the language of advantage': Setting, light, and language as production values in Danish television series. *Journal of Popular Television*, *1*(2), 259–265.

Kaptan, Y. (2013). Proximity or difference: The representation of Turkish melodramas in the Middle East and Balkans. *Global Media Journal: Mediterranean Edition*, *8*(2), 1–10.

Kaptan, Y. (2016). Marking differences, consuming identities: United Condoms of Benetton campaign and "global Turkishness." *Journal of Consumer Culture*, *16* (2), 447–466.

Kaptan, Y. (2018) Multiple proximities and national identities: Turkish audiences' perception of advertising adaptations. *Popular Communication*. doi: 10.1080/15405702.2018.1497800.
Kavoori, A.P., & Punathambekar, A. (2008). *Global Bollywood*. New York: New York University Press.
Ksiazek, T.B., & Webster, J.G. (2008). Cultural proximity and audience behavior: The role of language in patterns of polarization and multicultural fluency. *Journal of Broadcasting & Electronic Media, 52*(3), 485–503.
La Pastina, A., & Straubhaar, J.D. (2005). Multiple proximities between television genres and audiences: The schism between telenovelas' global distribution and local consumption. *Gazette: The International Journal for Communication Studies, 67*(3), 271–288.
Moran, A. (1998). Copycat television: Globalisation, program formats and culture identity. Luton, UK: University of Luton Press.
MacLachlan, E., & Chua, G. (2004). Defining Asian femininity: Chinese viewers of Japanese TV dramas in Singapore. In K. Iwabuchi (Ed.), *Feeling Asian modernities: Transnational consumption of Japanese TV dramas* (pp. 155–177). Hong Kong: Hong Kong University Press.
Marcus, B., Weigelt, O., Hergert, J., Gurt, J. & Gelleri, P. (2017). The use of snowball sampling for multi source organizational research: Some cause for concern. *Personnel Psychology, 70*(3), 635–73.
Navaro-Yashin, Y. (2002). *Faces of the state: Secularism and public life in Turkey*. Princeton, NJ: Princeton University Press.
Noy, C. (2008). Sampling knowledge: The hermeneutics of snowball sampling in qualitative research. *International Journal of Social Research Methodology, 11*(4), 327–344.
Punathambekar, A. (2005). Bollywood in the Indian-American diaspora: Mediating a transitive logic of cultural citizenship. *International Journal of Cultural Studies, 8*(2), 151–173.
Radway, J.A. (1991). Reading the romance: Women, patriarchy, and popular literature. Chapel Hill: University of North Carolina Press.
RTUK. (2010). Kadınların Televizyon İzleme Eğilimleri Araştırması. *RTUK*. Retrieved from https://www.rtuk.gov.tr/rtuk-kamuoyu-arastirmalari/3890/5234/kadinlarin-televizyon-izleme-egilimleri-arastirmasi-2-2010.html.
Savage, M. and Warde, A. (1993). Urban sociology, capitalism, and modernity. London, UK: Macmillan.
Straubhaar, J.D. (1991). Beyond media imperialism: Assymetrical interdependence and cultural proximity. *Critical Studies in Mass Communication, 10*(1), 39–59.
TodoTVNews. (2017, May 30). Korea's CJ E&M launches production unit in Turkey. *TodoTVNews*. Retrieved from http://www.todotvnews.com/news/korea-cjem-launches-production-unit-in-turkey.html.
Whatteverrr. (2014, March 31). Turkish Korean remakes that no one knows. *MyDramaList*. Retrieved from https://mydramalist.com/article/2014/03/27/turkish-korean-remakes-that-no-one-knows.
Yanardagoglu, E., & Karam, I. (2013). The fever that hit Arab satellite television: Audience perceptions of Turkish TV series. *Identities, 20*(5), 561–579.
Yilmazok, L. (2012). *Eurimages and Turkish cinema: History, identity, culture*. (Doctoral thesis, University of Amsterdam, Amsterdam, The Netherlands). *UvA-DARE (Digital Academic Repository)*. Retrieved from https://pure.uva.nl/ws/files/4316029/106667_thesis.pdf.

About the Contributors

Elaine W. **Chung** teaches Chinese history and culture at Cardiff University. She is also a Ph.D. candidate at the Centre of Media and Film Studies, SOAS, University of London. Her doctoral project revisits the transnational trajectories of South Korean film and TV stars in mainland China from 2000 to 2016.

Afonso **de Albuquerque** is a professor in the Department of Cultural and Media Studies and in the postgraduate program in communication at the Federal Fluminense University. He develops research on comparative communication and international media studies. He has published in the *International Journal of Communication*, *Media, Culture & Society* and *Journalism Studies*, among others.

Jennifer Rachel **Dutch** is an assistant professor of English and chair of the English Department at York College of Nebraska. She received her Ph.D. in American studies from the Pennsylvania State University. Her book, *Look Who's Cooking: The Rhetoric of American Home Cooking Traditions in the Twenty-First Century*, was published in 2018. Her research focuses on the intersection of innovation and tradition in food production and consumption, particularly related to cooking at home and on YouTube.

Yeşim **Kaptan** is an assistant professor in the school of communication studies at Kent State University. Her research interests are transnational media, global communication, identity politics, and consumer culture. She has published research in the *International Journal of Communication*, the *Journal of Consumer Culture*, the *Global Media Journal*, *Popular Communication* and various English and Turkish media journals.

Ann-Gee **Lee** is an associate professor of English at the University of Arkansas–Fort Smith. She received her Ph.D. in rhetoric and writing from Bowling Green State University. Her research interests lie in women's studies, covert rhetoric (secret codes/languages, non-verbal communication), civic discourse, popular culture (particularly television), ESL theory and pedagogy, multi-genre writing, as well as literacies and multiliteracies.

Min Joo **Lee** is a Ph.D. candidate in the gender studies department at UCLA. She received her BA in comparative literature and women's gender and sexuality studies at Williams College. She grew up going back and forth between the U.S. and South Korea and in the process, became interested in media and its influence on cultural rhetoric. Her research interest is the intersection of Korean television dramas, gender, sexuality, and race in the transnational context.

Tony Tai-Ting **Liu** is a visiting research fellow at the Institute for Advanced Studies on Asia, the University of Tokyo. He is also a research fellow at the Institute for Comprehensive Japan and Korea Studies, National Chung Hsing University. His research interests include international relations theory, international political economy, East Asia international relations, and Chinese foreign policy. His work can be found in *The Routledge Handbook of Global Cultural Policy* and *Education About Asia*.

Daniela **Mazur** is a Ph.D. student at the Postgraduate Program in Communication at the Federal Fluminense University. Her research focuses on Korean and *hallyu* studies, TV dramas and post–Western world. She is the honorary reporter for Korean Culture in Brazil by the Korean Cultural Center in Brazil (CCCB) in São Paulo. She also publishes articles on South Korean culture and media communication between Brazil and South Korea.

Melina **Meimaridis** is a Ph.D. candidate at the Federal Fluminense University. Her work analyses "Comfort Television Series" in American TV. She is researching the fictional representation of social institutions in television series. She has publications on fan studies, spoilers, Netflix, and gender politics in television series.

Sofia **Murell** received her BA in media and culture and her MSc in contemporary Asian studies. She conducts research about South Korean soft masculinities from the University of Amsterdam, the Netherlands. In 2016, she received a second master's degree in film studies focusing on Korean cinema from the same university. Her research interests include Korean cinema, gender, youth and culture, Korean visual culture, memory studies, and globalization.

JaeYoon **Park** is an assistant professor of media communication at the University of Arkansas–Fort Smith. Before coming to the U.S. to work on her doctorate, she was a writer and producer for two of the major broadcasting networks in Korea, and for a late-night talk show and music programs at SBS and MBC. Her research primarily focuses on the historical and ideological analysis of media communication, with special emphasis on the complexities of female subjectivity in a cross-cultural, interconnected context.

Mary A. **Sobhani** holds a Ph.D. in comparative literature from the University of Arkansas. She is the managing editor of the Spanish-language literary magazine *Azahares*, published through the University of Arkansas–Fort Smith, and is the head of the World Languages Department at the University of Arkansas–Fort Smith.

Murat **Tutucu** graduated from Ankara University's Faculty of Communication, Radio, Television and Film Department. He received his master's degree in media and communication studies from İzmir University of Economics. He is a doctoral student at Anadolu University in the Journalism Department. He also works as a screenwriter in the Distance Education Center, which belongs to a governmental institution.

Phyllis Wei-Lih **Yeh** is an assistant researcher in the policy research division of STPI, National Applied Research Laboratories in Taiwan. She holds a Ph.D. in economics from the Institute of China and Asia Pacific Studies, National Sun Yat-Sen University. She conducts research on cultural developments in Asia with a focus on the creative industry in China and Taiwan. Her research interests include the political economy of cultural and creative industries in Asia as well as cultural studies and international trade.

Index